The Great Festivals of Colonial Mexico City

A series of course adoption books on Latin America:

Independence in Spanish America: Civil Wars, Revolutions, and Underdevelopment (revised edition)—Jay Kinsbruner, Queens College

Heroes on Horseback: A Life and Times of the Last Gaucho Caudillos—John Charles Chasteen, University of North Carolina at Chapel Hill

The Life and Death of Carolina Maria de Jesus—Robert M. Levine, University of Miami, and José Carlos Sebe Bom Meihy, University of São Paulo

The Countryside in Colonial Latin America—Edited by Louisa Schell Hoberman, University of Texas at Austin, and Susan Migden Socolow, Emory University

¡Que vivan los tamales! Food and the Making of Mexican Identity—Jeffrey M. Pilcher, The Citadel

The Faces of Honor: Sex, Shame, and Violence in Colonial Latin America—Edited by Lyman L. Johnson, University of North Carolina at Charlotte, and Sonya Lipsett-Rivera, Carleton University

The Century of U.S. Capitalism in Latin America—Thomas F. O'Brien, University of Houston

Tangled Destinies: Latin America and the United States—Don Coerver, TCU, and Linda Hall, University of New Mexico

Everyday Life and Politics in Nineteenth-Century Mexico: Men, Women, and War—Mark Wasserman, Rutgers, The State University of New Jersey

Lives of the Bigamists: Marriage, Family, and Community in Colonial Mexico — Richard Boyer, Simon Fraser University

Andean Worlds: Indigenous History, Culture, and Consciousness Under Spanish Rule, 1532–1825 — Kenneth J. Andrien, Ohio State University

The Mexican Revolution, 1910–1940 —
Michael J. Gonzales, Northern Illinois University

Quito 1599: City and Colony in Transition —
Kris Lane, College of William and Mary

Argentina on the Couch: Psychiatry, State, and Society, 1880 to the Present — Edited by Mariano Plotkin, CONICET (National Council of Scientific Research, Argentina), and Universidad Nacional de Tres de Febrero, Buenos Aires, Argentina

A Pest in the Land: New World Epidemics in a Global Perspective —
Suzanne Austin Alchon, University of Delaware

The Silver King: The Remarkable Life of the Count of Regla in Colonial Mexico — Edith Boorstein Couturier, Professor Emerita

National Rhythms, African Roots: The Deep History of Latin American Popular Dance — John Charles Chasteen,
University of North Carolina at Chapel Hill

Series advisory editor: Lyman L. Johnson,
University of North Carolina at Charlotte

The Great Festivals of Colonial Mexico City

Performing Power and Identity

Linda A. Curcio-Nagy

UNIVERSITY OF NEW MEXICO PRESS
ALBUQUERQUE

To my father and mother, Nunzio and Viola,
for instilling in me a fascination with the past
and a passion for the present.

© 2004 by the University of New Mexico Press
All rights reserved. Published 2004
Printed and bound in the United States of America
10 09 08   2 3 4 5 6 7

ISBN-13: 978-0-8263-3167-0

Library of Congress Cataloging-in-Publication Data

Curcio, Linda Ann.
  The great festivals of colonial Mexico City :
  performing power and identity / Linda A. Curcio-Nagy.— 1st ed.
      p. cm. — (Diálogos)
  Includes bibliographical references and index.
  ISBN 0-8263-3166-1 (cloth : alk. paper) —
  ISBN 0-8263-3167-X (pbk. : alk. paper)
  1. Festivals—Mexico—Mexico City—History. 2. Mexico City
(Mexico)—Social life and customs. 3. Mexico—History—Spanish
colony, 1540–1810. I. Title. II. Diálogos (Albuquerque, N.M.)
  GT4814.M4C87 2004
  394.26972—dc22

                            2003026972

Typeset in Electra LH 11/14
Display type set in Amerigo BT
Design and composition: Maya Allen-Gallegos

Acknowledgments

Many individuals have assisted in the successful completion of this book, a project that lasted several years. Therefore the list is long of friends and colleagues who either read parts of the many permutations of this manuscript or who otherwise gave encouragement and constructive criticism. I wish to thank the members of my dissertation committee at Tulane University who supported the initial research for this project: Richard E. Greenleaf, Gertrude M. Yeager, Teresa Soufas, and Alain Saint Saens. I owe a large debt of gratitude to the Fulbright Hays Doctoral Research Committee for one of their generous grants, without which I would not have been able to travel to far-flung archives for my doctoral thesis. The University of Nevada, Reno, was also generous in providing a Junior Faculty Research Grant so that I might continue my research in Mexico.

I wish to thank Marina Pinto, Kathleen Myers, Sonya Lipsett-Rivera, Susan Deeds, Cheryl English Martin, Daniel Balderston, Alejandra Osorio, Alejandro Cañeque, Nancy Fee, John Frederick Schwaller, Stafford Poole, Susan Shroeder, and Jeffrey Pilcher for their support of this project and their friendship over the years. The staffs at various institutions were always helpful, cheerful, and encouraging. They made researching this project sheer pleasure. They include the many kind individuals at the Archivo General de Indias (Sevilla), the Biblioteca Nacional (Madrid), the Biblioteca Iberoamericana of the Universidad Cumplutense (Madrid), the Archivo General de la Nación (Mexico City), the Biblioteca Nacional de México (Mexico City), the Nettie Lee Benson Latin American Library at the University of Texas, the Manuscript Division and the Hispanic Division of the Library of Congress (especially Gorgette Dorn), the Bancroft Library of the University of California (Berkeley), the Biblioteca del Instituto Nacional de Antropología e Historia at the National Museum of Anthropology (Mexico City), and the Archivo Histórico del Antiguo Ayuntamiento de la Ciudad de México (Mexico City). A special thank-you must go to Roberto Beristaín for all his assistance and expertise.

Finally, I express my gratitude to my two editors, David Holtby and Lyman Johnson, who tirelessly and patiently encouraged this project and who provided their editorial insights to improve this manuscript.

To my good friend and colleague William Beezley, I thank you most sincerely for all your illuminating comments, for steadfast support and friendship, and for introducing me to Stephanie Plum, who kept me laughing during the more discouraging moments connected to this project. To my dear husband, Christopher von Nagy, without whom this project would never have been completed, I extend my overwhelming gratitude for your anthropological insights, your reading and rereading of the variations of this manuscript, and your loving support. And to my sweet Helena, I send many hugs because you show me how to fiesta every day.

Contents

Chapter 1: Introduction   1

Chapter 2: The Ideal Prince   15

Chapter 3: The Perfect Vassal   41

Chapter 4: Celebrating Apollo   67

Illustrations   86

Chapter 5: His Majesty's Most Loyal
and Imperfect Subjects   97

Chapter 6: Ritual, Satire, and
the Coming of Independence   121

Chapter 7: Concluding Thoughts   145

Appendix   155

Notes   159

Bibliography   193

Index   217

Chapter 1

Introduction

In early November 1624, the marquis of Cerralvo formally entered Mexico City and politely received the kind words and flattery of all the officials, who had not only despised his predecessor, the marquis of Gelves, but had led a successful revolt against him just months earlier. In 1621, Gelves arrived to take up his position filled with righteous zeal, determined to end corruption and enforce the law regardless of long established local political arrangements. In the process, he made few friends in the capital. Instead he alienated important officials at all levels of government, including the judges of the highest court in the land, the Audiencia. He offended and even exiled members of the powerful city council because they refused to attend the festival of Candelmas on February 2, 1622. His gravest error had been ostracizing and insulting the powerful archbishop, Juan Pérez de la Serna, by violating the sanctuary rights of the Church. The situation became so embattled that the viceroy eventually exiled the archbishop, who in turn ex-communicated the viceroy. Priests throughout the city incited their parishioners from the pulpit, claiming that the marquis was a heretic. Public sentiment quickly turned against the viceroy and led to the riot that sealed his fate.[1]

Relieved, emboldened, and feeling justified in their actions, Mexico City's ruling elite prepared to meet the marquis of Cerralvo, the new viceroy. They spent months preparing and planning for his entry celebration. It cost approximately 20,000 pesos, more than an average Native worker earned in a lifetime.[2] Average citizens in the capital watched the feverish preparations with great interest. All wondered what themes would be presented on the paintings of the triumphal arches in the Plaza de Santo Domingo and on the cathedral facade in the main square. Before a crowd of thousands, Native Americans, *castas* (people of mixed ancestry), Spaniards, and Africans, the painted narrative that decorated the cathedral arch justified the actions that the

1

Mexico City elite, especially the clergy, had taken against Gelves. The paintings symbolically depicted the Audiencia and the rest of the local elite as the noble senate of ancient Rome charged with the duty of protecting the republic from a crazed Caesar (Gelves).[3] There in the midst of the most expensive and most important festival in the colony, revolt was not only rationalized but glorified by the capital's most powerful residents. The festivities in honor of the new viceroy continued for weeks, flowing into the celebrations for Christmas. However, on the anniversary of the riot, Cerralvo ordered the city councilmen to fund a public ritual to counter any sense of pride that the local elite had taken from the revolt. On January 15, 1627, the anniversary of the rebellion, all officials, including the viceroy, dressed in fancy uniforms and paraded on horseback through the city. The city fathers hosted fireworks, jousts, and riding competitions. All this occurred so that "the city could demonstrate its loyalty to the Crown."[4]

The Theatricality of Power

Together the intertwined stories of the political demise of Gelves and the elaborate welcoming celebration for Cerralvo raise a number of issues about the unique and complex relationship between politics and festivals in colonial Mexico City. Festivals were pervasive, a defining characteristic of life in the capital. For most of the colonial period, inhabitants could witness a hundred religious and civil celebrations in a given year if they chose to do so. The five largest city-wide festivals, not coincidentally, were sponsored by the authorities and included the entry of a new viceroy, the oath ceremony to a new monarch, the celebration of Corpus Christi (the Holy Eucharist), the feast of the Virgin of Remedies (divine patroness of the city), and the Royal Banner festival. I became intrigued by how such festivals came to be purveyors of political concepts. Extending that central query led me to question what message the festivals set forth and how such concepts were actually performed and received by spectators. I also wondered how festivals and their message might reflect colonial realities and evolve over time, especially given the change in ruling dynasty from Hapsburg (1521–1700) to Bourbon (1700–1821).

It became clear that in Mexico City, these five large-scale spectacles were crucial media for modeling, presenting, teaching, and acting out political and social concepts. These festivals were designed as tools of cultural hegemony in that Spanish officials sought to utilize festivals and their message as a means of social control. The Spanish ruling elite sought to dominate subject peoples culturally, inducing submission, and encourage the acceptance of their political agenda.[5] The introduction of European public ritual occurred immediately after the fall of the Aztec capital, Tenochtitlan, to Hernán Cortés. Spanish priests seeking to evangelize the Native population brought the rich liturgical calendar of public festivals so characteristic of Early Modern Catholicism. Civil authorities also sponsored festivals designed to glorify the expanding empire and Spanish superiority. The military conquest completed, persuasion through music, dance, and public display, rather than the blasts of muskets, was now marshaled in a Spanish effort to maintain control of a newly acquired empire.

Large-scale spectacle became one tool in an arsenal of colonizing agents that included coercive force, discriminatory laws, religious institutions such as the Inquisition, and economic power. The elite believed, without question, that by virtue of their moral and racial superiority, they deserved to rule. Clifford Geertz has pointed out that every political authority requires its own "cultural frame" from which to define itself and claim its legitimacy, and festivals became just that for the ruling elite in Mexico City.[6] They utilized festivals to reassert periodically and bolster symbolically the values of the socioeconomic hierarchy that maintained their privileged position. And they were willing to spend large sums of money to accomplish their goals.

Demographic changes over time only seemed to make festival statecraft all the more necessary. The capital's very diverse population had an impact on the message and the design of government festivals. During the seventeenth century, approximately 100,000 people lived in the city, only a small percentage of whom were Spaniards. Native Americans constituted the largest percentage of the population. In the late eighteenth century, Natives still were a substantial percentage of some 137,000 city dwellers, although perhaps half were *criollos* (individuals of Spanish and Native American ancestry). In addition, a significant percentage of the population was African or Afro-Mexican, the result of the slave trade that brought tens of thousands of slaves to the colony after 1580. The majority of the African slaves brought to Mexico resided in Spanish urban areas, especially the capital, because Spaniards gauged prestige and wealth by the number of slaves they possessed as servants and workers. The manumission rate for slaves, especially women and children, was high compared to other slave-holding colonies in the Western Hemisphere, and consequently free blacks constituted an important percentage of the city's population. Racial mixing was also considerable, and the castas, individuals of mixed ethnic background, became the fastest-growing portion of the city's population (along with criollos) as time progressed. Ethnic relations in the capital were extremely complex as individuals intermarried, worked together, and created a unique popular culture that incorporated influences from various traditions.[7]

Officials were uneasy with the tremendous diversity of the capital. Viceroy Luís Velasco (I) as early as 1554 disparaged the plebe:

> The mestizos are greatly increasing and they all end up poorly inclined and susceptible to vices, and these people and the blacks you should be wary of. They are so many that coercion and punishment, even regular punishment, has no effect. The mestizos walk among the Indians. . . . They treat them poorly and serve as ruinous examples [of behavior].[8]

Officials would eventually develop the caste system, a legal system in which individuals were categorized by their racial and ethnic ancestry, each with certain rights and privileges and status. The caste system did not contain racial mixing by any means; authorities would eventually create over sixty categories.

Officials worried that the diversity of the population made it especially unruly and rebellious. In 1580, Viceroy Martín Enríquez de Almanza, writing to his successor, warned of potential instability due to the growing number of castas:

> It is the large number of the little people [the plebeians], the mestizos, mulattos, free blacks, and the frequency with which they mix with Spaniards born here or on the Iberian peninsula—and they all are so poorly inclined that I do not believe it would be a sin to presume of them whatever evil in the case of

a rebellion, and if there is something to fear, do not doubt, Your Lordship, that with them will be the majority of Indians.[9]

The fears of officials were justified in their minds because several uprisings and disturbances took place in the capital—during 1611, 1612, 1624, 1692, and 1697. In addition, fear of civil unrest permeated the city from 1608' to 1612 and in 1665, 1696, and 1701. Both the riots of 1611 and 1612 were connected to African-mulatto conspiracies to overthrow the Spanish. Although we know the reasons to be more complex, author Sebastián Gutiérrez explicitly stated that the cause of the revolt against Gelves in 1624 was the "instantaneous confabulation of so many different people, utterly hopeless, and subversive." The city councilmen claimed the same revolt was the result of the "unrest of the masses of mestizos, Indians and mulattos." In 1665, fears of a black rebellion again placed city officials on the alert. In the revolt of 1692, a large group of Native Americans and castas stormed the main plaza, forcing Spanish colonists and the viceroy to fear for their lives.[10]

Bourbon officials, during the 1700s, like their Hapsburg counterparts, were also concerned about the continued growth of the casta population and sought to reaffirm the caste system with such laws as the Real Pragmática de Matrimonios (1776), which fortified the *patria potestad* (power of the father) by granting the adjudication over disputed marriage proposals to royal courts rather than ecclesiastical ones. Young people, especially criollos, who wished to marry outside of their socioeconomic and caste group against their parents' wishes found the court unsympathetic to their claims.[11] In addition to concerns about lineage and status, Bourbon officials looked with a wary eye at popular culture and religion and found it in need of modernizing. This would lead to an entire series of civil and religious decrees designed to mandate changes in the average citizen's behavior.[12]

Government-sponsored celebrations attempted to promote a shared history and values among these diverse and potentially "dangerous" groups.[13] Through consistent repetition of the festival message over time, officials believed that they could influence the creation of a colonial identity.[14] At issue, then, was the ability of festival designers to reinterpret cultural experience for spectators and foster limited acculturation. Officials had the power to impose a new festival calendar and to conquer space, literally the streets of the capital, for their productions and their message. In this regard, they were quite successful. However, encouraging the acceptance of the message would prove more challenging. Festival sponsors believed that all these diverse individuals, largely unknown to each other, could feel united by an emotional inclination toward the city, the king, the Madonna, or the viceroy. According to Victor Turner, festivals by their very nature stand outside of the normal space and time of everyday life, creating unique spaces in which spectators and participants become more receptive to social, cultural, and religious concepts, serving as major event markers for individuals and society at large.[15] Officials sought to stir up emotions, to affect, attract, persuade the masses to their message. According to Antonio Maravall, the idea was to channel the will of the people in the proper direction to ensure the stability of the political system.[16] And festivals were designed as sensory experiences that included music, dance, rich costuming, drama and suspense, special effects, fireworks, weeks of performances, incense, displays of prowess, and temporary architectural structures that increased in size as time progressed. These events were feasts for the eyes and ears.

In addition to appropriating and designing the set for these political dramas, officials also created and refined the script—a highly sophisticated message designed to resonate with the general population. Within the festival (re)presentations, the organizers delineated the principles of leadership and envisioned the desired relationship between the ruler and the ruled. The festival patrons defined and objectified their idea of good governance. In the process, they posited the nature of the ideal ruler and his ever loyal vassal. They constantly evoked Christian virtues as measures of this good governance. In this fashion, officials promoted their values as sacred in an effort to bolster their legitimacy. Their "ruling mythology" (propaganda) emphasized that Spanish control would lead to prosperity for the benefit of all. In this scenario, vassals had to play their part and not merely serve as spectators. Thus citizens in highly choreographed performances appeared in the festival spaces.[17] As officials performed their power, citizens performed their identity as vassals. The large participation of Natives and Africans was a defining characteristic of state-sponsored festivals in Hapsburg Mexico City.[18] However, in the process, officials

imposed their own ideas about ethnicity and gender on those participants and the general public.[19] For the festival sponsors the desired
result was to create a vision of an idealized colonial polity where
everyone knew their place in the social hierarchy.

That colonial polity was uniquely Mexico City. First and fore-
most, Mexico City was the capital of a large viceroyalty, New Spain,
a territorial unit that eventually encompassed modern Mexico,
Central America, the Caribbean, the Philippines, and the greater
southwest of the United States.[20] All visitors and new immigrants to
the colony inevitably came first to the City of Palaces, as the capital
came to be called. From there, they traveled to other locals such as
the silver city of Zacatecas, Guatemala, Manila, or Lima. The city
attracted people from all over the viceroyalty as they attempted to
influence the powerful and improve their lives. Mexico City was
where officials reviewed law and policy, debated religious and moral
codes, granted favors, and forged business deals for the entire colony.
Those who became rich in the silver mines and on ranches built their
palaces and educated their children at the finest schools and at the
Royal Pontifical University. The bells of fifty-five elegant and lavishly
decorated churches announced mass; the nuns of twenty-two convents prayed for their city, nursed the sick, and gave food to the
hungry. Thirteen hospitals cared for those afflicted with a variety of
ailments from leprosy to madness, and thirteen schools educated the
young and reformed the fallen (prostitutes). It was by any standard an
impressive metropolis, and inhabitants claimed that it rivaled any
European city for beauty, marvels, and wealth.[21]

The focus of the city was the main square, or *zócalo*, the center
of power and prestige and home to the cathedral, the viceregal palace,
and the municipal offices. The zócalo was the hub of political, religious, and commercial activity. Even location within the city was
gauged in relation to the plaza. Under these circumstances, the
zócalo was the natural and logical setting for all major colonial rituals. The great square was capable of hosting 40,000 spectators, and
authorities could make use of government buildings to enhance their
productions. They decorated, adorned, illuminated, and re-created
the buildings by covering them with new temporary facades. They
made use of different neighborhoods, nearby smaller plazas, canals,
and the streets of the downtown area, but generally events included

a big finale in the zócalo. In all cases, spectators were reminded of the power and majesty of the colonial government. Yet each festival evoked the city and its grandeur, bringing it to life, remaking it each time as a meaningful cultural landscape in the eyes of participants and spectators.[22]

Of course, daily life in the capital was more complex and substantially less beautiful than that depicted in government propaganda. First, the city was never spared from the continued onslaught of disease and natural calamities. During the sixteenth century, epidemics killed millions of Natives. The third great epidemic (of smallpox), which raged from 1576 to 1581, was particularly devastating and caused the Native population in central Mexico to sink below 2,000,000.[23] At least twelve more epidemics afflicted inhabitants from 1587 to 1739. In addition, a number of natural disasters and poor agricultural years resulted in food shortages in the capital. Flooding occurred almost annually with the onset of the rainy season but was particularly severe during the 1620s and 1630s. Earthquakes racked the city as well, startling unsuspecting inhabitants and inflicting considerable damage to homes and businesses.[24]

Nor did economic development for the capital and its hinterland progress smoothly during the seventeenth century. The demographic collapse created a great labor scarcity even with the addition of African slave labor. Spanish farmers and ranchers sought to compensate for the loss of Native producers but were not always successful. A silver boom bolstered the economy from 1596 to 1620, but silver production then declined, especially during 1641–50 and 1671–80, and species, sources of capital, and businesses dried up as the mainstay of the economy faltered. At the same time, international trade contracted. Although regional trade and contraband with other European nations probably offset some of the decline in trade with Spain, the overall economy suffered from stagnation as producers attempted to diversify and recoup their losses.[25]

In many ways, the economy appeared to fare better during the eighteenth century. Another silver boom made New Spain the greatest producer of silver in the world by 1800.[26] However, a portion of the economic profits from that boom was siphoned by the Crown, which instituted new taxes and collected old ones with new efficiency. Thus growing silver production did not relieve the colony's shortage of currency, capital, and credit, and as a result, wages and per capita income declined. Trade did improve, and agriculture expanded to meet the needs of a growing population, especially the urban markets and the silver-producing cities. However, expansion of commercial agriculture combined with the increasing population altered land use and tenure, and legal disputes mounted. This caused an increase in the number of seasonal and day laborers, many of whom migrated from rural areas to the capital in search of work.[27]

Whether during the Hapsburg or later Bourbon period, the capital was a place of grueling toil and poverty for many inhabitants. Many slept in portals and doorways of government offices, churches, and businesses. Making a living in the capital was arduous, and many eked out an existence without permanent fixed employment. Citizens were frequently forced to pawn or sell their clothing to buy food. A floating population of beggars depended on the kindness of strangers and the generosity of the city's many convents.[28]

This lack of economic stability was keenly recognized by local officials, who occasionally included economic issues in the festival presentations. They also were mindful of the impact of epidemics and poor harvests and how such events could affect the mood of the public. This led city councilmen, especially during the Hapsburg period, to patronize more festivals because they were necessary "not only for the effect but equally . . . so the public would be happy."[29] The implication was that an unhappy populace might revolt.

However, for city councilmen during the Hapsburg era, festival patronage was more than just appeasement of potentially disgruntled citizens or a means to influence the mood of the public. It also was a means to demonstrate a government sensitive to the needs of the general population. For example, in 1640, city councilmen justified increasing festival expenditures by stating, "It is necessary to entertain the public because of the labors and sadness that they have experienced due to losses and other misfortunes." In the midst of the 1651 epidemic, they ordered the city government to host several days of bullfights to entertain the populace in addition to penitential processions seeking divine respite from illness. The councilmen even believed that government sponsorship of festivals was tantamount to a virtue. After all, they commissioned the 1642 triumphal arch celebrating the entrance of the viceroy, the count of Salvatierra, pointing out that when governor of Seville, he had hosted an eight-day city-wide festival because a malcontent had damaged a religious painting.[30]

Behind the Scenes: Collaboration and Rivalry

Behind the fanfare and ostentation, choreographed performances, and propaganda were the organizers and sponsors—government officials. The organization and design of these great festivals in the capital was the responsibility of local authorities, especially the city councilmen. They were primarily wealthy criollos, Spaniards born in the colony, some even descendants of the original conquerors. These men earned their living through a number of diversified enterprises and businesses, from ranches, to haciendas, to regional commerce. Some also had family connections to royal officials and to international merchants. They constituted the notables of the city and considered their participation in city government not only a privilege but a right. Being councilmen distinguished them from other citizens and other officials. Their business was the business of local politics, local concerns, and they developed a lively sense of patriotism for the capital city that, in a sense, belonged to them.[31] That identification with the city is clearly evident in the minutes of their council meetings. As the city matured into the capital of a far-flung colony beginning in the 1580s, its city councilmen increased their activities and festival patronage to better showcase their city.

Local artists and artisans aided the councilmen in their efforts to highlight the city and symbolize political concepts in the festivals. The city councilmen selected prominent local intellectuals renowned for their ingenuity and fine turns of phrase to design pivotal aspects of the festivals, for example, the triumphal arches used for the viceregal entries. Many of those chosen became, in essence, court artists and designed aspects of several festivals during their careers. Such a commission marked a high point for many of these authors because it signified their literary stature in the capital. The designers worked with their patrons, the councilmen, as well as the architects, painters, performers, and musicians who actually constructed materials or performed in the festivals. Local officials organized and reviewed much of the festivals themselves and had final approval of all aspects of the festival. They also paid the artists and writers handsomely for their inventiveness and paid for descriptions of the festivals to be published.[32]

The councilmen and their court artists in theory were to collaborate with royal and high-ranking ecclesiastical authorities appointed from Spain. That collaboration was based on mutual goals: performance of civic duty, maintenance of Spanish custom, desire to fortify the legitimacy of the government in the eyes of a very diverse population, and demonstration of personal prestige and wealth. However, local authorities were also working to establish their own identity as uniquely rooted in the capital and New Spain itself rather than in Spain. In addition to issues of identity, there were real rivalries among officials over jurisdiction, policy matters, and business and political opportunities. Differing perspectives affected festival statecraft as authorities negotiated the funding and the significance of festivals. Discord occasionally led to powerful breakdowns in these "negotiated scripts," as in the case of Gelves discussed above.

The fissures between authorities would widen under the Bourbon regime as a new political philosophy began to affect local interests in a more direct and negative fashion than had ever occurred under Hapsburg rule. The Bourbon kings and their ministers, influenced by certain aspects of Enlightenment thought, viewed the Hapsburg system of governing with great dismay and disdain. In their eyes, it was mismanaged and inefficient and in need of a drastic overhaul, a fact pointedly revealed after appointed royal investigators found colonial accounts in arrears, plagued by fraud and a general misuse of funds.[33]

These concerns necessitated more effective Spanish control and administration of its colonies in order to protect Spain's empire in the Western Hemisphere, a goal that would be extremely costly both financially and politically. Beginning with Philip V (1700–24) and reaching a peak with Charles III (1759–88), the Spanish Crown sought to preserve the empire, reassert monarchical authority, and increase the royal treasury through a variety of administrative and economic measures that have been referred to collectively as the Bourbon Reforms.[34] Authorities were joined by regalist bishops and archbishops, especially Archbishop Francisco de Lorenzana (1766–72), who agreed with their civil counterparts and energetically promoted religious reform of both the clergy and the laity.[35] The reforms eventually touched almost every aspect of life in Mexico City, including government-sponsored festivals and the concept of good governance that had been so meticulously crafted by Hapsburg officials.

The Audience

The authorities designed festivals with each other and the king in mind, but by their own admission, the stage and script of colonial government festivals mostly were aimed at the anonymous, heterogeneous citizenry. This, of course, raises the question of how those citizens perceived spectacles. Unfortunately, citizen perception of these festivals and the official message on good governance is most difficult to ascertain because of the limited number of detailed sources discussing their participation from both Spaniards and Native Americans. In general, the voices of average citizens of the past are always difficult to reclaim, if not impossible in certain circumstances. The surviving evidence is anecdotal, biased, fragmentary, or all too brief in its detail.[36] However, in this case, there is also the additional issue of how culturally diverse audiences understood such festivals, how they "read" the symbols and rituals, and how they both viewed and acted their mediated performances of perfect vassals. The festivals were historically and culturally dynamic entities in which symbols formed patterns of relationships that not only changed over time but were in essence fluid. Thus both the language utilized to describe and discuss them and the actual symbols codified in official rituals could be appropriated by spectators and participants and utilized for purposes different from, although not necessarily in opposition to, the goals of festival sponsors. The multiple uses and perspectives overlapped: any individual might attach several layers of meaning to such large-scale rituals. The fact that individuals could experience the festivals in different ways added to the power of such rituals of legitimacy because they had the ability to promote social cohesion utilizing symbols (and ritual acts) that held diverse, even contradictory, cultural meanings even among the official sponsors.[37]

The very pervasiveness of festivals, the power of the language of ritual and rulership, and its multifaceted interpretation created possibilities for individuals to assess and participate in a larger societal discussion of good governance. This was accomplished by exploiting the ritual forms themselves (the performative) and by referencing the ruling mythology through discursive means (such as sermons and satirical poems). Although official sponsors created a utopian vision of society and the government, their rituals were literally cultural constructions that sought to ignore and even hide the very real socioeconomic tensions that pervaded society, thereby forestalling any attempt to resolve them. It was at this disjuncture between the recognition of those problems and the requisite need for real solutions and their deferment via ritual propaganda and performance that vassals would attack festival organizers. Thus some vassals understood all too well the true meaning of the ruling mythology.[38]

In 1698, Agustín de Vetancurt claimed that

> the single greatest thing that the city can boast about is the frequency of its religious devotion to the Sacraments, its ostentation of so many festivals, and the generosity of spirit of all its inhabitants.[39]

It is well to remember Vetancurt's description. In his mind, pride in the capital was linked to festivals and piety. Hapsburg city councilmen would have applauded. In the next chapter, we meet those officials who first introduced to the capital the concepts of good governance and manifested those ideas in large-scale ritual. Chapter 3 focuses on the presentation of loyal vassals as ethnic representatives and discusses how festivals were perceived by certain citizens, such as Native American leaders and Franciscans. Chapters 4 and 5 discuss how Bourbon officials altered festivals in accordance with their goals and thereby redesigned the concept of ideal ruler and vassal. Finally, in Chapter 6, I analyze how anonymous satire directed against Bourbon officials referenced festivals and sought to reinterpret the concept of good governance in light of Bourbon policies and the coming of Mexican independence in 1821.

Chapter 2

The Ideal Prince

For Diego López Pacheco, the marquis of Villena, the most immediate task at hand was to thank God for his safe arrival.[1] The three-month voyage from Spain had been uneventful, literally smooth sailing, even though the passengers had suffered through the trials of an ocean voyage: bad weather on the high seas and worries about possible attacks from nefarious pirates, who, no doubt, would have rejoiced at the notion of capturing a Spanish flagship with a newly appointed viceroy on board. Finally, on June 25, 1640, he gazed from shipboard at the port city of Veracruz, the gateway to the great land of Mexico. He had only the vaguest notion of what awaited him, as he had never before set foot in the New World.

Once his welcoming festivities began in Veracruz, the marquis was feted continuously until November as he visited many towns and cities such as Jalapa, Tlaxcala, Puebla de los Angeles, Cholula, and Huejotzingo on his route to the capital, his new home. As he approached Mexico City, the sumptuousness of the welcoming festivities increased, yet these splendid events could only suggest the rich celebrations that awaited him in New Spain's premiere city. Finally, Villena arrived at Otumba, situated at the southern rim of the Valley of Mexico. Gazing down, he saw the lakes, at the center of which stood the jewel in the Spanish crown, the viceregal capital. Here Villena met his predecessor, the marquis of Cadereyta, royal officials, superiors of the religious orders, and members of the powerful international merchants guild. The viceroy then proceeded to the town of San Cristóbal, some twelve miles from Mexico City, where he met the entire city council (two aldermen representing the capital had traveled as ambassadors with the viceregal entourage since Jalapa).

The following day, the governor journeyed to the summer palace of the viceroys at Chapultepec. It was situated in the midst of a beautiful forest at the base of a large hill. The site had once been the location of the recreational palace of Aztec emperors. This palace, modest when compared to the viceregal residence in the city, was nonetheless impressive and included a large walled interior patio, used occasionally for bullfights.[2] The interior decor of the palace was sumptuous. For example, every room was illuminated by silver chandeliers and every wall was draped with tapestries, large paintings, or silk. In one room, the ceiling was covered with a blue velvet canopy and hanging silver artichokes, the leaves of which had been filled with perfume.

Once settled in, the marquis attended one event after another for several days. One afternoon, 400 Native Americans, wearing festival capes and feather headdresses, danced. Later, two men and a giant "serpent" fought a mock battle for control of a large castle with five towers. There were also religious sermons, banquets, plays, bullfights, and more dance performances.

Finally, on August 28 at three in the afternoon, more than two months after his initial debarkation in Veracruz, Villena entered Mexico City. At the entrance to the Native barrio of Tlatelolco, all the city's officials lined up in ascending order, the most powerful (the new viceroy) placed at the end. Twenty-five indigenous musicians, wearing uniforms and hats in the colors of the city (orange and purple), played trumpets, *chirimias* (flutes), and *atabales* (kettledrums). Next came the constables, porters, and deputies of the city, counselors, university professors, the city council, the royal tribunals, the Audiencia, and finally, the new viceroy.[3] He rode a white stallion and was seated on a sumptuous black velvet saddle that topped a crimson velvet and white satin cloth; the stirrups and bridle were gold.[4] The viceroy was dressed in garments of gold thread and appeared to be the very sun riding a horse. Carried high above his head was the palio, a sixty-foot tawny-colored canopy made of silver and gold thread.

This entourage paraded through the streets of Mexico City until it reached the Plaza of Santo Domingo. From behind the temporary fencing erected for the entry, the people shouted, "Viva!" and went wild when the viceroy appeared. At the plaza, the viceroy saw the great triumphal arch erected under the auspices of the municipal authorities. The arch stood ninety feet high and was sixty and a half feet wide and seven and a half feet deep. Decorated with large paintings, statues, and emblems, the gilded arch lauded the viceroy and likened him to the Greek god Mercury. The marquis swore an oath to defend and protect the city, and the councilmen gave him the gold key to the city. A costumed actor explained the paintings and symbols on the first side of the arch to the viceroy and the crowd. The city council then asked the viceroy to walk through the doors of the arch and view the canvases on the other side. At each step of this ceremony, the crowd cheered enthusiastically.

Next the city councilmen escorted the viceroy to the cathedral, where he was greeted by the archbishop and clergy. After another formal oath, this time to defend and respect ecclesiastical privilege, the viceroy was treated to an explanation of the arch commissioned by the city's religious authorities (the members of the cathedral council or chapter). The cathedral arch was much smaller than that of the city council and was not a freestanding structure but rather an elaborate *portada* temporarily attached to the facade of the cathedral. With the ceremony at this arch completed, the archbishop welcomed the governor into the cathedral as the Te Deum played. A high mass followed and marked the end of the ceremony. From there, civil authorities escorted the viceroy to his palace across the square.

The marquis of Villena was now to spend two more months as the guest of honor at many cultural events. There were five full days of bullfights, a mock joust, and a demonstration of horsemanship by the city's nobility and royal officials. This was followed by a parade of floats complete with music, poetry recitals, and theatrical performances in the main square. Evening entertainments included elaborate firework displays, dances by Native Americans, Afro-Mexican women, and student groups, and many banquets and a formal-dress ball. Although by today's standards, these months of celebration might seem excessive, by the conclusion of all the festivities, the viceroy had met and received counsel from all the significant quarters of viceregal society. He was uniquely aware of the pressing problems and the differing opinions over the possible solutions to those problems.

The average citizen viewing the entrance of the viceroy in Mexico City during this period would have been awed by its magnificence. And it was intended to be so. The inaugural entrance of the viceroy during the Hapsburg period defined the European Renaissance concept of magnificence. Magnificence was the physical realization and exemplification of the power and majesty of a prince and therefore was essential to the image of the viceroy.[5] Many rulers believed that surrounded by all the insignia of power, they could impress the populace with grand conspicuous displays, thus instilling a respect for the legitimacy of the government.[6] City councilmen believed that average citizens expected to see such grandeur from their rulers. In their minds, the entry was the perfect forum to present their definition of good governance, a concept that in turn hinged on a highly crafted image of the viceroy. Rulers also believed that such displays of wealth had to be accompanied by the image of officials as virtuous and pious.[7] The entry had to be elaborate and ostentatious, and it had to showcase the viceroy as a truly superior and virtuous individual—the ideal Christian prince. Furthermore, participation in and sponsorship of certain religious festivals allowed officials to reinforce the values of good governance presented in the entry and thereby continue to perform both their power and their piety in public on a regular basis. Although these ceremonies were ostensibly designed to celebrate the viceroy or some aspect of Catholic belief, at the center of these displays of wealth and power stood the city councilmen, the organizers and sponsors. Even though viceroys had significant roles to play in these large-scale spectacles, local officials, especially the city councilmen, fashioned a concept of good governance that in the end reflected their concerns and perspective.

Early History

Conquistador Bernal Díaz del Castillo gave the first indication that an entry ceremony would play a significant role in the viceregal capital. He recounted that when Hernán Cortés returned from Honduras in 1526, both Indians and Spaniards clogged the streets hailing his arrival because they viewed him as a savior from the abusive and corrupt officials who had ruled in his absence. Two years later, in 1528, the first Audiencia arrived to take over the administration of the colony, signaling the beginning of Crown efforts to assert royal authority over the unruly conquerors. The arrival of the new judges marked the first of many government-sponsored entry ceremonies, and the festivities included music, triumphal arches, and a mock battle.[8]

From 1531 to 1566, the entry remained a modest affair, consisting of a small triumphal arch, music performances, dances, and fireworks.[9] From 1566 to 1580, the councilmen expanded this basic festival with poetry recitals, banquets, a mock battle between "Christians and Moors" at Guadalupe (a village north of the city near the present site of the shrine of the Virgin of the same name), crimson velvet robes, a canopy of silver or gold thread, the key to the city, and formal oaths at the arches. Councilmen provided refreshments and sweets for prominent citizens and officials, lavishly draped the main streets with fancy cloth and tapestries, and illuminated their offices and homes with torches. They added three or four days of bullfights, elaborate fireworks for several nights, and demonstrations of military drills with rifles and flags. This new expanded entry cost the councilmen approximately 11,300 pesos.[10]

The years 1585 to 1700 marked the height of the entrance ceremony. By 1611, the events at Guadalupe no longer formed part of the entry because all such festivities had shifted to the viceregal palace at Chapultepec, thereby doubling the cost and length of the entry festival. The festival was now an elaborate, ostentatious months-long series of events like that which celebrated the arrival of the marquis of Villena. During this 115-year period, the entrance of the viceroy in Mexico City cost, on average, 23,300 pesos in gold, almost one and a half times the annual budget of the city. In 1603 and 1640, the festival reached highs of 36,800 and 40,000 pesos respectively.[11]

Magnificence and Power

Each of the costly component parts of the ceremony—the parade of dignitaries, costuming, arches, oaths—contributed to the job of representing good governance and magnificence. Consequently, the aldermen obsessed over every detail from the popular dance performances to the design of the formal gowns of office to the paintings that decorated the triumphal arches.

The parade of dignitaries, the actual physical entrance into the city, placed all the parts of the government on display before the people. One by one, each group passed in an orderly manner, arranged by rank and the strictures of protocol. They symbolized the perfect government—unified, efficient, organized, accessible. The procession idealized the relationship between the various government entities, because in reality there was considerable rivalry and conflict among them. The procession also allowed each segment to act out its dependency on the power of the viceroy, demonstrating his paramount location in the political order of the capital. The procession thus gave power a concrete presence because, although it idealized the relationships among officials, the parade exalted the colonial government.

In order to present this image of the government as power defined by magnificence, formal attire was essential; it was "the" marker of magnificence. The clothing each group wore reflected the business of holding office and had to be suitably rich and ostentatious. The aldermen were extremely concerned about their clothing for the parade, and pages and pages of city council minutes of meetings are filled with specific listings of materials for garments and accessories that the municipal government purchased for each councilman. The purchase of their crimson robes of office constituted a significant portion of total entrance expenditures and in some cases cost as much as 18,000 pesos in total.[12] Other government officials dressed in an equally sumptuous manner, completing the picture of an elegant, orderly, and wealthy government.

As stunning as the various officials looked, the focus of the parade was the viceroy. The viceroy's horse had to be one of the finest mounts in the colony, and with one exception, only he wore a suit woven from gold thread. Only the viceroy (the archbishop and the Holy Eucharist) entered under a canopy, a European tradition usually reserved for monarchs. The parade gave the inhabitants the opportunity to "meet" the ruler, and in many respects, the viceroy was both an actor in and the subject of this grand theater of the entry. During the parade, the viceroy maintained an image of "opulent composure," in that while he was surrounded by the height of sumptuousness, he remained aloof and refined. It was not unlike the image that also had been cultivated for the Spanish monarch. All of this, combined with the fact that the viceroy came at the end of the procession, was designed to build suspense and strike awe in the minds of the spectators, many of whom would be seeing the viceroy for the very first time.

The drama and suspense further heightened as the dignitaries halted at the arch in the Plaza de Santo Domingo. Looming more than five stories high, the triumphal arch was the most spectacular single component of the festivities. Gilded, decorated with bronze statues, covered with niches and giant cloth paintings, the arch amounted to a visual wonder. Under the Hapsburg government, no other urban building stood higher than the city council's triumphal arch during entry celebrations. City councilmen stated that the arch was "the most important item in the entry."[13] The cost of constructing the arch rose dramatically from 1580 to 1585, marking its increasing importance within the festival. From a very modest 62 pesos in 1580, the arch cost rose to 500 pesos just five years later. In the seventeenth century, the average cost of the elaborate arch was more than 2,000 pesos.[14]

The ceremony at the city's arch is particularly important in terms of the overall significance of the festival. The viceroy swore to defend the city and its traditional rights and to govern justly, and in return, the councilmen gave him the gold key, the symbol of the submission of municipal authority to royal will. At the arch, the viceroy listened attentively as costumed actors explained the images on the front of the facade, whereupon the city councilmen invited him to step through the arch doors. This was in actuality an invitation to set foot into the city officially for the first time as viceroy. Then before the religious hierarchy and their arch, he not only vowed to govern well but to respect the Holy Mother Church. He then listened to the explanation of the cathedral arch. Under no circumstances could the city or the archbishop refuse the king's minister. The viceroy's oath and the subsequent ritual submission of local and religious authorities formally represented the colonial hierarchies to the masses crowded nearby. Furthermore, the delivery of the oaths in such an important government ceremony was not merely a method of making propaganda before the general public; it was also an effort to legitimate the rule of a new viceroy and a means of acquiring popular consent for his government.[15] With these oaths, the viceroy signed in essence a social contract with local officials and the populace to govern within the expectations of the Church and political institutions of the capital. In addition, he accepted publicly (or at least appeared to do so) the ideas, requirements, and recommendations of the aldermen and the cathedral chapter as to the definition of good government for the colony expressed in the paintings on the two arches.

The arch designers and their patrons, the city councilmen and the cathedral chapter, aimed to make ethical, religious, and political truths accessible to all through the lure of the pictures on the arches.[16] But they also attempted to do much more. Arch designer Joaquín Velázquez de León stated that the "the intention of the arch [was] to make the Hero [in this case the viceroy] liked by the people."[17] Local arch designers always portrayed the viceroy as a hero, the Spanish king as a god, and their "divine" actions as symbols or examples of higher moral statements. The spectators' and the viceroy's understanding of the arch depended on their ability to "read the images" during "an age sympathetic to and indeed educated to symbolism."[18] Ephemeral architecture and decoration were part and parcel of many large-scale festivals, and over time, the repertoire of entry themes became familiar to the spectators. The same themes were also repeated in other entry performances sponsored by the authorities. An average city dweller might view five or more entries in his lifetime. The paintings were huge and showed a clearly recognizable viceroy busy performing great deeds. Nonetheless, many spectators no doubt were challenged to unlock the meanings of the more obscure pictorial images, the emblems, which consisted of a single image, such as bird that had taken flight to symbolize a more abstract concept such as liberty. It is not unthinkable that a "game" of sorts developed in which the public sought to solve the riddle of the emblems on the arch. They could have speculated about the connection between certain emblems and the biography or personality of the new viceroy, later comparing their ideas with those offered in the formal explanations delivered by the paid actor. When even these poetic descriptions failed to elucidate the meaning of the emblems, the arches did not necessarily fail to impress and intrigue the crowd. For example, in 1680, Sor Juana Inés de la Cruz wrote in her description of the cathedral arch:

> The arch [was] ostentatious in its colors, in the perfection of its design, in the resplendent gold that it burnished like rays; it was nothing less than a work consecrated to such a fine prince; the inscriptions impressed the knowledgeable as the colors impacted the eyes of the common person and [garnered] the cordial love and respect of all.[19]

The Ideal Prince Defined

With their awe-inspiring beauty and monumental size, the arches literally stood as symbols of good governance, and their message always represented the viceroy as the ideal Christian prince. The governor had a commanding presence as "the" king's minister in the viceroyalty, which facilitated the creation of an image of the viceroy as a type of father figure, a position cultivated by the arch designers and by festival patrons. However, viceroys were not only cast in a paternal light, personally responsible for the welfare of the colony and its inhabitants, but were also touted as deliverers. The ruler as *savior trope* began with Díaz del Castillos's description of the triumphal return of Hernán Cortés to Mexico City in 1528. The representation of the viceroy in this heroic style reached its apogee in the seventeenth-century entry.[20] For example, in 1640, author Gutiérrez de Medina described the public's reaction to the viceroy's appearance by stating that he saw "flocks of women and men, all yelling and clapping for joy most confusingly, [with] the happiness of those rescued after having been held captive." He also reported that the crowds yelled out:

> You've come just in time, Father of the poor, to cure this Republic; Take away the drought with the rain of your wisdom and benevolent prudence; With the heat of your fervent desire take away the cold and weakness of our hearts; You've come just in time with the light that banishes the shadows.[21]

There is no way to ascertain whether these are the actual words shouted during the entry. If such statements were truly made, it is possible that the comments were spontaneous, and it is equally possible that certain individuals led the crowd in such exclamations. Either way, these expressions correspond exactly to the theme of the viceroy as a deliverer so manifest in other aspects of the entry.

The actual arches presented the deliverers' deeds and virtues to the crowd, following the Spanish custom of utilizing ancient legendary figures as examples of virtue. The viceroys were compared to the Greek gods Mercury, Neptune, Mars, and Jupiter and to more mortal Greek heroes such as Prometheus, Perseus, Hercules, Ulysses, Aeneas, and Paris. On other occasions, famous figures such as the

Roman emperor Octavio Caesar, the Aztec emperors, and Joseph from the Bible served as examples for the viceroys.[22] The designers of the allegories on the arch took great pains in their published accounts to directly link the viceroy with his ancient mythological counterpart. In all the descriptions, authors presented the hopes that their patrons and ostensibly the people pinned on the new governor.

For example, in the 1624 entrance, arch designer Sebastián Gutiérrez represented the marquis of Cerralvo, Rodrigo Pacheco Osorio, as a descendant of one Lucius Iunio Pacieco, an officer of the imperial army under Julius Caesar, who supposedly founded the house of Pacheco. This supposition made it much easier to present the allegory of the marquis as Octavio Caesar. One particular event confirmed the accuracy of the analogy: the reign of Octavio was hailed by a beautiful rainbow, and a giant rainbow apparently had appeared in Mexico City and entered a palace window exactly when news of the new viceroy's arrival at Veracruz had reached the capital. The rainbow of Octavio was a portent of his successful administration of the Roman empire. He brought peace, expanded the empire, subjugated the bellicose Spaniards, promulgated new and just laws, and was known as the "Restorer" and "Father of the Nation." The author stated that this was exactly what was expected from Cerralvo, who would govern in the aftermath of the revolt against Gelves.[23]

The actual paintings on the arches always started off by displaying the nobility and the antiquity of the viceroy's family line and defining his sacred relationship to the king. Every arch of the period told a variation of the same story. The viceroy/hero was charged with a mission, the governing of New Spain, by a divine or morally superior being, always portrayed as the king of Spain. For example, in 1688, the arch showed Paris, the Trojan hero (the viceroy), receiving a world (New Spain) to carry on his shoulders from a giant imperial eagle sent by Zeus (Charles II).[24]

Just as the paintings linked a viceroy to his heroic counterpart and the king, they also were made to clarify the basic qualifications of a good viceroy. For example, noble lineage and successful experience on the battlefield were consistently portrayed as essential qualities of a successful ruler. The nobility of the viceroy presumed other virtues such as loyalty and integrity while battle experience connoted strength and valor.[25] Experience in arms and noble birth were not, however, enough to ensure good governance. In the opinion of the arch designers and their patrons, the viceroy had to serve as an example to his people. Author Pedro Fernández Osorio believed that a viceroy had to always be on the side of beauty and virtue because he was the soul of the people, "who [were] united in their love by the aura of his benign spirit."[26]

The authors were confident that a viceroy's personal religious devotion determined his ability to serve as a moral model to the people and defined his character as an effective leader. Over and over again the arch designers emphasized that the observance of religious sacraments, holidays, and teachings was "the most efficient means to prevent public harm."[27] Devotion to God gave the viceroy the strength and needed guidance to govern properly because, according to arch designer Sor Juana Inés de la Cruz, "only from heaven [came] success."[28] The level and intensity of a viceroy's devotion indicated the type of governor he would be. According to arch designer Alonso Ramírez de Vargas, a truly pious ruler would be "continuously successful . . . with complete rectitude regarding justice [and] a high degree of prudence, implementing the virtues of his heart against fear, discord, and even death."[29] The viceroy's piety would lead him to administer justice fairly, alleviate suffering, and maintain peace.[30] As might be expected, one of the most important virtues of a viceroy listed by entry patrons was wisdom because, according to Sor Juana Inés de la Cruz, "wisdom, and not gold, [was] what crown[ed] princes."[31] However, arch designer Agustín de Salazar y Torres warned that a viceroy, as a true Christian prince, also had to fight against "sin, [which was] drowning those who had been induced to error and had to act so that [those individuals] would not remain consumed by such deception."[32]

According to local officials and artists, such good Christian governance inevitably led to prosperity and abundance for the colony. This theme, so often repeated in the imagery, was connected to desires for a return to a utopian epoch. Arch designers made frequent references to the mythological phoenix that would rise again and usher in a new era when everything would be "of riches,/and blessings."[33] In the entry of 1640, the arch specifically made reference to the Siglo de Oro (the Golden Age), when Saturn ruled over the world, and included a large painting showing a land with rivers of milk and ambrosia, flowers and fruit, oak trees producing honey, and overflowing cornucopias. In 1642 and 1653, the city arches linked the return of a golden age to the development of mineral resources. This analogy was in direct response to the slowdown in colonial silver production that had depressed the economy during the decade between the two entry celebrations.[34] The 1688 city arch designer, Francisco de Azevedo, even claimed that material prosperity was "the best recompense [the viceroy could give] for the loyalty and love of the people."[35]

Arch designers and their patrons listed several specific policies that a pious governor could institute to generate that material prosperity. The most important of these was the effort to drain the lakes surrounding the capital, an issue almost since the Spaniards seized control of the city. Over the years, the plant cover of the valley had been stripped away on the nearby mountains in order to supply the capital with firewood, lumber, and charcoal. Consequently, there was little plant protection to hold the rainwater that rushed to fill the lakes. Flooding so plagued the city that Philip III twice ordered that it be relocated to higher ground. With the flooding also came epidemics. The *desagüe* (drainage) plan was to limit the threat of floods by diverting the waters of several small rivers that fed into the lakes surrounding the city. Various viceroys promoted the project, but it was an arduous task, requiring special technology, substantial financial resources, a large labor supply, and consistent management over decades. It is no wonder that in 1642, 1650, 1660, 1680, and 1688, the desagüe was represented in sizable paintings.[36]

In addition to completing the desagüe project, another, more abstract policy goal made a golden age possible—a viceroy's generosity. According to the arch designers, a generous viceroy not only did not hesitate to grant "favor" to worthy individuals, groups, or institutions but also had compassion for people in need.[37] Arch designer Salazar y Torres in 1653 believed that it was more important "to aid the unfortunate than to win battles against enemies." Furthermore, he claimed "that following Christian precepts, in politics/a prince should care for the unfortunate/because as there is no fruit without a flower/so there is no government without compassion."[38] The theme of compassion and generosity toward one's subjects was repeated twice on each arch for the years 1642, 1650, and 1673.[39] In the final analysis, many designers believed as Fernández Osorio did when he wrote that "the kind prince captured the hearts of his people."[40]

The paintings on the triumphal arches emphasized that the generous Christian prince could bring about a new era of prosperity only through hard work. Diligence and industrious were strong leitmotifs of the seventeenth-century arches because, according to Sebastian Gutiérrez, "laziness was the origin of all vices and an enemy of successful government."[41] The truly virtuous prince worked hard to further ennoble his family.[42] No feat was too difficult that it could not be overcome through hard work. Alavés Pinelo claimed that industriousness gave Perseus, the ancient Greek hero, the strength and intelligence to decapitate Medusa, the snake-haired infanticide-performing semidivine creature who with one glance turned men to stone.[43] Perhaps more important, arch designers believed that the diligent prince motivated his people to be industrious, and, when diligence was lacking, he chastised the lazy.[44]

The Pious Rulers

As we have seen, the entry showcased the opulence, wealth, and power of the state and put forth a particular concept of good governance. However, this good governance depended on the viceroy's moral character, his ability to serve as a model of Christian piety for his subjects. Only then would he be able to change society for the better (the golden age). The viceroy's commitment to Catholicism was highlighted by his entry oath before the archbishop to respect the faith and his subsequent attendance at a high mass in the cathedral. Theoretically, all good Christians desired to practice the essential virtues of charity, humility, and love of God, and in the case of the viceroy, even more was expected. Governors performed charitable acts, funding chapels, continued construction of the cathedral, orphanages, or religious shrines. However, as the ideal Christian prince, the viceroy was expected to attend religious services and festivals, actions specifically listed on the triumphal arches. Piety and festival participation had particular resonance in the strongly Christian society of Mexico because piety and devotion to God's word were seen as the requisite attributes of a moral person, and it was a belief in the basic tenets of Christianity that linked the very ethnically and religiously diverse population of the city. True believers sought to demonstrate their devotion to God both in private and in public. In this fashion, the image of the viceroy in the entry necessitated that a royal governor perform his devotion because it was woven into his legitimacy as ruler. Certain important large-scale religious festivals provided the perfect forum to do just that.

As with the viceroy's entrance, the city councilmen planned and sponsored most major citywide religious events (in cooperation with ecclesiastical authorities). Thus the councilmen were integral to both the creation and the maintenance of the viceroy's image as the Christian prince. Such demonstrations of piety not only provided for the eternal salvation of the aldermen but also became for them a matter of honor. Participation in religious festivals confirmed their status and enhanced their own legitimacy as local leaders, as did participation in the entry. It was not accidental that in many religious festivals, they were given pivotal roles and positioned near the viceroy.

More than any other festival, Corpus Christi allowed officials to articulate the piety so essential to the concept of good governance presented in the entry ceremonies. Religiously, the festival allowed spectators to witness God and experience his presence in the form of the Eucharist. In this respect, the festival celebrated the transubstantiation, the moment when Catholics believe that the bread and wine in the mass become the body and blood of Christ. Corpus celebrated the Last Supper of Holy Thursday, when Christ performed the first such miraculous transformation before his apostles.

Corpus Christi was the largest and most expensive annual religious festival in the capital, occurring usually in late May or early June, depending on Easter.[45] Hundreds of people participated in the procession, representing every parish, religious order, confraternity, government institution, and ethnic group. The procession was led by a rather carnivalesque group of individuals dressed as devils, giants, and big heads as well as dance performers and allegorical carts (decorated floats that carried actors who performed short plays about the lives of the saints) and a dragon (*tarasca*). Along the processional route at different intervals, prominent guilds erected ephemeral altars before which the procession would pause, allowing participants to pray and rest before continuing the celebration. Large public theatrical performances in the main square were also part of the festivities as were musical and dance performances inside the cathedral and witty and inventive sermons at the many churches of the city. At the focus of all these events was the Holy Eucharist, carried for all to see in the procession. Corpus Christi was a joyful festival that celebrated the Church, Jesus Christ, and the devout.

The compartmentalized and diverse nature of the procession reinforced group and ethnic identification as disparate and often antagonistic groups found themselves in the same location. Rivalries existed over clothing, banners, adornments for saints' statues, sermons, and the decoration of temporary altars. A good showing in the procession might lead a spectator to donate funding to a particular parish or religious organization. These distinctions also fortified and reflected the hierarchical nature of viceregal society. For example, the city councilmen carried the canopy over the Eucharist and the viceroy walked alongside it. In this way, the focal point of the procession, Christ incarnate, spotlighted officials and also manifested the values on the ephemeral arches of the entry. In the procession the viceroy (and other authorities) manifested their Christian virtue and their superiority to the rest of the population because, after all, they walked in the most prestigious position.

Even though it emphasized differences in society, the Corpus festival was also important because in no other annual religious festival did so many inhabitants participate together. Generally, individuals celebrated their parish, confraternity, and neighborhood saints among themselves, although anyone could attend and view their procession and celebration. Even at Easter, only certain confraternities participated in public activities, walking in processions on different days and times during the Passion. With Corpus Christi, officials and the populace were joined (literally walking as one) by their love for the greatest sovereign of all, Jesus Christ. They all humbled themselves before his higher moral authority (the Host).[46] Thus the Corpus festival encouraged integration and identification with a larger community and stirred a sense of civic pride in Mexico City while it reminded participants of their social place.

In this context, it is noteworthy that the marquis of Cerralvo made a particular point of walking in the first Corpus procession after the revolt of 1624, a tradition not entertained by his deposed predecessor, Gelves.[47] The aldermen were quite pleased by this decision and requested that a decree be issued ordering all future viceroys to walk in the procession (it had been optional), and future governors did just that. The presence of the supreme colonial authority in this particular procession was significant politically and spiritually. In theory, the religiosity of the viceroy would inspire his subjects and reaffirm the concept of a religious and cultural system shared by all. Officials could appear to be in control of the city once more and could claim that everything had returned to normal. In this case the viceroy's participation reaffirmed the image of a unified government and populace in a time of crisis by emphasizing the spiritual devotion and Christian zeal that theoretically linked everyone.

Performances during the Corpus procession and the published descriptions of events affirmed this depiction of a unified, pious, yet hierarchical Christian society. For example, during the procession of 1635, actor Diego de Cornejo recited before the crowd a poem that had been written by prominent local literati Pedro de Marmalejo.[48] In this poem, Marmalejo, using the idea of the Corpus procession as inspiration, described Mexico City, especially those streets along the route of the procession, and linked them to a spiritual journey. According to the poet, the very streets of the capital led individuals to a deeper understanding of Christ's message.

At the close of the poem, Marmalejo named those individuals who best epitomized the Christian virtues in the capital. They were none other than the viceroy, the marquis of Cerralvo, the judges of the high court, the members of the cathedral chapter, and the city councilmen. The latter in particular were lauded for the many "great deeds that they perform[ed]," especially their generosity in sponsoring the procession. The city councilmen also sponsored the publication of Marmalejo's poem, an act that he claimed further indicated their virtuous nature. Just like the actual Corpus procession, the poem emphasized the religiosity of the inhabitants and the city itself but singled out officials as true models of piety.

In addition to Corpus Christi, other festivals allowed viceroys and city officials to demonstrate their exemplary piousness. For example, the single most important occasional (as opposed to annual) religious commitment of the government was the devotion to the Virgin of Remedies, divine intercessor in times of drought, famine, and epidemic disease. Residents in Mexico City believed that she had performed many miracles for Spaniards, Natives, and Africans. For decades, she was primarily the patroness of local Native communities situated near her shrine. In 1574, the city councilmen from the capital became the official patrons of the shrine. They maintained the building and grounds, paid for special masses and her feast day celebrations, and provided for the resident priest. Although the indigenous devotion to the Virgin of Remedies continued, the aldermen, as members of the confraternity devoted to her, claimed her for the city. They escorted the statue in a procession of up to 40,000 people to the cathedral on eighteen separate occasions from 1577 to 1696. Inhabitants sought her aid during times of epidemics, poor harvests, and drought.

Although a number of devotions to various manifestations of Mary existed at the confraternity, parish, and personal levels, the Virgin of Remedies, the patroness of the city council during the sixteenth and seventeenth centuries, became the only image consistently utilized in large-scale spectacles to protect the entire city. People believed that the Virgin of Remedies answered their supplications, intervened on their behalf with her son, Jesus Christ, and brought relief to the capital. The aldermen and viceroys patronized the processions and walked next to the Virgin, thereby appearing to share in the afflictions suffered by the general populace. They demonstrated their devotion to Mary, and, just as importantly, they aided in the alleviation of the capital's suffering through their special relationship with the Virgin of Remedies. Each miracle performed by the Virgin confirmed the efficacy of the religious devotion of the inhabitants and also bolstered the legitimacy of the Hapsburg government because of the visible devotion of its officials and their personal connection to her.[49]

Other festivals allowed the viceroy to demonstrate his compassion or, alternatively, his righteous indignation. During the annual Saturday Easter vigil, the viceroy demonstrated forgiveness, another important Christian virtue, by freeing some prisoners from local jails, a common European practice introduced to Mexico by Spanish authorities.[50] Those who repented their criminal misdeeds were given a new opportunity to live more virtuous lives. The viceroy also played the role of judge in the autos-de-fé, or penitential spectacles, of the Holy Office of the Inquisition, in which prisoners convicted of heresy, bigamy, or other offenses to the Church were showcased to serve as examples of what would befall those who deviated from orthodoxy. The Inquisitors designed these spectacles, situated in the main square, to re-create the final Judgment Day, on which Christ would judge all and select those who were to reign with him in paradise. Those on his right would enter the kingdom while those on his left would be condemned for all eternity to the fires of hell. In actuality, the Inquisitors judged and selected the punishments for all the prisoners, depending on whether they had reconciled with the Church or not. The viceroy sat on a special chair in the center of the stage and the guilty sat either to the viceroy's left or his right, making the royal governor the symbolic representation of Christ on earth.[51] In this way the viceroy fulfilled his duty as a good Christian prince charged with fighting the demons of evil.

The participation of officials in state-sponsored religious festivals emphasized the unique relationship between religion and politics in the capital. Clearly, the primary significance of the festivals was a religious one connected to Scripture, the miraculous power of Mary, the transubstantiation, or some other aspect of Catholic theology. However, this fact did not preclude the viceroy or the city council from playing a central symbolic role in the theological presentation of such celebrations. Rather, quite the opposite occurred: these festivals afforded officials the perfect opportunity to place themselves in pivotal locations in an attempt to ensure that the people connected their piety to their political authority.[52] Furthermore, government officials could also emphasize their own privileged position in society because although they participated in these celebrations as Christians, they were more prestigious, powerful, and wealthier Christians than their much more numerous humble social inferiors: the Natives, castas, and poor Spaniards.

Local Interpretation:
The Ideal Prince and the Absent King

Local officials invested much planning, effort, time, and expense on presenting and representing good governance connected to the viceroy, the king's representative (and the city councilmen). The distant monarch is virtually lost in all these performances of power and piety. In more ways than one the Spanish king was conspicuous by his absence. Hapsburg colonial officials did recognize, however, that it was to their advantage if the highly diverse population of the capital could be brought to imitate their allegiance to the king of Spain. During the sixteenth and seventeenth centuries, a number of festivals were organized to directly glorify the king. Citizens were encouraged to celebrate the birth of an heir to the throne, the monarch's marriage, the queen's pregnancy, royal victory in battle, and even the king's birthday. However, these festivals were small in size and cost and usually included a solemn mass and an inspiring sermon at the cathedral. Although these events were designed to place the monarch in the lives of his distant subjects, they never rivaled the viceregal entry.[53]

The jura del rey (the oath to the king) was the largest and most expensive of royal celebrations. The jura was a public oath of allegiance to commemorate a new monarch's ascension to the Spanish throne. Oath celebrations took place in Hapsburg Mexico for Philip II in 1557, Philip III in 1599, Philip IV in 1621, and Charles II in 1666 and again in 1676. Little is known about the first juras performed in Mexico City. However, by 1621 the procedures of the festival were well established. Royal and local religious and civil authorities as well as Native American nobility sat on a decorated stage in the center of the main square. The royal ensign (a councilman elected to serve as official standard-bearer) recited, "Castille, New Spain, Castille, New Spain, Castille, New Spain for the King, Don Philip, our Lord." He did this three more times in different locations, representing royal, religious, and municipal officials. Guns were fired and fireworks exploded following each oath recitation. He then rode through the streets, carrying the royal banner. Once the entire ceremony was completed, the officials and public attended a mass at the cathedral. For the most part, the event remained a one-day affair.[54] Seventeenth-century oaths never cost more than 5,000 pesos, one-quarter the average price of the viceregal entrance and only 1,500 more than the annual average spent on the religious festival of Corpus Christi.[55]

Although the jura became more costly and elaborate as the Hapsburg era progressed, it received neither the resources nor energies devoted to the viceregal entry. Other occasional royal festivals were also modest in cost. Funeral services for the monarchs were expensive because they usually included the construction of an ephemeral funeral pyre displayed in the cathedral, but even when the cost of funeral commemorations is added to the oath ceremony that followed it, the combined sum does not equal that spent on the more frequent viceregal entries. Simply put, the king's premiere festival lacked the scale, richness, and repeated symbolic power of the viceregal entry.

Most inhabitants in Mexico City probably witnessed at least one jura during their lifetime, but it was a celebration that was dedicated to an individual who the average colonial citizen would never see. In Spain, public officials created and perpetuated an aloof, almost otherworldly aura around the personage of the king, but many Spaniards occasionally had the opportunity to view the actual royal person during events such as entrance ceremonies and coronations or informally as he traveled from city to city and palace to palace.[56] However, because the Spanish king never set foot in the New World, he was only present, in the case of Mexico, through decrees sent from Spain, through his likeness represented on a limited number of paintings or in these occasional royal festivals. One of the essential components of the jura ceremony in Mexico City was to display an image of the new monarch. Thus the oath celebration was designed not only to pledge allegiance to the king but to introduce him to his subjects for the first time. The presentation of the "absent" king before his subjects was in the hands of his officials, mainly the city councilmen. Inhabitants in Mexico City only received an image of the king, filtered through the rituals sponsored by colonial officials. In the viceregal entry, municipal and religious officials posited the king as a powerful otherworldly figure from whom justice and authority emanated; he was a divine ruler, above reproach. And in reality, demands for services and complaints about government policies and procedures were not blamed on the monarch (per se) but rather on his minister, the viceroy. Complaints about government policy and practices were certainly registered with the king after filtering through the Council of the Indies, but the royal person was seen as the final arbiter. All viewed the king as the one individual capable of righting an injustice perpetuated by colonial officials.

At the same time, the physical distance that separated the king from his New World subjects facilitated the use of the bureaucratic formula *obedezco pero no cumplo* (literally, I obey but do not comply). Decrees from Spain could be set aside, disregarded, until other, more favorable laws were issued, pending legal appeal. Authorities, and on occasion the populace, were allowed some latitude in interpreting laws to fit local needs and circumstances. Those who failed to comply could invoke the *composición*, whereby a nominal sum was paid to the royal treasury in order to receive a dispensation allowing one to sidestep a law. The very nature of colonial life—vast expanses of territory, communication and transportation systems based on the horse and carriage, different ethnicities, conflicting bureaucratic authorities—bred a certain flexibility in the approach to royal decrees and policies. In some cases, the Spanish colonists objected to the royal will, claiming that certain laws were unsuitable because of the very nature of colonial society. Laws could be put aside because the king, though a just monarch, did not know and understand life in the colony. However, disregard of the royal will did not constitute disloyalty. Distaste for a particular law or political policy did not necessarily lead to disenchantment with the concept of kingship that the Hapsburg jura celebrated, but it did affect the city council's prioritization of festivals.[57]

We need look no further than the disputes over funding entry ceremonies to see how local interpretations might subvert royal directives. The aldermen borrowed huge sums of money for the viceregal entries from the royal accounts, usually the *sisa del vino* (wine tax) account, and by 1686, the debt accrued was 206,000 pesos.[58] Clearly many viceroys assisted the city councilmen by allowing them to borrow funds from accounts designated for other purposes, such as public works or even defense. But other viceroys and the Spanish monarchs themselves attempted to stop these raids on funds needed for other purposes. As early as 1598, royal officials became concerned that the entry celebration "feted the minister as though he were the king."[59] In 1607, the viceroy, the marquis of Montesclaros, refused to lend 30,000 pesos to the city councilmen in order to properly celebrate the second term of Luis de Velasco. He even decreed cost-cutting measures that greatly displeased the city fathers. The aldermen claimed that the city's reputation "would be ruined, and that their personal honor and that of all their descendants would be tarnished" if the ceremonies were diminished. Disregarding the ban, they spent an estimated 25,000 pesos from various other accounts. Four years later, in 1611, Viceroy Velasco limited the cost of the entry of Archbishop/Viceroy García Guerra to

14,000 pesos.[60] City councilmen again worried about the potential damage to the image of the government, complaining that

> it would be very inappropriate and would diminish greatly the said entry. . . . The natives and vassals of his Majesty . . . equate the majesty of that which is represented [in the entry] with what it stands for . . . [namely] the public authority and the joy and happiness, approval and respect with which the viceroys have usually been received and obeyed.[61]

A royal decree intended to put an end to all this overspending arrived in Mexico City on October 20, 1620. The king decreed that the viceroy should not be received under a canopy and that the festival should be toned down because, the decree stated, "after all, the viceroy was not the king."[62] Removing the canopy severely affected the image of the government because without the canopy, public figures could not wear the crimson velvet robes because the festival lost its premiere designation as one of royal authority and sanctity. The city councilmen worried about the impression the indigenous inhabitants would have of the reduced celebration. They pointed out that Viceroy Velasco had also been concerned about excess spending but gave considerable funding for the entrances because he was "[a] person quite experienced in the nature of the Indians and he knew what best suited this event."[63] Summing up the necessity to fully patronize the festival, one councilmen stated, "It is less inconvenient to spend the money than give the public some motive [for rebellion] being so distant from the eyes of his majesty."[64] Another alderman rather bluntly stated that the city council should disregard the king's ban because the monarch simply did not understand the role of the entry in the colonial capital.[65] In fact, the riot against the marquis of Gelves occurred during this period of strict royal fiscal controls. The marquis of Cerralvo arrived in New Spain carrying a new decree allowing the councilmen to spend as much as they deemed appropriate for future entrance ceremonies. Obviously, the authorities in Spain recognized that the image of the government in Mexico City had been seriously damaged by the fall of Gelves. They therefore renewed earlier levels of financial support for the celebration, hoping to shore up the image of the imperial government.

The Spanish monarchs once again attempted to rein in costs in 1638 and 1666. These decrees were either rescinded or proved otherwise ineffectual due to the actions of the city councilmen.[66] In 1690, Charles II decreed a 12,000-peso spending limit and ordered new viceroys to spend only eight days, not two weeks, at Chapultepec Palace. Furthermore, he demanded that viceroys be made personally responsible for any expenditures beyond the stipulated amount.[67] The last Hapsburg viceroy, the count of Montezuma, did not stop at Chapultepec Palace at all; however, the cost of his entry still remained high because events in the city proper multiplied to compensate for the loss of the Chapultepec venue. Despite the excesses, he apparently did not pay for the extra expense.[68]

Clearly, the entry celebration was central to the city council's conception of the image of the state. They were more than willing to overrule viceroys and even ignore the king's decrees in order to "properly" sponsor the festival.[69] Where some viceroys and monarchs saw excess, the councilmen saw a festival absolutely essential to maintaining and reinforcing the political and social status quo in the colonial capital. After all, the responsibility of actual governing, of enforcing one decree or another, fell squarely on the shoulders of the viceroy. To the local elite in particular, his decisions, at least in the viceregal capital, usually had immediate consequences. While the monarch was a distant, almost mythic, figure, the viceroy, who represented the king, wielded "real" power, power that could be identified easily by inhabitants and that could perhaps be influenced and molded to local goals and needs by the city councilmen. Consequently, the ascension to the throne of a new king was celebrated for one or two days, but the arrival of a new viceroy was celebrated for months. The city councilmen prioritized festivals, arranging them in order of importance based on local realities and needs.

This local perspective also led councilmen and ecclesiastical officials to criticize viceroys who did not live up to their vision of good governance, albeit implicitly. They, after all, delineated the principles of leadership and set the parameters for officialdom's uses of power. They constantly asserted the same virtues over and over again and by doing so pointed out the inadequacy of previous viceroys. For example, the 1624, 1642, 1650, 1653, 1664, and 1688 triumphal arches warned new viceroys not to engage in corruption. Local authorities alluded to the fact that some seventeenth-century viceroys had not been effective rulers and some had been indeed quite corrupt and unscrupulous. Viceroys assumed their office accompanied by a large number of family and retainers who they quickly appointed to major administrative posts. Because of the short duration of any given viceroy's reign, his appointees viewed these plum positions as means to quickly reap profits from the districts under their control. *Corregidores* were quick to oppress Native Americans, demanding increased tribute payments, which occasionally led to revolt. In addition, many viceroys allowed their associates to dominate the commercial affairs of the colony, displacing or sidestepping established entrepreneurs. Combined with poor decisions on major policies and/or poor harvests or epidemics, the interference in the local economy could result in disaster for colonists.[70]

For example, the count of Baños (1660–64) was considered by many colonists to be tyrannical and vindictive. He jailed, attempted to murder, exiled, and acted harshly against his perceived enemies when they complained about his appointees, his misguided policy decisions (for example, meddling with the supply of mercury during a time of decline in silver production), and his efforts to extract heavy tribute burdens from the region of Tehuantepec, an area that had just rebelled over exorbitant tribute demands. In 1663, matters were so out of hand that the king suspended Baños and appointed his archenemy, acting archbishop Diego Osorio de Escobar, as viceroy. Baños refused to step down and even destroyed the royal decree that fired him. Osorio de Escobar fled the city, fearing for his life. Eventually, the king's wishes prevailed.[71]

Clearly not all viceroys were as extreme as Baños, nor should we fail to mention that the city councilmen themselves were not always paragons of virtue. Their positions allowed the unscrupulous among them to take advantage of commercial opportunities (such as food hoarding or price fixing) that were in opposition to their own professed notions about good governance. For example, in the 1650s, several councilmen were deposed from office and arrested for having taken bribes from the bakers guild in an effort to manipulate bread prices.[72] The actions of less than honest viceroys and councilmen hurt the concept of good governance so meticulously crafted in festivals but also made such festivals all the more necessary to maintain the legitimacy of the colonial government in the eyes of inhabitants.

Conclusion

In the inaugural entrance of a new viceroy, the city councilmen (with the aid of commissioned local literati and most outgoing viceroys) marshaled all their public (and occasionally their personal) resources to create a magnificent vision of the perfect government, all aimed to impress the general audience (and incoming viceroys) with the power and majesty of the colonial system and their colonial capital. They meticulously prepared and considered each detail and were more than willing to engage in deficit spending. Their desire was to create a vision of an urban utopia ruled by an exemplary governor, an ideal Christian prince, ever aware of his duties and responsibilities to the populace. The entry charged the governor with being wise, prudent, charitable, diligent, dedicated to the care and welfare of his people. Inspired by his Christian faith, he was to labor like a benevolent patriarch to create a more just and prosperous society. The viceroy's devotion to God was the foundation for this good governance, but placing the public welfare above personal enrichment, generosity, and industriousness would ensure success. Local sponsors and their commissioned intellectuals posited that government legitimacy was dependent on the demonstration of religious devotion and commitment to Christian precepts. Thus performing power became linked to performing piety.

Consequently, the political mythology represented in the entry did not disappear when the entry festivities came to a close but was referenced and reaffirmed regularly by official patronage of and participation in major citywide public religious festivals. With Corpus Christi and the Virgin of Remedies, officials sponsored major devotional events on behalf of the populace, and their positions alongside the Host and Mary gave a physical manifestation to their position as pious rulers. In other festivals, they demonstrated their empathy and compassion and their unwillingness to suffer the wicked. They sought to model religiosity for the citizenry and seek divine aid and protection for the city.

Although festivals dedicated to the Spanish monarch formed part of ritual statecraft in the capital, they were not the main focus of local festival sponsors, who had substantial control over the imagery, level of ostentation (or magnificence), and performative details of an official spectacle. They countered attempts to alter the entry, sidestepped decrees, and spent their own funds to impose their vision of what was necessary for the colonial context. The entry would be celebrated in a manner appropriate for the capital of the viceroyalty, inhabited by a highly diverse population. The oath to the king would also be celebrated but without the extravagance that characterized the viceregal entry because in the end, the viceroy was more important to colonial political reality than was the distant king. The aldermen, perhaps rightly, posited that the general population's direct experience of the imperial system was in the immediate person of the viceroy.

Interestingly, this local prioritization of political spectacle had the effect of deflecting criticism away from the Spanish Crown by focusing attention so consistently and heavily on the viceroy's personal virtues. The distant semidivine king, above reproach, displayed in the oath and the entry ceremonies, symbolized the imperial system. Thus in 1624 when the angry mob (and high court judges and archbishop and city councilmen) rebelled against Viceroy Gelves, they had at their disposal a means (a language) to justify their actions, justifications that later appeared on the ecclesiastical arch to Cerralvo. They could claim that the viceroy lacked the personal virtues and sufficient understanding to effectively rule the colony. And they could criticize the royal government without yelling down with Phillip III.

Chapter 3

The Perfect Vassal

I n the 1640 viceregal entry, the marquis of Villena and his official parade entourage stopped at the main square of Tlatelolco, one of the indigenous neighborhoods in the city, before reaching the triumphal arch commissioned by the city councilmen in the Plaza de Santo Domingo. Here Native leaders greeted Villena, hosted a reception in his honor, and commissioned triumphal arches to celebrate the new viceroy. With an interpreter by his side, Villena listened to an explanation in Nahuatl of each painting from a richly costumed performer. More dances and musical performances rounded out the entertainment. Before leaving Tlatelolco, the viceroy passed under a traditional indigenous arch, a towering thatch construction that bore the heraldic symbol of Aztec Tenochtitlan, the eagle seated on a cactus.

After the ceremonies at the triumphal arches at the Plaza de Santo Domingo and at the cathedral, the viceroy and the spectators were entertained by a variety of performers. Native Americans, wearing elaborate traditional attire, danced, sang, and fought in mock battles, showcasing their prowess with pre-Columbian-inspired indigenous weapons. The indigenous *voladores* were the true crowd-pleasers of these festivities. Men dressed in elaborate Native costumes climbed a pole erected thirty feet or more. Attached by long ropes to the top, the men jumped from the pole, swirling around it upside down as they slowly descended to the ground. They appeared to be flying; hence their designation as voladores (or flyers). One performer remained at the top of the pole, playing music on a flute as the others "flew" downward.

Later that evening, beautifully dressed Afro-Mexican women danced for the new governor, stopping at distinct points in their performance to present very large paintings to Villena and the assembled crowd. A male actor, speaking as though he were one of the women, explained each painting as it was brought forward. The paintings lauded the viceroy, proclaiming him to be handsome, virtuous, and resplendent like the sun. The paintings also emphasized the women's loyalty and devotion to the Spanish ruling system.

The Perfect Vassal

These performances of Native Americans and Afro-Mexicans were only a small sampling of the many citizen performances that constituted the entry (and to a certain extent the jura). Such performances were just as essential to the overall official message of the entry as the paintings and rituals of the triumphal arches. As we saw in the previous chapter, local officials created festivals that glorified the state and focused on the virtuous and pious nature of the viceroy as a means to define and promote their concept of good governance. They hoped to impress their message on the general public's mind with the sheer magnificence of government-sponsored festivals. The official promise or depiction of good governance justified continued Spanish rule, placing the authorities, the white male elite, in positions of overwhelming power and wealth. Yet Native Americans constituted the largest segment of the population of the capital during the Hapsburg period, and their perception of festivals (and government legitimacy) was a central concern for the city councilmen. Mexico City was also home to the colony's largest African population. Both ethnicities were connected to several rebellions or threats of unrest in the capital. Thus festivals such as the entry and the jura had to persuade citizens to accept not only the concept of rule by a virtuous and divinely inspired Spanish colonial government but also the social and ethnic hierarchy of the capital that reinforced Spanish control.

One of the most effective means to encourage this acceptance was through citizen participation in the festivals. In the entry and the oath, certain individuals were singled out as "the perfect vassals" and performed in a highly choreographed and scripted fashion. They "acted" as representatives of their ethnic identity, as Native Americans and Africans who honored the viceroy and the king. These presentations were designed to present the hierarchical nature of society and encourage Native Americans and Afro-Mexicans to recognize and accept their subordinate position. However, the presentation differed for each group, reflecting official conceptualizations of distinct ethnicities and gender. The male Native ruling elite participated as Indians who were historically distinct leaders whose authority derived from a pre-Conquest imperial past but who were now part of the colonial governmental system. Africans were conceptualized as part of the Spanish cultural sphere, a distinct racial group that was supposedly hispanized and removed from their traditional African roots. In both cases, the rituals alluded to real political and social circumstances. The Native elite were the symbolic heirs of pre-Columbian political traditions and served as intermediaries between their own Native vassals and Spanish officials. Africans, whether slaves or free in the capital, usually were found as servants and workers in Spanish factories, shops, businesses, and homes and with each passing generation lost cultural connections to Africa, especially after the slave trade began to decline after 1640, diminishing the number of recent arrivals from Africa. African women like those who danced in 1640 also performed the official stereotype of black females as submissive yet sexualized persons.

The participation of representative Native Americans and Afro-Mexicans in the festivals reaffirmed the official vision of an idealized colonial polity that was both hierarchical and unified, much like that presented in the compartmentalized Corpus Christi procession. In this case, different groups participated as separate entities but were joined by their acceptance and recognition of Spanish superiority. The message embedded in the festivals suggested that to do so would benefit spectators personally. In this fashion, participants were put forth as a type of colonial "success story." They represented select and privileged groups who through their participation bolstered their own positions, solidified patronage ties to the city councilmen and the viceroy, and earned the esteem of their own ethnic groups.

However, Spanish privilege and control did not necessarily benefit all citizens or even the actual participants in these events. Tensions, problems, and hostility lay just under the surface of these festivals and their depiction of harmonious ethnic relations. Natives were forced to pay heavy tribute and engage in labor service for Spaniards. Many Africans were slaves who were treated harshly by their masters. Laws codified the privileges accorded to wealthy male Spaniards. Festivals washed over these issues and instead idealized colonial society as an organic reality. Many citizens no doubt noted the disparity between the self-serving elite political and social messages embedded in festivals and the reality of colonial life. Some Native Americans and clergymen noted the hypocrisy of the Spanish elite and questioned whether officials had lived up to their promises of exemplary rulership. Because the official message was so well articulated, pervasive, and embedded in the festivals, the rituals themselves provided the perfect format for interpretations and messages different from those presented by local officials.

Native Americans in the Viceregal Entry

In the early sixteenth century, Spaniards, especially priests who engaged in evangelizing the Native population, were aware of the important role that ritual had played and would continue to play in Native society. The Aztec had regularly celebrated important deities through large-scale spectacle. Pilgrimages, processions, mock battles, dances, ephemeral architecture, songs, and prayers formed part of many of these events.[1] Chronicler Alonso de Zorita pointed out that if Native rulers failed to sponsor fiestas, their people would neither hold them in esteem nor obey them.[2] In a declaration that could just as easily have been applied to colonial spectacle, chronicler Fray Diego Durán claimed that the Aztec coronation feast "was designed to bewilder and make [spectators] see the grandeur and abundance of jewels and gifts. . . . All of this was based upon ostentation, vain gloriousness, in order to show that the Aztecs were the masters of all the riches of the earth. This is why they celebrated their feasts so splendidly."[3] This recognition of the pivotal role that festivals played in the lives of indigenous peoples combined with Iberian festivals of statecraft and official concern about the image of the government in the eyes of the Natives. Consequently, as early as 1531, during the celebration of the arrival of Sebastián Ramírez de Fuenleal, the president of the colony's second Audiencia, indigenous leaders participated in the entry festival.[4] And, as we have seen, this belief in the importance of ritual to Native Americans served as the city councilmen's justification for resisting royal attempts to alter and decrease the sumptuousness of the entry.

Spanish authorities recognized that pre-Columbian rituals could serve as the foundation for state festivals of legitimacy immediately after the Conquest. Parallels did exist between Aztec and colonial ritual statecraft that facilitated the introduction of Spanish rituals. For example, the concept of vice-king (viceroy) existed during the pre-Columbian period and would not have been viewed as an anomaly by indigenous inhabitants. Under the Aztec, powerful *cihuacoatl*, second only to the emperor, handled the daily operations of the empire, such as organizing military campaigns, managing finances, advising the emperor, and ruling the city proper. Thus, the cihuacoatl was a position not so unlike that of a Spanish viceroy in New Spain. Although both had great authority, they received their orders from and obeyed the king.[5]

Furthermore, Spanish and Aztec ritual statecraft shared similar traditions in regard to the perceived duties of rulers, the manner in which the populace was to view their leaders, and ritual forms such as ephemeral architecture. For example, the ideal qualities of the Mexica, or Aztec, ruler were similar to those posited for the viceroy and the Spanish monarch in colonial rituals. In both eras, the supreme rulers were seen as semidivine, and the emperor and the viceroy had to demonstrate their expertise on the battlefield. Both the Mexica behavioral code and Spanish Christianity emphasized moderation and held rulers, in theory, to the highest standards of behavior, believing that rulers should serve as models for their people.[6] Each system posited that the fair and impartial dispensation of justice was one of the central responsibilities of a ruler.[7] Aztec and viceregal leaders were expected to be merciful, kind, and generous and were charged with promoting the welfare of the people. Both political cultures claimed that governing was an arduous task. To rule for the Aztec was to carry "the great bundle, the great carrying frame, the governed. On [his] back, on [his] lap, in [his] arms our lord placeth the governed, the vassals, the common folk, the capricious, the peevish." In 1580, Viceroy Martín Enríquez wrote to his successor, the count of Coruña, summarizing the responsibilities of rulership under the colonial administration: "There is no matter, however small or big, nor person of whatever status that does not go to the viceroy with all manner of business that it frightens, because even in the case of the fights and childishness that takes place in the privacy of their homes, citizens believe that, if they do not give account of it to the viceroy, they will not be successful. And seeing that this land requires this . . . I have been forced to do it."[8]

Spanish and Aztec official discourse also utilized similar allegories to describe how vassals viewed a new ruler. Extant Aztec coronation speeches, composed and performed by the nobility, claimed that the masses were apparently filled with joy, "thirsting and starving, as one person, crying, saddened, longing for his mother, for his father, so the governed desire to be ruled." The common folk wished to reside under "his [the emperor's] shade, his shadow, become rich and be prosperous."[9] As we saw in the previous chapter, the viceroy in the entry ceremonies was represented as a hero and savior, an allegory that appeared in all triumphal arches. In addition, it was posited that through his superior moral character and governing expertise, a viceroy would rescue the population from bad government, economic woes, and injustice.

Each political system also relied on state patronage of entertainments, believing that it was an essential part of rulership. When Aztec leaders became aware that the citizenry was anxious about some event or issue, they commanded that a ball game be played "to animate the people and divert them." In addition, "the ruler was greatly concerned with the dance, the rejoicing, in order to hearten and console all the peers, the lords, the noblemen, the brave warriors, and all the common folk and vassals."[10] In Mexico City, the city councilmen believed that it was a good idea "to occupy and entertain Indians with festivals because they needed some relaxation and merriment." In 1611, the authorities hosted two parades "in order to please the inhabitants." According to the city councilmen, public festivals "were necessary to keep the people happy."[11] Viceroys were very visible participants in major religious festivals, and these actions were expected and considered virtuous by the city councilmen and the populace.[12]

Both Mexica and Spanish rituals utilized ephemeral architecture. For example, the Aztec festival Panquetzaliztli included a race (Ipaina Huitzilopochtli) in which a runner carried a large image of the Aztec patron deity along a route shaded with arches and decorated with flowers, featherwork, and banners. The festival also included the performance of rituals at Chapultepec, where, at the base of the hill near the site of the future viceregal summer palace, the images of Aztec emperors had been carved into rock. Ephemeral architecture also played an important role in the celebration of Quetzalcoatl, in which Native Americans danced and performed farces on decorated stages.[13]

Some pre-Columbian festivals, such as Huey Tozotli, dedicated to Tlaloc, the god of rain, included the re-creation of a virtual forest with trees, flowering plants, and animals in the courtyard of the deity's temple. Native forest re-creation became an important part of early viceregal entry ceremonies in the zócalo.[14]

The parallels between pre-Columbian and colonial rituals of statecraft would have been evident to early-sixteenth-century Natives who lived in Tenochtitlan, even though the moral values attached to leadership had been recontextualized and dramatically altered by the Conquest and the rituals themselves were different. To Native Americans of the Conquest generation, the inconceivable had occurred: their once great capital had fallen. They suffered a profound sense of loss as they viewed their city in rubble and watched its central core (the sacred precinct) redefined as the center of Spanish power and elite residence. Because Hernán Cortés chose Tenochtitlan as the capital of the Spanish colony, Native residents there had their experience of the Conquest more directly mediated by constant contact with Spaniards than did Natives elsewhere in the colony. In addition, they had the overwhelming task of both maintaining some continuity with their pre-Columbian past and making sense of their post-Conquest present. Both Spaniards and Natives entered into a cultural process in which they sought to understand each other. The fact that they independently shared a number of beliefs and rituals about imperial festival statecraft may have facilitated that process, although it also generated misunderstandings and false assumptions.[15]

By the late sixteenth century, however, pre-Columbian rituals resonated less powerfully with the Native population. A great deal of Native historical memory had been lost due to the passage of time as well as the sheer number of deaths from epidemic disease. By the 1580s, few Natives had been directly socialized by way of the Mexica educational, religious, and state systems. In addition, the creation of the colonial political system and its institutions had the effect of fragmenting the pre-Columbian political framework. As a consequence of these changes, Natives in the city were becoming more acculturated.[16] Furthermore, efforts to rebuild the city, not only in terms of its physical appearance but also its image as the capital of a colonial empire, had reached a pivotal juncture.[17] These circumstances created the opportunity for the viceregal government to encourage identification with the colonial system among the Native population in a more formalized manner. Rituals reflected this changing demographic and cultural reality and responded to it. It is no coincidence that Native participation in state-sponsored festivals increased substantially beginning in 1580 with the entry of the count of Coruña.[18] The entrance and the jura took on new resonance for Native Americans in the capital, becoming the only rituals of imperial statecraft that they would know and experience firsthand. They became colonial celebrations rooted in the city's multicultural reality, not merely rituals imported and imposed by Spaniards. This could be seen in the 1640 Tlatelolco entry, in which Spanish ritual forms (the oath and modified triumphal arches) were combined with Native performances in Nahuatl and the use of the traditional indigenous arch (made of thatch and decorated with foliage and flowers and the heraldic seal of Tenochtitlan).[19] City scribe and local scholar Arias de Villalobos proclaimed this new era when he wrote that "the Natives with the new political situation of the times . . . burst with joy and, recognizing that their relationship with the King our Lord, as his ministers and vassals, [believe] that they too should be represented in good form in yet another fantastic and dignified festival that will be forever remembered."[20]

The Native elite who participated in and patronized portions of government festivals reflected this acculturation. They were the group most integrated into the Spanish system. They were bilingual and most likely to have established economic and political ties to local Spanish civil and religious authorities. For example, during the pivotal last quarter of the sixteenth century and into the early seventeenth century, the governorship of Tenochtitlan was held by Antonio Valeriano, followed (after an interim governor) by his grandson of the same name. Valeriano had been an Indian Latinist who was Spanish educated and highly so. He had an excellent command of both Spanish and Latin in addition to his native Nahuatl and had worked with Fray Bernardino de Sahagún and Fray Juan de Torquemada, famous Spanish priests who researched and wrote extensively on pre-Hispanic culture. Noblemen like Valeriano were very often chosen by the Spanish to serve as interim governors in other Native jurisdictions during times of dispute over governorship because of their loyalty to and expertise in colonial government.[21]

Thus, Native leaders like Valeriano served as local (and sometimes regional) officials and constituted the first level of the Spanish ruling system for the majority of the inhabitants of the colony. Native participation in ritual gave a symbolic form to the Spanish ruling concept of a colonial world consisting of Indian republics and Spanish towns, each separate yet united by loyalty to the Crown. Throughout the entry, Natives appeared in pivotal roles, yet roles that were always subordinate and complementary to official Spanish presentations. At Chapultepec, indigenous dancers, musicians, and warriors shared the limelight with Spanish dancers, fireworks, plays, acrobats, banquets, and bullfights.[22] As the viceroy's entourage left Chapultepec and traveled toward the city, Native Americans elaborately dressed as ancient warriors positioned their canoes along the causeways and bowed in deference to the new governor.[23] Before formally entering the city proper at the Plaza de Santo Domingo, the viceroy and the parade of Spanish officials first stopped for the entry at Tlatelolco.[24] In the zócalo, Natives performed before Spanish parades, jousts, and horse races. The sixteenth-century Native forest re-creations in the center of the zócalo were surrounded in turn by expensive European tapestries hung from the balconies of government buildings and the cathedral's triumphal arch, signaling Native inclusion and subordination.

This emphasis on complementarity and hierarchy extended to the manner in which Native leaders performed in the festivals. Although they were acculturated and formed part of the Spanish government, the Native elite always performed their official identity as individuals whose ancestors had been subjugated by the Spanish during the Conquest. This point was emphasized by their manner of dressing in pre-Columbian festival clothing and the fact that they always spoke publicly in Nahuatl although they were bilingual and rarely wore such costumes in their duties as Native colonial elite. To the spectators and other participants, they appeared as an other (Native American) from the past that was readily identifiable and known, yet different because they were singled out as such. To emphasize the theme of subjugated Natives, city councilmen even commissioned special firework displays. For example, after the 1621 Native American oath to the king, firework experts set ablaze two large floats in the shape of canoes (filled with fireworks) and decorated with figures of Montezuma and other pre-Columbian leaders kneeling before the royal lion (a symbol of the Spanish Crown). The fireworks symbolized not only the submission of Native Americans to their Spanish overlords as a result of their defeat during the Conquest but also the destruction of the pre-Columbian political system. Natives no longer lived in independent polities outside the Spanish colonial system, a fact emphasized by the real-life presence of indigenous leaders on the stage during the ceremony.[25]

Post-Conquest power rules necessitated that Native leaders accept this crafted image of themselves as representatives of their conquered ancestors in the entry and the oath. Their participation was an essential ceremonial duty. But they also had to embrace such rituals as a means to legitimize their role and power vis-à-vis the colonial government.[26] Their participation and festival sponsorship can be seen as part of a larger political strategy through which Native leaders attempted to manipulate Spanish customs and institutions to ensure their own continued political survival as well as that of their indigenous vassals. This Native approach to Spanish ritual forms paralleled similar approaches on the more traditionally economic and political front. For example, Native elites allied with local friars made alliances with local Spaniards and engaged in select participation in the market economy in order to maintain control of and aid their communities.

Native American leadership may have used their ritual sponsorship to demonstrate and prove their status as loyal vassals and as a means to gain political positions, prestige, and high status in their own communities. Firsthand contact with new viceroys allowed indigenous leaders to establish direct political relationships with the new governor, thus providing the opportunity to gain influence and court his patronage.[27] Native annalists (historians and scholars) recorded with great interest the activities of Spanish officials, particularly the viceroys, because of the Spanish officials' impact on Native communities. Indigenous nobles and intellectuals certainly were aware of and quite interested in the titles and personal dynastic histories of incoming viceroys. This was especially the case when high-ranking officials visited indigenous towns. For example, in a 1612 journal entry, Domingo de San Antón Muñón Chimalpahin, a prominent Native historian and intellectual, commented on the first time that the marquis of Guadalcazar entered the capital, providing the details about the titles and social rank of his entourage.[28] During the viceregal entry, indigenous leaders hoped that Spanish officials would be impressed with all that they saw; thus civic or community pride played a role in such elaborate festivals.[29] From early years, the ostentation of these festivals was utilized to prove Native loyalty, a tradition that was continued during eighteenth century.[30] Furthermore, such performances would have provided perfect ritual spaces to play out Natives' own traditional rivalries (for example, that between the neighborhoods of San Juan de Tenochtitlan and Tlatelolco in the capital).[31]

The indigenous nobility's connection to the viceroy was further enforced by the fact that newly elected Indian officers traveled to the viceregal palace to receive imperial confirmation of their positions (just as in Aztec times leaders had journeyed to Tenochtitlan). In the colonial era, Native leaders swore an oath to govern honorably, treat their vassals well, promote Christianity, deliver tribute payments, and refrain from corruption.[32] Thus the Native oath of governing mirrored the oath that the viceroy gave as he traveled from town to town on his way to the capital.

Entries and oaths were at the top of a festival hierarchy that began with local ceremonies. All these festivals shared similar goals of promoting alliance, allegiance, and legitimacy for officials. The Native leadership held court at the local level, and feasting and festivals, especially those connected to their investiture in office, were important to their legitimization as ethnic rulers. Native leaders patronized festivals and also made large donations, repairing chapels or for major new construction projects. For example, the rulers of Tlatelolco rebuilt an entire new municipal complex with gardens, lodgings, and salons between 1576 and 1581 with funds generously provided by a previous Native governor.[33] Furthermore, the oath ceremony in particular appeared to reference Native rituals by having the representatives from the subject Indian towns of Tenochtitlan and Tlatelolco publicly give gifts and pay homage to their own leaders as part of the oath ceremony. This act therefore presented a hierarchy of ritual submission that began when the Native nobility expressed their allegiance to the Spanish Crown and concluded when their own Indian vassals did the same.

The fact that Native leaders performed in Spanish rituals in highly stylized Native costumes served to reaffirm their cultural distinctiveness and emphasized their special rights and privileges. These Native leaders also retained information and traditions from the pre-Columbian period in a systematic way. They and other Native scholars and intellectuals actively recorded and maintained the history of their communities.[34] The Native leadership in the two Indian neighborhoods recognized their position as the political heirs to the great Aztec capital and probably had retained substantial knowledge of the history and past rituals of their communities. In effect, in these festivals they asserted their "ethnic royalty." Whether spotlighting noble leaders or performers dressed as warriors, the rituals showcased Native men of high rank. Even Native musical performers were most likely higher-status Indian intellectuals.[35] The connection to the pre-Hispanic past was emphasized repeatedly. This was clear from the manner in which the Native elite dressed and the constructed arch that showcased the symbol of the Native city (the eagle perched on the cactus designating Tenochtitlan). There were constant references to the Aztec: the Native traditional music, dances, costuming, language, and warriors dressed in regalia who impressed the crowd with their martial abilities, thereby alluding to the military prowess of their ancestors.[36] The presence of Native leaders, especially in the jura, where they symbolically were portrayed as equal to the Spanish officials (on the same stage, performing a separate oath), served as a point of continuity with the pre-Columbian rituals.[37]

The political and social benefits of festival participation and sponsorship were substantial for the Native elite. But the financial costs were quite high because Native leaders funded parts of these festivals. The city councilmen paid for Native performances at Chapultepec and in the main square, but the indigenous leaders funded the entry at Tlatelolco and sometimes paid for their participation in the oath ceremony.[38] The entry at Tlatelolco may have cost Native communities as much as 14,000 pesos because Native leaders often hired Spaniards to design their arches, a costly endeavor.[39] To fund the festivals, Native officials collected funds from their own vassals.[40] These festival taxes were paid in addition to regular tribute payments that already burdened the indigenous poor. Festival collections often jeopardized Native ability to pay tribute for a number of years. In the cases of Tlaxcala and Huetzotzingo, the Spanish Crown allowed indigenous communities to waive the payment of tribute in lieu of celebrating the entry.[41]

However, tribute reprieves from the Crown were not always forthcoming. For example, in 1621, Tlatelolco governor Don Melchor de San Martín participated in the oath to Philip IV. The Natives paid for the construction and decoration of the stage, possibly costing as much as 1,000 pesos, collecting funds from subject villages. Later Don Melchor was jailed along with one of his alcaldes (councilmen) for failure to provide full tribute payments. Native governors were often held personally responsible for tribute payment failure and were frequently jailed in response. Unfortunately, in this case, he died in prison in 1623. It seems likely that Natives would have had the funds to pay tribute if not for this heavy ritual obligation.[42]

Tensions resulting from tribute burdens and the treatment of Native Americans could not always be glossed away by festival fanfare. Although these real-life issues rarely surfaced during the meticulously organized city council entry and jura, the entry as a ritual form lent itself quite easily to reinterpretation as some inhabitants linked better treatment of Native Americans and less onerous tribute demands to the ideal of good governance predictably highlighted in the viceregal entry ceremony.

For example, in 1543 Native Americans protested high tribute payments by re-creating (perhaps lampooning) the viceregal entry. In this case, large groups of Natives from towns near the capital feted a French Franciscan priest, claiming that he was a new viceroy. The cleric was treated to a processional fanfare, a triumphal arch, and a feast in imitation of Mexico City's official entry. During this entry, the priest (and other Franciscans who accompanied him) claimed that he brought word from France of an impending invasion of Mexico. Once the French were victorious, he claimed, the king of France would abolish Native tribute and labor requirements. The priest promised to protect them from mistreatment from the Spanish and to "return them to how they had been before [the arrival of the Spanish]."

The city councilmen were quite upset by these actions and feared it signaled an Indian revolt. Immediately calling for an investigation of the whole affair, they even considered formulating an official explanation of the long animosity between Spain and France for the Natives. In short, the councilmen sought to persuade the Natives to remain "good" vassals of Spain. Although there is no further record of this event, this alternative entry attests to the power of ritual to serve as political protest during the colonial period.[43] In this case, the ritual form of the entry served as a powerful tool to question the Spanish government and point out the hypocrisy of government's claims of "pious" rulership by drawing attention to abusive tribute payments and labor drafts. Unfortunately, it does not appear to have lessened Spanish demands for either.

The role of the Franciscans in the 1543 incident, a religious order that in Mexico historically characterized itself as a protector of Native Americans against Spanish abuse, is unclear. We can suspect that they encouraged Native leaders to use the entry ritual as a means to protest Spanish government abuse and neglect. Although their religious zeal waned over the colonial period, many Franciscans continued to see themselves as defenders and protectors of the Natives against labor drafts, burdensome tribute payments, and poor treatment. This was still evident in the late seventeenth century, when prominent Franciscan theologian Manuel de Argüello delivered a sermon that challenged the message of the viceregal entry.

In 1696, during the entrance of the viceroy, the count of Montezuma y Tula, Argüello described an imaginary arch, an arch that presented not the ideal government but the real one.[44] Argüello purposely chose the triumphal arch metaphor because the viceroy had already seen the actual ostentatious arch constructed by the city councilmen. Argüello pointed out the hypocrisy of the entry ceremony that sought to present a perfect city to the new governor by means of constant festivity and, in so doing, shielded the viceroy from the less than perfect reality of life in the capital. In order to learn about the real Mexico City, Argüello believed that the viceroy had to speak with those who suffered—the indigenous population. In fact, Argüello accused the Spanish elite of attempting to influence the viceroy by painting a picture of the city amenable to their own self-interests.[45] He criticized both the entry's false utopia and the unwillingness of officials to rule justly.

The cleric highlighted five illnesses (fever, blindness, limp, dehydration, and anxiety), each representing a political injustice that afflicted the city and required immediate attention from the viceroy.[46] Argüello presented each malady as though it were a painting on an imaginary triumphal arch with himself as the actor explaining each one. First, he expounded on fever, a physical ailment that afflicted the downtrodden and the humble because they lacked food, clothing, and shelter. Argüello described an imaginary painting in which a large group of Native Americans, suffering from hunger, went from house to house, searching for aid, until they were finally helped by a poor Franciscan priest in Tlatelolco. In this case, Argüello claimed to be describing an event that had actually occurred some weeks earlier in the capital. He pointed out that

> there was not one rich man, of the many that parade about in the capital, with millions [of pesos given over] to greed, with thousands to gambling, and hundreds to vanity, who would aid these Natives.[47]

He claimed that such a lack of charity and compassion on the part of the wealthy damned them eternally. In this fashion, the priest questioned the faith of the ruling elite because they lacked these essential characteristics of a good Christian.

In his depiction of blindness, Argüello focused his criticism on the city government, the very patrons of the viceregal entry. He believed that the councilmen were men of little vision who were so consumed with politics and self-interest that they were blind to the consequences of their actions or inaction. To prove his point, he singled out the poorly managed drainage project that had failed to end the constant flooding that afflicted Mexico City. On the real triumphal arches, the city councilmen had asked incoming viceroys to drain the lakes, implying that the failure of the desagüe project was due to neglect on the part of royal governors. However, Argüello blamed the lack of progress on the councilmen's own mismanagement of funds. What the friar called a "holocaust" of Natives (because their neighborhoods, especially Tlatelolco, were hardest hit by flooding) was due to "corruption." He was clearly aware that the city councilmen characteristically used funds designated for public works (that might have been utilized for the desagüe) to finance the viceregal entry.

In the third painting on the imaginary arch, the theologian used the idea of physical disability to attack the *alcaldes mayores,* the local officials who collected Native tribute. They also used the *repartimento,* a custom in which they forcibly sold unwanted and unneeded goods at exorbitant prices to Native communities in their jurisdiction.

According to this critic, these petty officials were corrupt and cruel. He pointed out that the alcaldes mayores swore an oath on the Bible to obey the law and not mistreat the Natives. Nonetheless, these officials knowingly took the oath with the "opposite goals," lying both to the king and God. In what must have been one of the more dramatic moments of the sermon, he asked his audience: Who had the greater faith? The heathen who swore true allegiance to false gods or the Spaniard who swore false allegiance to the true God?

With the fourth infirmity, dehydration of the body, Argüello claimed that the regular droughts that afflicted the Valley of Mexico were the direct result of Spanish abuse of the Native Americans. In his eyes, debt peonage, forced labor, low wages, and poor working conditions all were responsible for destroying Native lives. The priest claimed that such blatant disregard for Jesus's teachings literally kept seeds from growing in the fields "because it [was] impossible that ground where God [was] offended with infidelities [could] bear fruit."[48] No matter how many times officials sponsored processions to the Virgin of Remedies to alleviate drought, it would be pointless because other droughts would occur due to the moral depravity of Spaniards.

The fifth and final illness, expectation or anxiety, was psychological rather than physical. According to Argüello, Mexico City "waited like a man about to be hanged, dreading the feel of the noose tightening around his neck, overwhelmed by a deceptive, furtive yearning for freedom." He believed that all the problems of the city could be solved by decisive action of the viceroy. Without such action, Argüello predicated that the capital would continue to be "aflame in avarice, emaciated by neglect, made barren by a lack of faith that was measured in lies, [and] suffocated in hopeful anticipation."[49]

Felipe de Colina, head of the Franciscan province of San Diego (encompassing all of central Mexico), and Nicolas Massías, theological expert for the Inquisition, both commented on Argüello's sermon, finding it well grounded in the Scriptures, truthful, and inventive. They pointed out that because the viceroy was the only individual capable of resolving the issues at hand, Argüello had acted wisely to inform the "good physician" about the symptoms of the patient. Argüello's commentary on these imaginary paintings stood in stark contrast to the opulence and extravagance of the actual arches and viceregal entries. Argüello's imagined arch was conceived to point out the hypocrisy of the ruling mythology depicted on the real triumphal arch and that of the government as well. According to Colina, God instructed the prophets to raise an arch as a symbol of their commitment to remain true to an oath. In this sense, the oath at the viceregal arch was never truly kept.[50] Argüello believed that the oath of the viceroy to govern wisely had to be removed from the world of mere symbols; it had to be made real. The ideal government espoused on the paintings of the real arches had to be made manifest so that the real-life afflictions on his imaginary arch could finally be remedied.

Although his sermon was innovative, Argüello still relied on the standard metaphor: the viceroy as deliverer and savior. Argüello never explicitly attacked the royal government or mentioned the incompetence or corruption of previous viceroys. Perhaps he did not have to, for it was implied in every statement. His most stinging harangues were all directed at local authorities. Argüello, whose authority rested on the Scriptures, sought to change local elite behavior through appeals to the Christian precepts that the authorities themselves had made the dominant themes of the entry. Just like good governance in the entry, Argüello's ideal government was defined by charity, justice, and compassion. However, his golden age clearly hinged on fair treatment of Native Americans. Unfortunately, Native Americans continued to be abused at the hands of alcaldes mayores and wealthy Spaniards, and flooding, grain shortages, and famines continued to plague the metropolitan area. Nevertheless, for one small moment, he forced the ruling authorities to consider the plight of the Natives and the gap between their festival propaganda and their actual policies.[51]

The disparity over time between the real government and the imagined utopia represented in the festivals created a space by which vassals could question and judge the Spanish government, utilizing its own forms and language. In other words, alternative rituals, whether actually performed like the 1543 entry or imagined like that of Argüello, could be created and become politically effective weapons for those who were marginal to the power structure or who sought to change it. Although conceived as overt challenges to the established social order, alternative rituals were cloaked in the custom and tradition of the ritual form itself; during the sixteenth and seventeenth century, such rituals appear to have been viewed by authorities as an affront or a cause of concern. For example, Argüello's sermon caused quite a stir among the elite, and he himself expected to be dragged forth blindfolded to bear public humiliation for his controversial sermon.[52] However, such plays on official rituals were rarely seen as direct a challenge as outright rebellion. This accounts for the willingness of Hapsburg authorities even to endure parodies and satirical parades lampooning the government and officials.

Afro-Mexicans in the Hapsburg Entry

Although Native Americans constituted the majority of the population in and around the capital, a sizable portion of the city's inhabitants were African and Afro-Mexican. The increased presence of Afro-Mexicans in festivals coincided with their increased presence in the capital, because after 1580 the importation of African slaves to New Spain rose dramatically. The inclusion of Africans in certain government-sponsored rituals dates from the early 1500s.[53] By the end of the sixteenth century, their participation was much more regular and pronounced and included female dancers.[54] The capital was home to at least one Afro-Mexican female dance troupe that often danced in the Corpus Christi procession at the behest of city councilmen. Unfortunately, very few detailed descriptions of these dances were recorded, making this 1640 performance so important to our discussion.

Not only the increased presence of Africans in the population factored into Afro-Mexican participation in the entry but politics as well, because increasing discord defined Spanish-African relations. Especially during the early seventeenth century, officials feared that Africans conspired to revolt, and rebellions did take place in the capital and surrounding area. In fact, one of the paintings in the 1640 performance directly addressed Spanish fears of Afro-Mexican revolts. It depicted a dark rain cloud looming over the city that was in the process of being dissipated by the sun (the viceroy). The actor, who spoke on behalf of the female dancers, claimed that the viceroy had nothing to fear, so constant was the loyalty of performers. Thus officials utilized the rituals at their disposal to present a submissive and loyal Afro-Mexican vassal to the audience and sidestep the society's very real racial tensions.

The performance of the Afro-Mexican women before Villena illustrates how city councilmen and court artists may have manipulated performances to create their image of the perfect vassal.[55] The performance, paintings, and poetic explanation presented to the crowd all appear to have been designed by a well-educated male author, although it was all purported to be the opinion of the female dancers. The themes presented on the paintings are consistent with those connected to the triumphal arches. It is possible that the women helped design their own performance, but unfortunately, city council records rarely listed the specifics of commissioned performances.

Both the paintings of the triumphal arches and those presented by the dancers represented the viceroy as savior and a phoenix rising to create a new golden age. However, in this case, instead of receiving his authority to rule from the Spanish king, the viceroy received his power from a mythical African queen, thereby justifying his rule over Afro-Mexicans. However, in contrast to the paintings on the triumphal arches, the focus here was not truly the viceroy but a vision of the women submitting to Spanish rule and demonstrating their loyalty as representatives of their race and their gender. They were made to emphasize this fact when they knelt before the viceroy as each painting was presented.

The paintings repeatedly emphasized the fact that the women were representatives of black Mexicans. For example, in one image, the women presented themselves as a canon fuse from Guinea, the original African homeland for many blacks in the capital, in the process of being ignited by the rays of the sun, the viceroy. The fuse produced a gentle haze of black smoke, representing the love that the women felt for the viceroy after he had touched them with his rays. Furthermore, the actor, speaking as though he was one of the women, claimed, "Although the color white limits who I am/if my love is great, [this lack] is not a hindrance." Apparently, he was suggesting that the women could compensate for their black skin by their love for the viceroy or loyalty to the Spanish ruling system.

Another painting displayed Apollo, the ancient Greek sun god, burning a phoenix, the mythological creature then reborn, announcing the dawn of a new era. The women, compelled by their love of the viceroy, voluntarily entered into the flames and thereby were reborn. This was necessary because the women were "black ash/ already of injurious lineage, a charred pot." According to the explanation, they were blemished and defective, and only through union or consummation with the viceroy could they be reborn to a superior state, or, put another way, only through their acceptance of Spanish authority could their lives and the status of their race improve. In this fashion, the painting alluded to racial mixing in which lighter skin color translated into a higher position in the caste system.

As with the two paintings discussed above, most of the images linked race, submission to Spanish authority, and romantic love. This was further emphasized in a painting that showed a heart (symbolizing the women) physically moved by a large moon surrounded by a starry night sky. The spoken explanation by the actor claimed that these black women were so enthralled with the handsomeness and valor of the viceroy (the moon) that they had lost their senses and fallen madly and hopelessly in love. In an ironic sidelight, the poet cast doubt on the validity of this sentiment, stating that "when it comes to love, there was no trusting a woman."

Popular beliefs also were woven into this complex presentation of race, loyalty, and romance. In one painting, the women offered the viceroy the *higa*, or black hand charm. People believed that the black hand, originally a symbol of fertility from Africa, could ward off the effects of the evil eye. According to the actor, the amulet, here a symbol for the spoils of conquest, was given to the viceroy because he represented the Spaniards, the conquerors of the New World. However, the painting also alluded to men as conquerors of women, this during an era defined by the culture of Don Juanism (the male reputation based on the seduction of as many women as possible). In the accompanying poem, the actor pointed out that the hand of the higa must be black in order to truly ward off the evil eye. It was as though the women were presenting their own hands (symbols of their labor) to the victorious Spaniards, in this case represented by Villena. They did this apparently in order to ensure that his reign would be successful.

The paintings and accompanying explanation emphasized the ideal qualities such as fidelity, devotion, humility, industriousness, and obedience that every woman was expected to possess in colonial society, according to Spanish Catholic moralists of the time.[56]

However, the constant emphasis on romantic themes such as swooning at the sight of the viceroy, being conquered by his actions, and fusing with him created, at least within the poetic explanation, quite an eroticized view of the women. This presentation was further heightened by the fact that the language utilized in the actor's explanation was more intimate than that used in official performances presented at the triumphal arches. The women, via the actor, did not call the viceroy "Su Excelencia" (Your Excellency) as was customary but rather utilized the more informal "tú" (you), an address in Spanish reserved for friends, family members, or lovers. This romantic discourse played on common stereotypes of the period that claimed that black women were more sensual and licentious than Spanish or Native women and that female slaves welcomed illicit relations with their white masters.[57] Such relationships between white men and their black slaves did exist, but many slave women were physically and psychologically abused by slave owners. They sometimes had their children and husbands sold away (and thus were forcibly separated from them) or they were not allowed to marry a man of their own choosing. The horrors of slavery were clearly ignored by this entry performance. As might be expected of an official presentation, slavery was mentioned directly in only one instance. The women presented an image of two black men in chains pleading for their freedom. The viceroy, according to the women, was renowned for his love of liberty, and they beseeched him to free the men depicted. The actor claimed that by doing so, the viceroy would demonstrate his valor and gallantry and forever "enslave" the men spiritually. In short, his virtue would secure their loyalty without the need for chains. The crowd apparently cheered after the actor explained this painting.

This depiction of the manumission of slaves by a benevolent and virtuous Spaniard had limited basis in fact. Indeed, among manumitted slaves most had their freedom bestowed by Spaniards because of loyal service or because they had managed to purchase their liberty once an agreement over price was reached with the slave owner. However, women and their children were much more likely to be manumitted than males. The performers were called morenas criollas, a term that during the seventeenth century usually meant a black woman of some status, usually free and born in Mexico. Thus the dancers literally represented those women (and their children) who constituted the majority of manumitted slaves, the free people of color in the capital and their descendants. They appeared as living examples of the benefits of loyalty to the Spanish.

The exact identity of these perfect vassals is unknown. However, the author did compare the women to a fine necklace of jet and glass beads. This was an important reference to the colonial dress code, issued as early as 1598 and then reiterated in 1607 and 1612, which expressly forbid women of color from wearing pearls because these expensive white beads were to be limited to white women.[58] That the decrees were totally ineffectual was suggested by seventeenth-century traveler Thomas Gage, who commented at length about the rich dress worn by *mulata* and black women in Mexico City, finding it both striking and scandalous.[59] In this "script," invented by white authors, the perfect black female vassal of official propaganda was made to wear more humble black beads, beads appropriate to her status and race required by race-based sumptuary laws.

In the end, the women appeared as loyal and submissive, accepting of their subordinate social and legal position in the colonial hierarchy. The presentation washed over a history of tension, abuse, unrest, and injustice that were all subsumed in an image of black women celebrating their inferiority and loving their oppressor. But the performers also represented acculturated free people of color who culturally were part of colonial society with only limited connection to Africa. The women did not wear traditional African clothing but wore dress suitable for Afro-Mexican women, albeit fancy enough for the occasion of a viceregal entry. References to African heritage included the ancient queen who appeared only long enough to give her ruling scepter to the Spanish viceroy, the reference to Guinea, and the higa, which had been integrated into the larger popular culture of the capital. Thus in contrast to the Native elite, the Afro-Mexicans did not celebrate their African heritage but rather their relationship to Spaniards in the colonial milieu. It is true that not all Africans or people of African descent shared the same language, history, culture, and nationality, possibly making it difficult to present one performance to represent them all. But this more personal and intimate colonial image of Spaniard and African alluded to real relationships because Africans worked for individual Spaniards as domestic servants and laborers in the capital.

We may never know how the Afro-Mexicans of 1640 viewed their elaborate performance for the viceroy. We can surmise that they garnered substantial distinction from a performance in such a prestigious venue as well as earning a sizable sum from the city councilmen. If nothing else, their performance could have served as a marketing tool to acquire more business and further patronage from the local and royal elite.

Not only performers but other citizens benefited directly from government-sponsored festivals, which no doubt affected their perception of those events. Festivals such as the entry led to a sizable transfer of wealth from the city government to certain residents.[60] Day laborers, construction workers, cleanup crews, bakeries, tailors, and other artisans all benefited from city council largesse. Businesses such as taverns, not directly involved in festival preparation, also benefited because of an increase in clientele: all of the visitors who came to the capital and all those citizens who got off work for the festival. Citizens did have a choice in where, when, and how they would engage the rituals. Their interaction with government festivals could change from one festival to another, depending on where they lived in the city, their level of acculturation, and their personal preferences in entertainment. A large percentage of the city's inhabitants did attend these festivals (if Spanish estimates, for example, of crowds of 40,000 in the zócalo are to be believed), although a certain number of the spectators would have been visitors from the hinterland. Other inhabitants probably disregarded the fanfare and used the days off from work to celebrate privately at home, at taverns, or at *pulquerías* (taverns that sold the traditional indigenous alcoholic beverage made from maguey), disregarding, if not dismissing, the festival altogether.

Conclusion

In colonial rituals of statecraft in Mexico City, the ruling elite (the city councilmen) expended enormous effort to create a complex set of performances that would animate the city and turn citizens into political performers. Although Native Americans and Afro-Mexicans did indeed become actors in these dramas, in real political terms their power was limited. Overall, the message of festivals such as the entry and the oath was one that emphasized the separate (never equal) racial components of colonial society. Performances of these vassals affirmed one of the most important points of government propaganda, namely, the idea of hierarchical unity. Individual ethnicities were to know and maintain their place in society but were joined by their submission to (and dependence on) the Spanish governmental system. More important, they would benefit by doing so. The African slave would garner his freedom, and indigenous elites would procure prestige and continued local control of their communities. Thus the ritual and the message embedded within it bolstered the colonial system by emphasizing hierarchical unity and providing "spaces" for Native leaders and prominent Afro-Mexicans to act as ethnic representatives. The entry and the jura, to a certain extent, were festivals in which social and racial difference was identified, even celebrated, yet these differences were subsumed under common images and symbols of Spanish ruling authority.[61] In other words, Hapsburg Mexico City was a world in which the Spanish ruling elite could publicly accept Native and African traditions only when they stood refashioned and recontextualized by the official Spanish-derived ritual.

Colonial festival statecraft not only identified ethnic representatives but differentiated between different groups, in this case, Afro-Mexicans and Native Americans, based on how each group was conceptualized via white elite stereotypes and realities. For example, the entry and the jura initially played on the fact that both Native and Spanish cultures emphasized festival traditions that presented complex religio-political concepts to impress spectators and manipulate their acceptance of the political and religious elite. Festivals provided continuity between the pre-Columbian and colonial eras during the sixteenth century. The Native and Spanish elite appeared together publicly at pivotal junctures, demonstrating in this manner their loyalties and ethnic identifications, and gave symbolic form to the colonial political framework. Although the Native elite were part of the Spanish governmental system and very hispanized, they were consistently asked to portray themselves in terms of the Conquest period, as the living legacy of subjugated ancient rulers.

For the hispanized Native American nobility, participation in and sponsorship of the oath and the entry served to cement their position in the eyes of the Spanish elite. It also gave them the opportunity to impress and gain influence with the viceroys, whose patronage was essential to their success as legitimate rulers of their own people. Their participation also enhanced their status vis-à-vis their own community as they wined, dined, and parlayed with the highest Spanish official in the land, and such festivals formed part of a sequence of festivals of legitimation within their own communities.

Afro-Mexicans performed as hispanized free people of color, living examples of Spanish manumission policies and trends. They did not celebrate their African heritage to the extent that Native leaders performed theirs but rather were made to emphasize their place in the Spanish sphere of colonial society. They had no official place in the political system as the Native governors did and therefore did not swear a separate oath in any African language to the king of Spain during the jura ceremony. The Afro-Mexican was made to celebrate a more personal relationship with Spaniards, emphasized by the very language ascribed to the performers. As Afro-Mexicans they performed their loyalty, but as black women they performed as females romantically linked to and interested in elite male Spaniards.

Hapsburg festivals of statecraft created a language of governing built around ritual that served the colonial state, yet at the same time, it also created an acceptable (or less dangerous) means by which citizens could consider good governance and their role as vassals. Woven within the very fabric of the festival were the elements of potential social critique because anyone could judge the effectiveness of the government and the moral character of the viceroys. Ritual, so pervasive a medium for the discussion of political concepts and societal values (and religious beliefs), became an important public forum by which different citizens made known their views on such matters. They, like the Franciscan Argüello, consistently sought to connect the idealized concept of good governance to actual policy at the local level.

In the final analysis, Spaniards, Afro-Mexicans, and Natives each experienced the festivals in a unique fashion, and therein lay the power of such rituals of legitimacy because they could promote social cohesion utilizing symbols (and ritual acts) that held diverse (even contradictory) cultural meanings. In this instance, the common action of witnessing or participating in the festivals and acceptance of the general parameters of the Spanish ruling system fostered certain aspects of societal unity, even though a citizen's perception of the event was determined by his ethnicity, socioeconomic position, attitude toward the Spanish system and authorities, and location as spectator or participant in the ritual sequence. Average citizens expected such grand displays and considered them a necessary part of life in the capital. Public spectacle framed the lives of the city's inhabitants, and certain points of commonality in and shared assumptions about government-sponsored spectacles united the rulers and the ruled.

All the inhabitants of the capital, if they desired to do so, could "read" these spectacles and interpret the concept of good governance in light of their own perspective and thereby interpret their own identities as loyal subjects. Although the fluidity of the symbols and their various meanings appeared to bolster the Spanish system under the Hapsburgs, these spectacles provided the language and the means to express dissatisfaction with the system in some fashion. As we have seen, rituals such as the entry and the jura never resolved social tension and ethnic conflict but merely presented Spanish elite schemes to defer real resolutions to such conflict.

Chapter 4
Celebrating Apollo

In 1747, Mexico City celebrated King Ferdinand VI's ascension to the Spanish throne. During the ceremony the royal ensign performed the oath in three locations as was customary. The Native governors of San Juan, Santiago Tlatelolco, Texcoco, Tacuba, Coyoacan, Xochimilco, and Mexicalizingo were in attendance on the palace stage. After the ceremony, indigenous dancers performed and the city council sponsored fireworks. Among the pyrotechnical wonders was a giant fountain, 157 feet in diameter, crowned by a bronze eagle, that became a "spring, not of crystals but of flames" that remained illuminated for three hours.

As part of the ceremony, the city council showcased three specially constructed stages that provided seating for episcopal, municipal, indigenous, and royal authorities. The city council's round stage was thirty feet in diameter, forty-two feet high, and shaped like a medieval castle. All the stages displayed paintings that were the focus of great curiosity and interest. One painting showed Jupiter, king of the ancient Greek gods, graciously relinquishing his lightning rods to Apollo (Ferdinand VI), who showered sunshine on Europe and the Americas. Other paintings depicted Apollo controlling the seasons, receiving praise from Mother Nature, and being honored by figures representing Asia, Africa, Europe, and America. One image referenced the legend of "Non Plus Ultra" (No Further), wherein the ancient Greek hero Hercules erected two pillars at the mouth of the Mediterranean Sea. These pillars limited seafaring traffic in the ancient world. To go beyond the pillars of Hercules (the Strait of Gibraltar) meant to venture into the unknown and to court disaster. Now Hercules was forced to remove the pillars because of the Spanish discovery of the New World. The painting celebrated the Spanish because they had single-handedly broadened the horizons of Europeans.

Other associations and guilds erected temporary architectural structures in or near the main square to celebrate Ferdinand VI. The cathedral chapter commissioned an arch on the facade of the archbishop's palace. The lace and thread makers guilds commissioned a giant solid stone column some thirty-three feet high on which was placed a five-and-a-half-foot statue of Ferdinand VI, painted purple and trimmed with gold. The painters guild erected an arch over a section of the facade of the viceregal palace. It was eighty feet high and thirty-six feet wide and showcased two Atlantean figures representing the ancient Greek painters Timantes and Apeles. Three engraved panels of silver depicted the tools utilized by painters in their trade, namely palettes, paints, tints, and brushes.

Some blocks away, the members of the Real Protomedicato, the professional medical association, decorated and illuminated the Church of the Hospital of Our Lady of the Conception and Jesus Nazareño. They also hosted two evenings of fireworks in the main plaza and constructed a triumphal arch in the cemetery of the church. This arch depicted Apollo (as the sun) standing above a giant rainbow that reached across the Atlantic Ocean, uniting the two parts of the empire, Spain and the Americas.

Twenty-seven guilds paraded with their ingeniously devised floats, providing entertainment for nine nights. In front of the palace, designated individuals (in some cases professional actors from the Coliseo, the main theater in the capital) performed a poetic recital explaining the allegorical theme of each float. After the performance before the viceregal palace, the floats moved through the streets of the city. Although the parades began in the late afternoon, the *pulqueros* (owners of pulquerías, which sold the traditional indigenous alcoholic drink), the *curtidores* (leather tanners), and the *obrajeros* (foremen of colonial workshops/factories) continued their merriment until dawn. Some 1,500 individuals, all elaborately costumed, accompanied wheeled floats that varied in size and shape depending on the theme being presented. Generally, they were at least nineteen feet long and eight feet wide. Some of the floats were *tableaux vivants* with real people representing different historical figures, including the monarch. All the floats were illuminated by hundreds of large votive candles and were quite spectacular to see. For example, hundreds of candles on the float of the silversmiths caused the panels of silver, weighing 652 pounds, to literally sparkle like the sun.

The confectioners, candle makers, and dye masters specialized in pyrotechnic displays. One night, they debuted a beautiful float filled with fireworks. This "chariot of fire" was ignited in two stages: first, giant flaming letters, *VIVA EL REY FERNANDO SEXTO* (Long Live King Fernidand VI), excited the crowd, and then the entire float exploded on cue. The second evening, the three guilds presented a giant wooden horse and, reminiscent of the legendary Trojan horse of antiquity, ten men jumped out of its belly, all carrying lit sparklers. Finally, the equestrian marvel was set ablaze. Not content with this, the three guilds then commissioned a pyrotechnic naval battle, a large fountain of fire, a giant made of reeds, and three large castles that all exploded in sequence.

Mexico City's educators and students also celebrated the coronation of Ferdinand. The teachers guild (*maestros del arte de escribir, contar y leer*) sponsored a special mass at the Church of Jesús María. Three hundred children dressed in costumes, wearing precious stones and pearls, participated. The university professors held poetry contests, encouraging all citizens to submit works for consideration by a panel of judges. A significant number of learned individuals responded, and on the designated day, the winners recited their work in the elaborately decorated halls of the university. The event was followed by yet another firework display, featuring an exploding obelisk topped with a large statue of Ferdinand VI.

For ten days matadors tested their skill against ninety-eight bulls. There were horse and even rabbit races and other games sponsored by the city councilmen. The elite of the city demonstrated their horsemanship and starred in jousts and the *sortija*, where each rider, at full gallop, attempted to throw a lance at a target displayed on an arch especially constructed for this competition. Gentlemen riders carried large leather shields with emblems that lauded the monarch and declared the participant's devotion to him. Many shields depicted a united Europe and America in the form of a lion (the royal symbol) holding two globes. One shield showcased a lion, a horse, an elephant, and a camel, representing the four parts of the world, subjugated by the powerful arm of Ferdinand.[1]

As this description of 1747 demonstrates, the ascension of a Bourbon monarch to the Spanish throne produced a spectacular response in Mexico during the 1700s and marked a dramatic change from the jura celebrations of the previous century. The eighteenth century in Mexico (as in Europe) was an age of monarchical absolutism, when kings sought to make themselves as powerful in practice as they were in theory. The Spanish Crown emphasized the role of the monarch, and Bourbon officials in Mexico placed emphasis and primacy on royal festivals in an effort to bolster the image of the monarch and make his presence more resoundly felt in the daily lives of inhabitants. Given this new focus, officials reprioritized government-sponsored celebrations, emphasizing, creating, or eliminating them in line with their new political philosophies. In the process, they reconceptualized the idea of good governance, the ideal prince, and the perfect vassal so specifically articulated by their Hapsburg predecessors. To these officials, many of whom were newly arrived *peninsulares* (Spaniards born in Spain), the oath ceremony was the perfect medium for vassals literally to display their loyalty to their sovereign.

The Bourbon Oath Ceremony: Architecture and Illumination

During the eighteenth century, most citizens would probably witness at least three juras in their lifetime. Mexico celebrated Philip V (1701), Louis I (1724), Ferdinand VI (1747), Charles III (1760), Charles IV (1789–90), and Ferdinand VII (1808 and again in 1814). In 1808, Ferdinand VII ascended the throne as Napoleon Bonaparte invaded Spain. Napoleon held Ferdinand prisoner and named his brother, Joseph, as ruler of Spain and its dominions. In 1814, after Napoleonic forces were defeated, Ferdinand regained the throne and Spanish officials in Mexico celebrated a second oath ceremony.

In the 1700s, the oath ceremony grew from a one- or two-day event into a four-week display of pageantry. The elaborate public entertainments usually associated with the seventeenth-century inaugural entrance of the viceroy now came to characterize this festival devoted to the king. Detailed published descriptions with pages numbering in the hundreds recounted and memorialized the oath celebrations, whereas in the previous century the jura had rated only limited descriptions of not more than ten pages, most of these never published.

The focus of the Bourbon jura, like its seventeenth-century counterpart, was the ceremony in the main plaza. Bourbon officials continued to follow the basic format well established under the Hapsburg authorities but dramatically increased the ostentation of the stages where officials were to be seated. The stages now took the form of triumphal arches with officials seated at the ground level.[2]

The larger and more numerous stages also provided festival planners with new locations for paintings in order to develop official jura propaganda. Bourbon authorities viewed ephemeral architecture much the same way that Hapsburg authorities did when designing arches for the viceregal entrance. One eighteenth-century author expressed the political importance of arches and other monuments when he wrote:

> The natural Reason of Republics of greater maturity and Government invented these MONUMENTS in order to instill the glory of the Nation. With these [structures] they hope either to inform of some interesting event or inspire (as in the oath to the King) a Magnificent, and Loving Idea, of the sovereign. The result is always of some noble public utility, ministered by means of EDUCATION.

The architectural components of the oath ceremony had to be erudite "in order that through education, the people [were] made pleasant and cultivated, because these works [are] not worth their cost, if they [do] not better those who enjoy them."[3]

Illumination and fireworks were essential and ubiquitous because officials wished to impress the inhabitants. An anonymous eighteenth-century author wrote, "The nighttime illumination forms the most eloquent Language with which one can persuade the People." Public reaction to these Bourbon light shows was apparently very positive. The same author continued, "The commoners of New Spain have such a passion for this type of nighttime Spectacle that it can form one of the tenets of their character."[4] The effective use and control of light suggested the power of the government and its servants. For a preindustrial society, where schedules were controlled by the rising and setting of the sun, the Bourbons had the ability to change nature on a grand, albeit temporary scale.[5]

The Bourbon profligate use of light can also be connected to their suspicions of the plebe and of popular customs. Colonial officials felt that rebellious and licentious behavior was encouraged by darkness. They believed that streets with lighting discouraged illicit and illegal activities. For example, although the plaza was lit with 656 street-lamps during the oath of 1747, authorities also placed guards at each entrance of the zócalo during the nighttime revelries.[6] Here ceremony and the desire for order were neatly conflated. Eventually, they installed street lighting in the capital as part of their concept of modernization and to ensure public safety.

Apollo and His Kingdom

The powerful role of illumination and fireworks in these ceremonies only underscored the metaphorical depiction of the king as the sun god Apollo, controller of light. The depiction of the royal person had almost always been associated with the divine beings of mythology. The Hapsburg era triumphal arches for the viceregal entries had portrayed the kings of Spain as any number of ancient gods granting local authority to their servant, the viceroy/hero. However, in the Hapsburg oath ceremonies, the monarch was never presented as a mythological being; he was simply introduced to the populace via his own portrait. The allegorical connection to Apollo was not new, however, in Spain. Beginning with Philip II, Spanish monarchs had been portrayed as the Greek sun god. Nevertheless, this analogy was something of a novelty for colonial Mexico because on only one occasion, in 1640, had the king been represented as Apollo during a large public display.[7]

Almost every facet of the Bourbon jura depicted the Spanish monarch as Apollo. Festival designers and officials claimed that as the sun ruled over the other planets and gave them light, so too did the Spanish king govern and aid his realm.[8] For example, during the 1808 jura, Ferdinand was in fact a king without a throne. Consequently, paintings showed the sun hidden behind clouds or shielded from view by mountains, analogous to Ferdinand's inability to exercise fully his royal will. Nonetheless, his "rays" were shown reaching New Spain. The paintings promised that the sun would shine brightly in the future since Ferdinand would scare away the dark Napoleonic clouds and regain his throne.[9] New Spanish inhabitants would always be loyal regardless of political problems and the thousands of miles that separated Spain and the Americas.[10]

Cast as the celestial giver of light, the king of Spain became the ideal prince in the eighteenth-century oath ceremony and his actions became the basis for a redefined concept of good governance, one that emphasized the power, grandeur, and innate virtues of the Spanish monarch. The king, it was asserted, was a morally superior and truly virtuous individual, divinely preordained to rule. However, the floats, arches, and platforms also clearly defined the actions and responsibilities of the monarch to his subjects.

First, the imagery consistently presented the Bourbon monarchs as the living repositories of virtues such as prudence, wisdom, and justice, which were considered the fundamental pillars of the art of governing. These superior qualities in essence justified the monarch's ascension to the throne and his right to rule America even though divine will chose the man who would be king. Officials claimed that the king could right wrongs, calm raging rivers, and even temporarily stop death. He was depicted as being extremely kind and an avid patron of the arts.[11] The king was so virtuous that in the 1760 arch of the medical doctors he was shown attracting his vassals to his cause like a bright light attracted moths.[12] Paramount among all the many virtues of the monarch was the ability to administer justice wisely.[13]

The monarch's personal actions and policies were connected to the popular well-being in the here and now. Expectations ran high at the news that a new monarch had ascended the throne, as paintings depicted rainbows, abundance, and the still desired golden age.[14] The theme of abundance first appeared in the 1724 paintings celebrating Louis I and was continued in later juras. Artists and festival sponsors depicted the king causing fields of wheat to grow and entire valleys to bloom, verdant and radiant.[15] Paintings also emphasized that the monarch's generosity to his subjects was vital to economic prosperity. He was expected to give resources and wealth to his colony. Paintings of the physicians guild showed that the king would quickly console and aid his subjects in their time of need in the same manner that a good doctor would treat an ailing patient.[16]

Fiscal Concerns

The Bourbon officials who organized a magnificent spectacle to honor this Spanish Apollo were also fiscally conservative, concerned with the efficient and appropriate use of government funds, characteristics that they believed had been severely lacking under the profligate Hapsburg colonial administration. They had clear notions regarding the utility and cost of festivals. Although they recognized and actively encouraged a sumptuous oath ceremony, they were not willing to go into debt to fund it. This was in marked contrast to their Hapsburg predecessors.

Early in the Bourbon period, the aldermen continued deficit spending policy for ceremonials. For example, the 1724 oath to Louis I was funded by 9,750 pesos procured from auctioning the right to collect the rents of tenants leasing city council buildings.[17] However, after 1727, officials rarely engaged in deficit spending in order to finance festivals. This resulted from a royal decree suggesting that the city council auction the right to host the bullfights to the highest bidder (a private entrepreneur), who would then charge admission. Bullfights, with about 18,000 to 20,000 people in attendance, soon became the cornerstone of Bourbon festival patronage. The oath festivities of 1747, 1760, 1789, 1808, and 1814 all would have been very different without revenues from the *corrida*.[18]

Details of these bullfight *remates* (auctions) are limited. Still, extant data demonstrate how successful the new policy was since the remate more than paid for essential state contributions to the jura. For the 1760 oath, for example, the city council collected 22,515 pesos from the remate, more than enough to cover the cost of the stages, illumination, and fireworks. Bullfights for Ferdinand VII's ascension (1814) generated 47,953 pesos, allowing the city council to spend 46,090 pesos on the festival and keep a small profit.[19]

The success of the bullfight remate explains how officials could increase the ostentation of the state-sponsored aspects of the ceremony and still keep pace with inflation at the end of the century. Expenditures for the jura steadily increased over the century. The oath to Philip V cost 6,469 pesos, while the ceremonies for Louis I twenty-four years later were almost double, at 11,148 pesos. The cost of the festivities for Ferdinand VI is unknown, although extant detailed descriptions demonstrate that it was similar to that of the later oath for Charles III. The festivities (for Charles III) reached at least 22,515 pesos. The oath to Charles IV cost an extraordinary 108,571 pesos. Finally, the festivities for Ferdinand VII (1808) came to 10,846 pesos and (1814) 46,090 pesos.[20] The remate was so successful that city councilmen began to utilize public funds previously committed to the public ceremonies to host private events such as banquets or masked balls for themselves and their social circle. Although the oath to Charles IV was exceptional in terms of its overall cost, it represents this larger trend and is worth further analysis. The public segments of the oath totaled 29,801 pesos, only one-third of the cost of the festival. Much of the rest of the cost went to banquets, dances, plays, dinners, clothing, stipends, and servants for the elite.[21] Thus most of the public entertainment was not provided by officials (who used the funds to finance their own events) but by the guilds and associations of the city.

The Virgin of Remedies: From the Madonna to Conquest Virgin

Although the Bourbon oath ceremony was extravagant and worthy of the many published descriptions, it was an occasional festival tied to the unpredictable life cycle of royal leaders. As a result, officials and the populace were limited in their enjoyment of these celebrations of the monarch. This was unacceptable to the Crown. Therefore colonial officials were forced to either create or appropriate other celebrations in order to maintain a denser ceremonial calendar. In fact, authorities did just that. They used the Virgin of Remedies, the capital's most important Marian image, and the celebration of the feast of Saint Hippolytus to accomplish their ceremonial purposes.

By appropriating the premiere Marian image of the capital for their purposes, Bourbon officials sought to capitalize on popular devotion to the Virgin of Remedies, renowned for her miraculous powers. The Virgin of Remedies was the primary protectress of the city against drought, famine, and epidemic disease and had only traveled by procession to the city to serve as intercessor for the entire capital population during crises. However, eighteenth-century royal officials began to claim her as the personal patroness of the Spanish Crown, thereby usurping the authority of the city councilmen.

Eighteenth-century royal officials appropriated the Virgin for royal festivals, the safe arrival of the fleet, and even to intervene during the illnesses of viceroys. From 1700 to 1810, Remedies was brought to the city on thirty-two occasions, and one-half of those processions were for royal events or the fleet.[22] During this same period, the city council only brought out the image for traditional local religious reasons, such as drought and famine relief, while the viceroy only organized a procession to the capital for political (imperial) reasons. Royal processions were in stark contrast to the more traditional penitential processions asking for intervention on behalf of the city. For example, in 1708, the Virgin of Remedies traveled to the cathedral in honor of the birth of Louis, son of Philip V. Remedios had apparently protected the royal family and guaranteed the good health of the mother and child. Instead of the traditional solemn novena, nine days of bullfights, plays, fireworks, and a parade with floats characterized the event, resulting in a festival not unlike the oath to the king.[23]

Increasingly royal officials became unwilling to share her with the city council. In 1719, for example, a severe drought afflicted the central valley, but royal officials refused to give their permission for a procession. One month later, however, they brought the Virgin from her shrine to the city to pray for the welfare of the monarch.[24] In addition, royal festivals took place with increasing frequency at the shrine itself with little regard for the established devotional calendar of nearby Native American communities.[25] In fact, royal authorities sometimes refused to return the Virgin to her shrine once their festivities were completed at the cathedral. In some instances, she remained at the cathedral for years. The city councilmen objected, believing such actions disrespectful to the image. In 1720, the aldermen in desperation sent a secret missive to the king, decrying this situation. Unfortunately, the viceroy learned of their duplicity and forced them to apologize for their effrontery. They did so rather reluctantly and immediately instituted an investigation to learn who among them had leaked this information to the governor, with the expressed purpose of chastising that individual. Even with the dressing-down by the viceroy, the city council did not back down on this issue and conflicts continued. Finally in 1750 a decree from the king pronounced that Remedios was the royal Virgin, naming her the Conquistadora (conqueror).[26]

This association of Remedies with the conquest had not been made for over a hundred years. The original apparition histories on the Virgin of Remedies had discussed her pivotal role during the conquest of the city in 1519. Apparently Cortés had placed her image in the Aztec Templo Mayor, beseeching her to bring rain. A miracle occurred (she caused it to rain), thereby proving to the Aztec the superiority of the Christian religion over their own, especially the rain deity, Tlaloc. Later, during the Noche Triste, when the Spanish were routed from the city and suffered heavy casualties, Remedies appeared at their side to throw dirt into the eyes of Indian warriors. Thus she became the conquest Virgin, fighting to implement Catholic Spanish rule in Mexico. However, in the late 1500s, this bellicose version of Mary was repackaged and altered. She became associated with Native Americans and with African slaves, not just Spaniards. Many miracles (curing the sick and lame, for example) were attributed to her. Right about this time, the aldermen gained control of the image and the shrine. Remedies in the seventeenth century had become the Madonna aiding all, and it was this benevolent, more universal interpretation that served as the basis for the city's widespread devotion to her.[27] However, with the 1750 decree, the battle between the city councilmen and royal officials over the meaning of the image was settled in favor of the latter.

As a result of this decision the city councilmen began to disassociate themselves from the Virgin of Remedies. Although the aldermen continued to host processions for traditional reasons, they had begun to claim lack of funding to support such events. They attempted to convince the Consulado of Cádiz (the international merchant guild) to patronize at least some of the processions because many were dedicated to the safe arrival of the fleet.[28] In 1789, a popular clamor arose for a procession of Remedies in response to an earthquake, but the city fathers claimed that they were too busy dealing with the disaster to host a procession. They even stated that they were doing their real job and did not have time to attend festivals. And when others hosted the procession that year in their place, they did not attend. Clearly, the city council no longer viewed the Virgin of Remedies as "their" patroness, and they were unwilling to expend municipal funds for the Virgin, now co-opted by royal authorities.

Instead they became devotees of the Virgin of Guadalupe. She saved the city during the plague of 1736 when Remedios had failed to do so. In 1756, the city celebrated a huge festival to Guadalupe in honor of her designation as patroness of the viceroyalty.[29] The Virgin of Guadalupe was a particularly attractive image as she was considered uniquely Mexican.

The Raising of the Royal Banner

Bourbon officials sought to encourage identification with Spain and the monarchy, hence their appropriation of the devotion to the Virgin of Remedies and the celebration of the oath, but both of these festivals did not occur annually. Therefore royal officials resurrected an annual festival that Hapsburg officials had ceased to celebrate decades before the Bourbons took control of Spain and the Americas.[30] The feast of Saint Hippolytus on August 13 had been a festival that glorified the Conquest, the empire, and the subjugation of Mexico to the greater glory of Spain. On this date in 1521, Cortés had been victorious against the Aztec and took control of the city. The festival originally commemorated the death of Spaniards during the Noche Triste (July 11, 1519), when the Europeans had been expelled from the city. The church of Saint Hippolytus sat on the location where many had lost their lives. The festival had both extolled the monarchy and the conquerors who had labored and died in honor of that monarchy. Bourbon officials labeled the festival the celebration of the raising of the Royal Banner (*el alza del pendón real*).

Royal officials ordered the city councilmen to commemorate the event with a parade of dignitaries on horseback, led by the royal ensign, who carried the royal banner aloft through the streets to the church of Saint Hippolytus. Afterward, all the officials returned to the cathedral for a high mass service. In 1721, royal authorities sought to take advantage of the 200th anniversary of the festival, believing that it could serve as a model for future celebrations. With this in mind, the viceroy instructed Gabriel Mendieta Rebollo, city council secretary, to research the festival in the city archives in order to ascertain how it was celebrated in the past.[31] Officials felt that only through an appropriate level of splendor could they "motivate and persuade the general public."[32] Based on the results of his investigation, the city councilmen hosted bullfights, a joust, dances in the cathedral, and fireworks. They illuminated the downtown area, ordered the guilds to parade, and decreed that citizens decorate their houses. They even reestablished the religious procession that had characterized the very early sixteenth-century celebrations. However, the most unique aspect of the 1721 festival was the inclusion of Native American leaders and confraternities in the festivities. The indigenous elite paraded and attended the religious service at the cathedral. In both cases, they immediately followed the city council, apparently a great honor.[33] The Hapsburg version of the festival had rarely included Native Americans; thus for the first time in almost 200 years, Natives celebrated the king and indirectly the conquest of their own ancestors, thus reaffirming their own continued subjugation. Although later festivals lacked the tremendous sumptuousness of this anniversary celebration, city inhabitants were asked to commemorate the monarch every year.

The Entrance of the Viceroy

Bourbon officials in Mexico selectively created a new hierarchy of festivals in the capital that complemented and articulated their ideas about the importance of the king in the lives of colonial vassals. As one might expect, there was little room in their conceptualization of good governance for an elaborate viceregal entry ceremony. As a matter of fact, new Bourbon officials of the eighteenth century saw the overwhelming authority of the viceroy, in theory and in practice, as contrary to their desire to enhance the authority of the monarchy. The establishment of the intendant system in 1786 struck a severe blow to the viceroy's traditional authority. New intendants, or governors, young men sent directly from Spain, accountable only to the king, now ruled in the provincial areas. Consequently, in those areas the viceroy lost much of his authority. However, well before the creation of the intendant system, the Crown sought to alter the symbolic status of the viceroy via a reform of the entry ceremony.

First, Bourbon officials reiterated the old Hapsburg decrees demanding that the cost of this ceremony be reduced dramatically. Unlike their predecessors, they strictly enforced these decrees. In 1701, a decree arrived limiting the cost of the entire viceregal entry to 8,000 pesos, 12,000 pesos less than the average cost in the seventeenth century. City councilmen attempted to sidestep the decree as they had others in the past, but repeated correspondence from Spain demanded that the entrance not exceed the stipulated amount. Municipal authorities heeded the royal warning, and the entrances of 1710 and 1716 appear to have cost approximately 8,000 pesos.[34] However, in 1722, city councilmen spent 12,000 pesos, agreeing to pay the extra 4,000 pesos themselves. They were severely chastised by the king.[35]

Such bold disregard of the royal will led to an investigation of previous entry celebrations. Royal officials found out that the city councilmen had spent large sums of money on the festivities at Chapultepec Palace and had excluded the cost of those events from the 8,000-peso total because they had technically taken place outside the city. Some councilmen defended the traditional expensive entry festivals, claiming that "it was an established custom and that any decrease [in ostentation] would damage the city council."[36] Such a statement during the seventeenth century usually caused the Spanish royal government to bow to local custom and opinion. In this case, it had no such effect. The king ordered the councilmen to hold all events in downtown Mexico City and abide by the 8,000-peso ceiling.[37]

Naturally, the 8,000-peso limit drastically reduced the magnificence of the entry ceremony. The viceroy no longer entered under the canopy even when, as was the case in 1702, he had been given special permission to do so.[38] Therefore the crimson robes, the elaborate gowns of office, disappeared. Until 1722, the city council continued to furnish a horse and ornate saddle; after that date, however, the governor formally entered the city in a carriage.[39] Popular displays of homage to the new governor declined as did jousts, parades, and artillery shows.[40] Not even the arch remained unaltered by Bourbon budget cuts. The arch changed also because of the elite's growing predilection for the neoclassical architectural style, where elaborate ornamentation, gilding, and complex designs and emblems fell into disuse.[41] Thus fiscal concerns combined with a new aesthetic to chip away at the magnificence and the awe-inspiring appearance of the arch. From a huge, elaborately gilded structure costing 2,000 pesos, the eighteenth-century arch was a smaller structure costing less than 1,200 pesos.[42] In the second half of the century, the public oaths before the arches were discontinued. Without the oaths at the arches, the festival itself lost significance.

The themes of the arch were still inspired by Greek and Roman mythology and history, but the allegorical cohesion and close connection between myth and biography so evident in the seventeenth-century structure were sacrificed.[43] In addition, the Bourbon descriptions made little attempt to demonstrate a direct link between the entering viceroy and the mythological figure chosen on the arch. In 1756, the marquis of Amarillas was compared to a pair of eyes. Other arches did present mythological heroes but mixed different allegories or mythological heroes on the same arch, altering the cohesion of the overall presentation. This decline in scale and ambition was clearly visible in the published descriptions commissioned by municipal and ecclesiastical officials. The descriptions of the previous century were commonly 100-folio tomes and included detailed drawing of the paintings and an explanation of their meaning. Most eighteenth-century arch descriptions were much shorter, some five pages, and written in rather sparse language. Some consisted of no more than the poetic recital of the actor. Some descriptions only included information on one facade of the arch, deeming the second facade of no interest to the reader. Others indicated that only one facade had been constructed. Increasingly, it appears that the arch was maintained as tradition rather than as an essential representation of political values.

As a further bow to tradition, many of the themes included on eighteenth-century arches remained consistent with those presented in the 1600s. As before, the king was depicted conferring authority to govern to the viceroy/hero.[44] The governor's qualifications for leadership remained his noble lineage and battle experience. Representations of the viceroy continued to offer him as an example to his people: he was prudent, forgiving, fair in the administration of justice, compassionate, incorruptible, and hardworking.[45] However, the themes of generosity and compassion did not dominate, and a golden age was not included at all.[46]

By 1761 the viceroy had begun to lose his semidivine quality in his representation in the entry decorations. The characteristics of lineage and nobility were no longer as important as they had been in the Hapsburg viceregal arch. The celebration of heroic deeds on the battlefield became a recitation of bureaucratic service. In 1771, it was pointed out that the Egyptian pyramids might be admired for their magnificence, but they were merely monuments to vanity. The irrigation projects of the Nile, however, were the stuff of true leadership. The magnificence and splendor utilized to glorify the viceroy, defining qualities of the Hapsburg entrance, were rejected by the Bourbons in favor of a new pragmatic philosophy of governance focused on public projects that promoted prosperity and modernity.[47] The good governor was no longer a demigodlike prince. Instead he was a competent administrator judged by his record in office. This new set of values is particularly clear in the last triumphal arch, dedicated in 1783 to Matias de Galvez. The paintings depicted the new viceroy's earlier administrative accomplishments in Guatemala and Santo Domingo.[48] The viceroy was now represented as a highly efficient and effective governor who followed royal directives. The ideal Hapsburg prince had become the practical and dutiful Bourbon bureaucrat.

After the entry of Galvez, the city councilmen and episcopal authorities ceased to build triumphal arches.[49] There was little left of the original Hapsburg viceregal entry ceremony. Yet spending on the festival during the second half of the eighteenth century actually rose well beyond the 8,000-peso limit. The average Bourbon entry cost 18,973.2 pesos. But some entries were extraordinarily expensive. For example, the entrance of Matias de Galvez in 1783 cost 60,350 pesos.[50] As was the case in the jura del rey, the councilmen auctioned the right to host bullfights to private entrepreneurs, and with the revenue from the auction, they funded the entrance.[51] Although it is not clear whether auctions took place with each entrance, a remate was held in 1783, 1785, 1798, and 1803. In some years, the state apparently even made a profit on the entry. Yet it was private elite functions, not public entertainments, that accounted for 65 to 75 percent of government expenditures.[52] For example, in 1783, the city council expended 60,350 pesos on the celebration but earned 73,735 pesos from the remate, netting a profit of 13,385 pesos. However, the majority of expenditures made for the entry ceremony went to private banquets, balls within the palace, and evening *paseos* (by carriage around Alameda Park) followed by refreshments, theatrical performances, and music recitals. With their admission ticket to the bullfights, the average person paid for all these elite extravagances. By the close of the colonial period, the entry had virtually turned into a nonevent. The author of the Gazetas (the capital's periodical) remarked that stores even stayed open in 1808 when Viceroy Pedro Garibay entered the city.[53]

Conclusion

During the eighteenth century, royal decrees and viceregal directives brought immediate change to state-sponsored festivals in the capital. In all respects, the jura del rey was to Bourbon officials what the entrance of the viceroy had been to Hapsburg authorities. Although they recognized the value of sumptuous display and special effects, eighteenth-century officials dramatically changed the significance of imperial festivals in the capital. Their festival policy reflected equally dramatic political and economic reforms, overwhelmingly designed to benefit the king. In short, public festivals became concrete ritual manifestations of Bourbon monarchical absolutism. A powerful and elaborate allegiance ceremony, positing the monarch as the ideal prince and the repository of the highest virtues, became the focus of four weeks of highly choreographed adulation. Although Bourbon officials are usually connected to the elimination of popular religious festivals, they were not above appropriating an enthusiastic public devotion to the city's protectress (the Virgin of Remedies) in order to further royal allegiance. They also addressed the fact that royal festivals had been only occasional events in the capital. By resuscitating and repackaging an old festival, they gave the public the opportunity to laud the Spanish monarch every year.

Although the viceregal entry remained part of Bourbon ritual statecraft throughout the eighteenth century, it was dramatically altered, becoming a nonevent. The viceroy was symbolically transformed into a servant of the Crown, a loyal vassal carrying out the desires of his sovereign. He was not the king and consequently did not merit a sumptuous and costly public festival. The "perfect vassal," so meticulously crafted for the Hapsburg entries, had disappeared from the festival completely. Now colonial subjects did not perform for the viceroy. Their only duty to the government was to pay the admission price to attend the bullfights and there view the new viceroy.

As a telling testament, we turn to an anonymous painting now hanging in the Museum of National History in Mexico City. The work dates to the second half of the eighteenth century and depicts the inaugural entrance of the viceroy, the marquis de la Croix, in 1766. What is striking about the painting is that the entry of the viceroy by carriage is one scene among many depicted in the zócalo. The painting is more an exposé on the residents of the capital, showing them going about their daily business of shopping and chatting with friends rather than witnessing and applauding the arrival of a new governor. The entry is presented as merely one more event in their lives, one that receives only scant notice. We can imagine how different the entry would appear if a painter had captured the entry of the marquis of Villena one hundred years earlier.

The perfect vassal did play a significant role in the oath to the king (as can be seen in the description that began this chapter and will be the focus of the next). However, unlike the Hapsburgs, eighteenth-century authorities did not believe that it was the duty of the government to engage in deficit spending in order to celebrate the monarch or the viceroy and ceased to patronize popular participation in both festivals. Rather, citizens were to share in the burden of funding events; most would do this via the admission price to the bullfights. The income generated at the corrida paid for government displays and for elite functions to which the general public was not invited. Whereas once the rulers paid many to celebrate their rulership, now citizens paid the rulers to celebrate the elite, that is, themselves.

A shift had also taken place in terms of who controlled the festival hierarchy. Under the Hapsburgs, the city councilmen had shaped ritual statecraft as they deemed fit, selecting those festivals that they believed had more resonance in the capital. They had successfully sidestepped, outsmarted, and occasionally engaged in direct confrontation with royal officials and the king in order to have their interpretation prevail. Under the Bourbons, city council struggles with royal authorities proved unsuccessful. Royal officials appeared to be inflexible and did not bend to or respect local custom such as when they appropriated the devotion to the Virgin of Remedies or enforced the 8,000-peso limit in the entry. Certainly the councilmen benefited from all the private soirees, providing more opportunities to gain influence with viceroys, but now they were in the position of implementing festival policy rather than creating it. Struggles such as these pitted the local against the imperial and reflected larger political rifts between peninsulares and criollos that loomed on the horizon.

In the end, Bourbon festival policy weakened both the symbols of the viceroy and the king. Without a powerful symbol of the viceroy, the king became personally responsible for the welfare of his vassals, subject to constant popular expectation, sentiments encouraged by the official propaganda itself. The Bourbon emphasis on the king symbolically made him more accountable for government mismanagement during a time of political and economic change that was not always greeted with applause by colonists. It is of interest to note that political dissatisfaction with the government increased after 1790, the same year that the largest and most expensive festival (the oath to Charles IV) took place in the city. The governor's claim to esteem based on good administration and public works occurred during an era of increasing economic difficulties in the capital for a majority of the citizenry. The viceroy, as he did under the Hapsburgs, could not deflect criticism against the Crown. Now when discontents would shout, "Down with bad government," they would increasingly think of the king, not a less virtuous viceroy who had poorly administered the king's will.

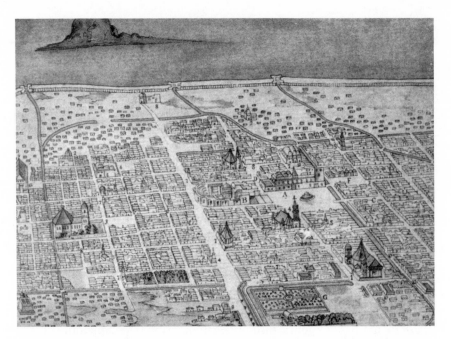

1. Overview of Mexico City in 1628. Map of Juan Gómez de Trasmonte.
Salvat Editores.

2. La Plaza Mayor in 1695 (Zócalo). Cristóbal Villalpando. Salvat Editores.

3. Viceregal entry of the marquis de la Croix in carriage during the eighteenth century. Anonymous. Museo Nacional de la Historia.

4. Voladores perform. Anonymous, eighteenth century. Salvat Editores.

5. Eagle and jaguar dancers during a festival.
Anonymous, eighteenth century. Salvat Editores.

6. Strolling in Alameda Park. Anonymous. Salvat Editores.

7. Fiestas at Chapultepec. Dancing and costumed revelry. Anonymous. Salvat Editores.

8. Fiestas at Chapultepec. Anonymous. Salvat Editores.

9. Fiestas at Chapultepec. Bullfight. Anonymous. Salvat Editores.

10. Fireworks. Anonymous. Salvat Editores.

11. Drawing of triumphal arch
submitted by Ignacio
Castrera to city councilmen
for review. Eighteenth century. Archivo del Antiguo
Ayuntamiento de la Ciudad
de México.

12. Drawing of illumination
device for the oath to
Charles IV in 1794. Archivo
General de la Nación.

13. Drawing of an auto-de-fé in a zócalo.
Anonymous, seventeenth century. Salvat Editores.

14. Religious procession for San Juan Nepomuceno.
Anonymous, eighteenth century. Salvat Editores.

Chapter 5

His Majesty's Most Loyal and Imperfect Subjects

During the oath to Charles III in 1760, the silversmith guild astonished city inhabitants with its triumphal arch. Perhaps arch is not an adequate word to describe the members' creation. They had cordoned off their entire street, and at each end, they had erected a triumphal arch. Each *arch* was sixty feet high and linked by means of two balustrades spanning the length of the street. The silversmiths decorated the balustrades with fifty-four emblems, tapestries, mirrors, and even fountains.[1] When it was time to celebrate the oath of Charles IV, citizens waited with great anticipation to see what the silversmiths had in store for them.

Everyone knew that the silversmiths were "inspired by the most laudable punctiliousness and lively desire to distinguish themselves in public displays." The *plateros* (silversmiths) were the wealthiest guild in all of New Spain, and their processions and feast-day celebrations were renowned for sumptuousness.[2] Their expertise with festivals was so well recognized that one observer noted: "Their political acumen understands how to infuse the most tender sentiments of love and loyalty toward our heroic monarch." Championing Saint Hippolytus, symbol of the Spanish conquest of Mexico, as (one of) their patrons, it was only logical that the silversmith guild would play an important role in the Bourbon allegiance ceremonies. This year they had outdone themselves and hired none other than Don Antonio Gónzalez Velázquez, the prestigious director of the Architecture Department of the newly established (art) Academy of San Carlos, to design their street arches.

The plateros inaugurated their creation on January 31 and continued to dazzle crowds for two weeks. Once again two balustrades, on both sides of the street, spanning 102 yards (the entire length of the street), joined two triumphal arches. The two double-tiered balustrades rose thirty-two feet from the ground and showcased emblems depicting the seven known planets. The number of emblems on the balustrades was limited so that attention would be focused on a central platform called "*el templo*" (the temple) that was thirteen feet wide and forty-one and a quarter feet high. Inside the templo was an eight-foot-high statue of the king that sat atop a five-and-a-half-foot pedestal. The statue depicted the king in his regal court garments with cape, scepter, and laurel crown. On the roof of the templo stood a statue of "Obedience" (also eight feet high) depicted with a yoke around his neck. On the yoke was engraved the word *gentle*. Obedience held part of the yoke in his right hand, and in his left hand he held a scepter with the words *Filial obedience [is] the most heroic*. In an accompanying engraved poem, the statue also warned: "Learn, Potentates of the world,/to dominate mundane pride/Look at the obedience of the Great Charles/the filial respect he always had." Charles IV could command the obedience of his vassals because he had been a perfect model of filial devotion to his father, Charles III.

Although the entire construction had few paintings and architectural details, the silversmiths managed to turn their creation into a major attraction by including 102 silver panels. The silver was illuminated by 400 candles placed on forty silver chandeliers strung between the arches and in the "temple." Another 7,600 candles illuminated the large triumphal arches at each end of the street, which were engraved with a number of poems. The plateros illuminated the arch ensemble and temple for weeks so that inhabitants might view the arch construction. The light from all the candles was so bright that it "made the street appear as though it were daytime and gave new brilliance to [the term] illumination."

Special performances and a formal explanation of the arches also took place. Entertainment included a specially choreographed dance. Sixteen young men who wore red vests of polished satin and sashes woven of silver thread performed before the statue of the king. Their hats were each decorated with a letter as well as the coat of arms of the guild. At the end of the dance, they arranged themselves in such as way that the letters spelled out *Viva Carlos Quarto* (Long Live Charles IV).[3] Once the performance was over, orchestras serenaded the spectators, who were astonished by the latest platero creation. One observer noted that

> so entertained [were] the eyes by such brilliant illumination and the ears with such pleasant and pleasing melodies [that] people were not only entertained but rather entranced in such a manner that soldiers were necessary in order to remind them and encourage them to leave by one door in order to make way for the infinite number of people of all classes who wished to enter by the other [door] to see and hear that which had captured all their attention.[4]

Extravagant, breathtaking, and all in the service of the Crown. The silversmith arch ensemble was clearly a marvel. The time, effort, and cost of such a construction must also have been tremendous. Hapsburg imperial festivals (both the entry and the oath) had included the participation of vassals who served as representatives of ethnic groups, each of whom performed their obedience and paid homage to the government. A quick glance at the 1747 oath description that began the last chapter demonstrates that Bourbon officials also incorporated select groups of colonial subjects into the oath ceremony. Parades, triumphal architecture, and performances by vassals far outshone that of royal and municipal officials. For it was paramount in an allegiance ceremony that citizens demonstrate their loyalty in some fashion. For the 1760 oath, vassals actually performed or commissioned paintings, floats, or shields that presented images indicative of their loyalty or did both. They became living examples or representations in art in order to establish and maintain both the legitimacy of the festival and the Crown. However, the exemplary vassals of the eighteenth-century oath festival consisted, for the most part, of wealthy Spaniards. Native Americans participated in the ceremony only, and people of color performed only if they belonged to a guild, not as a separate group.

Local notables played a starring role as loyal subjects with their jousts and games in the main square and in the bullring during every oath festival. As the bullfights took place for ten straight days, the city's well-to-do were always in the limelight, in effect parading their abilities and their extravagant costumes and handsome mounts. The city councilmen, among the riders, personally selected the participants for their "conscientiousness, occupation, status, and nobility," thus holding them up as examples to the rest of the inhabitants.[5]

The participation of several professional organizations marked the oath, illustrating new Bourbon cultural preferences. For example, the Real Protomedicato, the professional medical association, became an important provider of entertainment for the Bourbon jura festivities, an understandable fact given the government's emphasis on practical science and on public health and sanitation.[6] The increased role of the architecture guild also complemented a new regard for that field and its importance in terms of city beautification programs and urban planning. The increasing professionalization of this group eventually led to the founding of the art academy in the capital. Given the official focus on education, it was important to include university professors and to showcase intellectual achievement through poetry contests as well.[7] All three professions consisted of Spaniards, and all tended to share the political philosophy of government officials or at least had benefited from government patronage.

However, the plateros more than any other group represented the perfect vassal in this new era. They created and defined a special festive space of sumptuous display and wealth that left crowds entertained and even awestruck, all in the name of the king of Spain. The plateros, more than any other group and even more than the city council, worked to strengthen the legitimacy of the monarch, serving therefore as the finest example of the ideal subject of the new era.[8] The power of the silversmiths, a minute fraction of the population, to represent themselves as the most loyal vassal rested on their economic success and their privileged position in the colony. The Crown had actively promoted the silver-mining industry and aided it by establishing a tribunal, school, and bank while offering fiscal incentives for miners, including a decrease in the cost of mercury, needed in the refining process. The profits from the silver boom filled royal coffers as well as the pockets of miners and silversmiths.[9] It was natural for the beneficiaries of the Crown reforms to celebrate the majesty of the king.

The Price of Celebrating Apollo

The tremendous wealth generated by silver mining, trade, and commercial agriculture, when it was not siphoned off by the Crown in taxes, was distributed very unequally. The gap between the rich and the poor widened in the midst of eighteenth-century prosperity. Most of the century's economic growth apparently occurred before 1750. By the time of Charles III (1759–88)and the implementation of most of the Bourbon reform program, Mexico had begun to experience an economic slowdown. During the last quarter of the century prices rose and inflation set in as the Crown engaged in deficit spending to maintain the empire and finance its wars.

In addition, from 1650 to 1750, the colonial population increased by 50 percent and then increased again by the same percentage from midcentury to 1810. This rapid population growth exacerbated land tenure issues and generated great tension in the countryside. Many landless peasants migrated to the capital, seeking work, but found little success. Yet the economic difficulties of many colonists did not deter officials from raising taxes and demanding that large sums of money be spent to celebrate the king.[10]

The Real Hacienda (the ministry of accounting and revenue collection) was revamped in order to improve efficiency and eliminate corruption, to the detriment of many a colonist, who now had to pay taxes in full in a timely manner. The Crown took complete control of the collection of the sales tax and increased the number of items that could be taxed under the law. A new tax on shopkeepers, liquor sales, and playing cards and a new royal monopoly on cigarette and cigar production were instituted. Native American tribute levies were raised as well. In addition, the royal government only supported colonial industries that did not compete with Spanish products, discouraging, taxing, or prohibiting those that did. This devastated many Mexican domestic industries.[11]

Disregarding increasing economic hardship for the citizenry, Bourbon officials felt justified in passing the financial burden of the festival onto private citizens because, in their view, colonial subjects ought to celebrate the new monarch and therefore contribute. They also believed in the educative value of citizens watching their fellows proclaim the monarch. This, they claimed, was for the "betterment of the national culture."[12] The eighteenth-century coronation and entrance ceremonies in Madrid were almost completely funded by professional organizations and private citizens, namely the nobility.[13] Bourbon officials expected the same from the king's Mexican subjects. Consequently, the authorities did not sponsor participation in any way, except for donating funds to joust participants who came from their own social circle.[14] Those groups who were unable to meet official expectations for ostentation eventually disappeared from the festival.

For example, Native Americans were still part of the ceremony, but their role in the jura declined as the century wore on.[15] Taken in conjunction with the elimination of Native performances from the Bourbon viceregal entry, the lack of Native participation in Bourbon imperial celebrations presents a striking contrast to Hapsburg ritual statecraft. Problems began in 1760, when a dispute occurred over indigenous participation in the festival. Some officials felt that Native Americans should do more to celebrate the monarch. They had traditionally sat on the stage in the main square, delivered the oath in Nahautl, and then presented what were called at the time "inventions," such as releasing doves from a specially constructed papier-mâché globe. Royal officials now wanted Native leaders to sponsor additional entertainments such as a parades, fireworks, or a triumphal arch, as other groups did. However, the indigenous neighborhoods did not have the financial resources to do this. Appearing to accept that fact, authorities then decided that if Natives were unable to perform additional public displays, they should contribute funds toward the government-sponsored stages erected in the main square. This was, in effect, penalizing them for their financial inability to perform dances or organize parades on a grand scale.

Natives formally complained to Charles III, and he ordered officials to stop demanding these funds from the Indians.[16] In the end, eight towns put together a processional party of some 250 Native officials, musicians, and honor guards. But they did not sponsor additional activities, nor did they present their traditional inventions.[17] In subsequent juras, Native governors sat on the palace platform and performed the oath but provided no entertainments at all, not even the historic release of doves.[18] It is not even clear whether the oath was performed in Nahuatl, as had been the Hapsburg custom. It is also uncertain whether Indians participated in 1808, but they were

not present at all, not even to swear the oath, during the second ceremony to Ferdinand VII in 1814.[19]

During the eighteenth century, the traditional guilds were primarily responsible for the costly evening parade.[20] The guild parade
of 1747 had been stunning. However, in 1760 the parade was modest
and the guilds were unable to put on a spectacular show. Only ten
guilds (420 individuals) presented very simple floats that lacked the
ornamentation of 1747. Almost all the guildsmen dressed in military
uniforms or as Romans in long togas.[21] In 1790, the guilds hosted
another parade but made such a poor showing that city officials
demanded they pay for one of the official stages for the ceremony.
The councilmen decided against the measure because it was obvious that if the guilds lacked the resources to fund a sumptuous parade,
they certainly lacked the money to pay for a stage.[22] There is no mention of the guilds in descriptions for the two oaths to Ferdinand VII
in 1808 and again in 1814 after his release from French prison. The
decline in guild participation reflects the very real economic woes
experienced by this economic sector. Inflation, a decline in real
wages, and a general economic slowdown at the end of the century
hurt many artisans. Bourbon decrees also undermined the guild tradition by encouraging an open wage system, bypassing the need for
the formal apprenticeships and examinations common in the guild
system. Officials hoped to encourage a more modern labor market
and stimulate commercial establishments, but in the process, the
guilds were condemned as backward.[23]

The financial burden of the parade was substantial for artisans
even without Bourbon attempts to dismantle the guild system.
Although the exact cost is unknown, the minimum expense for the
nine-day parade (based on the oaths to Ferdinand VI and Charles III
and excluding the additional activities of the plateros) easily could
have equaled 45,000 pesos. In 1760, a member of the *pulqueros'* guild
asked the viceroy for an exemption from paying his 40-peso contribution required to fund his guild's float. He claimed that these 40
pesos were merely for the float's decoration and did not include the
cost of a costume and the rental of jewels for adornment that he also
was required to pay.[24] Individual contributions for a float depended
on the number of guildsmen, the financial status of the guild, one's
position within the guild, and the theme and design of the cart. The

carts submitted by several collaborating guilds may have required less expense from individual members than those carts funded solely by a single guild. In addition, the silversmiths had to contribute a great deal to produce a silver-plated cart. In the 1747 jura, some 1,500 individuals marched with the floats.[25] If each had submitted a minimum of 30 pesos, the cost of the fiesta for these participants would have been 45,000 pesos. In many cases, the float contribution required for these ceremonies may have equaled the monthly wage of an artisan.[26] Thus demonstrating one's loyalty to the king in a Bourbon jura was a costly proposition and became more so as inflation increased.

Attempts by citizens to limit their participation by claiming financial hardship placed their loyalty in question. Guilds who collectively complained and sought to excuse themselves from these imposed festival duties were told bluntly that they were "obligated in proper just demonstration to proclaim our sovereign, not only because it corresponds to the nature of the occasion and its importance, but also [because it is] appropriate of vassals that prize themselves on [being] loyal."[27] In 1760, the candle makers, dye masters, and confectioners objected when municipal officials demanded that each guild contribute 400 additional pesos to the jura. The city council wanted them to pay for firework displays above and beyond what they usually contributed. The guilds appealed to the viceroy, but he ordered them to pay 300 pesos to fund additional fireworks. He claimed that the guilds "want to bargain and litigate about something that others of less resources have offered with so much good will and honesty."[28] This additional sum was above and beyond the cost of the chariot of fire provided by these artisans, which equaled 2,140 pesos, an amount that had already required an emergency collection among the guildsmen.[29] Some officials, such as viceroy, the second count of Revillagigedo, justified such demands for increased expenditures because they equated a vassal's loyalty to the amount of ostentation they were willing to pay for.[30]

With pyrotechnic feats of wonder, impressive ephemeral architecture, and large-scale performances, Mexico's loyal subjects lauded the virtues of the king and pledged him unremitting loyalty. It was their duty as loyal vassals to do so, and they had to be willing to expend large sums of money to fulfill that duty. The city government funded the stages, the bullfight, the firework displays, and the illumination of the plaza through the bullfight remate. It even generated a profit in the process. Sufficient funds were available to come to the aid of Native communities and guildsmen, but colonial officials spent those funds on private functions that benefited the elite. Officials tried to fine some guilds for the lack of sumptuousness in their displays, demanding that they pay for a government stage that, in fact, was already paid for by the bullfight remate. If the guilds or Native Americans could have been forced to pay for a stage, then officials would have had more funds at their disposal for elite banquets and balls.

The desire to generate a profit also lay behind efforts to encourage the use of fireworks as a means of demonstrating loyalty. Many groups turned to fireworks to celebrate the king and express their loyalty because fireworks were less expensive than commissioning an ephemeral arch or staging a mock battle. But government pressures also account for the increased use and more elaborate nature of firework displays by vassals during the era because these forms of display directly benefited the government. The Crown held monopoly rights on the sale of gunpowder, the essential ingredient for all fireworks. Especially after festival reform began, officials encouraged vassals to turn to fireworks to celebrate major events. In 1780 the viceroy issued a decree demanding as much. He claimed that fireworks increased revenue for the state and were also a good source of employment for Indians and other poor people.[31]

His Majesty's Most Loyal Subjects

Not only did officials mandate ostentatious displays by citizens but they, like their Hapsburg predecessors, also closely scripted the political message presented by those performers. This accounts for the striking thematic cohesion of the separate parts of the celebration. Royal authorities reviewed drafts of ephemeral architecture and themes of floats in order to ensure that cohesion. For example, the viceroy, the second court of Revillagigedo, personally reviewed and revised the 1790 silversmith arch ensemble before any construction could take place.[32]

The vassal's loyalty to the king was the central theme of every jura celebration in the eighteenth century. For example, loyalty was the focus of one-third of the paintings presented on the platero arch of 1760, and four of them specifically claimed that loyalty to the monarch even gained one a place in heaven.[33] Paintings, floats, and shields depicted vassals consumed by admiration and love for their sovereign. For example, the arch of the painters guild in 1747 depicted all the guildsmen with hearts literally afire for Ferdinand VI.[34] Loyal vassals defended their sovereign even if it entailed great personal sacrifice. Female images representing America ripped their hearts from their breasts and offered them to the Spanish kings.[35] Images of the Mexican eagle sacrificing itself were also commonly portrayed as symbols of loyalty. For example, in the oath of 1808, the Mexican eagle was depicted as willingly spilling her blood to nourish her young, Mexican artillerymen readying to fight the forces of Napoleon if necessary. The message was clear: the vassal had to be prepared to give everything, even his life, for the king.[36]

If citizens ever doubted that sentiment, the oath mythology delivered a direct warning about popular uprisings. The populace was reminded that the king could both bestow love and dole out punishment.[37] The silversmiths depicted Charles IV leading troops against the masses during a popular rebellion in the Spanish possession of Naples. Six other paintings showed the swift action the king would take against any popular uprising. Of particular interest is a painting portraying the legend of Phaeton, who stole Apollo's chariot and died for his effrontery: "The same will happen to the vassal that may wish to take the reins of sovereign government, worthy only of the hands of Monarchs."[38] This warning was not issued by government officials directly but appeared on the arches of the silversmiths. The threat against rebellious vassals was issued by His Majesty's most perfect vassals, the silversmiths.

Closely linked to the theme of loyalty and rebellion was the image of Native Americans in the Bourbon jura. Native loyalty and affection for the Spanish monarch were the best guarantees against widespread popular rebellion since Native Americans constituted a significant percentage of the city's population. Consequently, they were consistently shown in a position of homage to the monarch or as subjugated vassals from the Conquest era. For example, in the 1747 guild parade, two floats represented Conquest-era indigenous rulers paying homage to the eighteenth-century monarch. Guildsmen, who were for the most part not Native Americans, wore costumes and acted the part of Indian rulers and "fierce" Chichimec warriors.[39]

One of the most interesting images of the Native population is found on two large paintings of the archiepiscopal arch of 1760. Here Native Americans were shown destroying their old idols while Religion (a female figure) was shown stomping out idolatry. The second painting showed "Política" (or government, another female figure) driving the chariot of the goddess of wisdom, Minerva. Along her route, the ignorance that had plagued the lives of indigenous peoples disappeared. On the road, two indigenous men were presented in "before and after" scenes. First, under the delusion of ignorance, they were blind men with donkey ears. After encountering the Spanish "Política," they were returned to human form and were pictured with instruments of the arts and sciences, symbols of their newfound knowledge.[40] Thus Natives appeared as either subdued rebellious natives (the Chichimec- or Conquest-era leaders) or semibeasts in dire need of Spanish education to become fully human. In reality, the actual participation of Natives in the festival itself was constrained by the poverty of their communities, caused by government economic policies.

The Civil Fates of Libertinage and the Breakdown of Morals

The notion that Native Americans (and castas) required improvement in order to create a better society was not merely an artistic device but a key Bourbon social policy. Formal education was of great interest to officials, and especially after the 1750s, they decreed that all villages establish Spanish language schools for children (including Native American boys and girls). Behind this emphasis on Spanish language instruction lay a belief in the benefit to the colony of a large population of highly acculturated bilingual Natives.[41] To late-eighteenth-century officials a hispanized and educated Indian was the natural complement to a more "modern," efficient New Spain.

The Bourbon desire to educate the plebeians led high-ranking clerics and civil authorities to evaluate the comportment and piety of the general populace. These new peninsular bishops and archbishops tended to emphasize education, religious instruction, moral living, and a quiet, modest form of religiosity. Civil authorities equally sought to educate the population to new, more modern modes of behavior. Bourbon officials felt that they had to work against the "civil fates of libertinage and the breakdown of morals."[42] Bourbon officials used the term *"urbanidad"* (civility) to explain their social policies, implying that they had some clear criteria to determine what was culturally acceptable.[43] Modern values apparently included gentlemanly behavior, affability, veracity, modesty, generosity, industriousness, and a retiring personality, qualities that now were attributed to the Bourbon viceroys and defined the Spanish monarchs. As a matter of fact, inhabitants were to take their cue from the king (especially Charles III), who could remain uncontaminated and pure even in the midst of a "Garden of Delights."[44]

It was inevitable that the new emphasis on education and modern behavior would lead to a reappraisal of popular religious festivals. Historically the Church's teachings served as a vital link for all the disparate ethnicities and also legitimized both the societal order and the government. During the sixteenth and seventeenth centuries, priests had initially encouraged and then accepted (or resigned themselves to) local interpretations, traditions, and festivals that did not always coincide with Catholic orthodoxy. But attendance at mass was good, and individuals enthusiastically supported public and private worship, taking great pride in local churches that they maintained and renovated through time. Most citizens fulfilled their annual Easter duty, and many went to confession regularly. Confraternities were numerous (eighty-five in the capital), and although they varied in terms of resources, they all managed to celebrate in some fashion their patron saints annually.[45]

Now those very same festivals and traditions came under review because of their excessive exuberance or supposed superstition in what amounted to a Bourbon moral crusade that had its greatest impact on the capital, the viceregal home of Bourbon absolutism. In general, reformers sought to separate the sacred and the profane and in the process gain control over the very streets of the capital by decreeing the proper way for residents to behave at religious feasts and processions. Festival reform provided the perfect opportunity, along with an increased emphasis on parish schools, to educate the population. Beginning at midcentury and intensifying under the tenure of Francisco de Lorenzana (1769–71), the most regalist of arch-bishops during the century, reforms abounded.

In addition, Bourbon fiscal policy had an impact on this new piety and ideas about public behavior and education. In general, officials believed that festivals cost too much and led to deficit spending, explaining the meager status of so many municipal government accounts.[46] In 1750, the transfer of parishes from regular orders to sec-ular clergy intensified, bringing local churches under the direct con-trol of bishops and royal authority. Authorities began championing the Spanish language schools, and, in some cases, the cost of main-taining the schools and providing a salary for the teacher came from community funds previously destined for the feast day of the patron saint. Bourbon officials believed that schools were a more laudable use of such monies than excessively patronizing a religious festival.

At the same time, royal authorities decreed reforms (and the confiscation of funds) of confraternities. Confraternities, organiza-tions of laypeople devoted to a particular saint, manifestation of Mary, Christ image, or the Holy Eucharist, served as a unifying force in towns, neighborhoods, and parishes. In these communities, members donated lands, livestock, and other property as well as their time and money to maintain the organization and to fund public religious cel-ebrations. Regardless of ethnicity and location (rural or urban), con-fraternity members in essence controlled the administration of sizable amounts of resources, although in theory local priests reviewed such accounts and supervised their activities. In the 1770s and 1780s, royal officials began a review of these accounts and demanded that con-fraternities demonstrate their official charters or titles. As a result, many confraternities were suppressed, their properties confiscated and sold because they were "illegal." Those that passed muster were more closely supervised by priests and royal authorities in order to ensure that funds were not squandered on excessive feasts or other costly (and apparently unnecessary) expenses.[47]

For example, neither religious zeal nor loyalty to the monarch served Native leader Ambrosio Ferrer Montes of Irapuato very well. As a matter of fact, these attributes produced the opposite effect. On behalf of the indigenous confraternity of Saint Joseph, Ferrer wanted permission to celebrate the oath to Ferdinand VI as a means of assert-ing the prestige of his confraternity. The viceroy not only said no, he stated that only *cabeceras* with city councils could perform the jura. (Cabecera towns were head towns, a special royal designation that denoted special privileges as well as the seat of Spanish authority in the provinces. They were juxtaposed to regular villages and pueblos.) The viceroy then chastised Ferrer for attempting to use pious funds for a civil function. The confraternity then fell into new trouble because royal officials had realized that it was not an officially approved organization. The viceroy now ordered an investigation.[48]

In addition to strengthening official supervision of popular religious festivities and controlling funding for such events, religious and civil leaders publicly condemned those forms of worship that they deemed superstitious in edicts and sermons. Similar reform efforts occurred in Madrid under the direction of the count of Campomanes, a minister of the Council of Castilla, who believed that "such [religious] spectacles, instead of being edifying, fomented a lack of devotion, disorder, irreverence, and a lack of respect and veneration of sacred places and objects."[49] Rather presumptuously, Bourbon officials believed that the commoners' grasp of the Catholic faith was superficial and was based solely on the ostentation and display of religious festivals rather than on deep spirituality. Eliminating time-honored traditions that reformers considered profane was designed to educate the masses to "proper" spirituality. The popular, almost carnavalesque nature of many festivals was viewed as irreverent and inappropriate for the occasion. Elements that had been acceptable at the time of the Conquest in order to attract Natives to the faith and to Spanish customs had reached their limit of usefulness and could no longer be tolerated. Native American festivals were of particular concern because they apparently were too licentious and unseemly for the now desired code of behavior:

> The first goal . . . ought to be to take a look at the Indians, with the end of making them rational, cultivated. . . . Whatever they acquire with their personal labor, they spend on the aforementioned festivities and in banquets and drunken parties with which they solemnize those [festivals] that more appropriately merit the term bacchanalias than refined and religious [events].[50]

In 1769, Archbishop Lorenzana prohibited various Native performances that he regarded as superstitious and idolatrous; in 1771, the Fourth Provincial Council prohibited the inclusion of new festivals in the liturgical calendar and in essence outlawed banquets during religious festivals and profane fiestas during the Easter and Christmas seasons.[51] In Mexico City, officials closely monitored large festivals and especially those in Native barrios[52] In 1789, civil authorities reduced the number of festivals that could be officially celebrated in the viceroyalty. By the close of the century, those who wished to hold a procession or public fiesta were required to obtain permission from the Church and a license from the city council. Stipulations on such festivals included that there be no fireworks of any kind, no mixing of genders in dances, and no alcoholic beverages and the termination of the event by the hour of vespers (late afternoon/early evening). These festivals could no longer last for several days because people were now expected to return to work the following day.

Nonetheless, more than a desire for enlightenment or the instilling of genteel manners and proper piety was at the heart of the Bourbon festival reform. During the second half of the eighteenth century, royal officials in Spain clearly became more obsessed with the possible relationship of festivals and revolts against the Crown. This concern partially reflected the experience of Charles III and his fear of and personal distaste for popular festivals. Apparently, he only valued hunting as a suitable pastime. However, Spanish officials generally believed that multitudes of anonymous commoners assembled during festivals and wearing costumes that increased anonymity represented a potential threat that had to be prevented at all costs. This fear stemmed from the 1766 Esquilache revolt in Madrid, which had occurred during Easter week. Disgruntled noblemen dressed as commoners had acted to defy the government. Subsequently troops were always on hand during festivities in the Spanish capital and Easter was one of the first religious festivals to be reformed by the Crown.[53] Beginning in 1791, the same would occur in Easter celebrations in Mexico City and its surrounding villages.[54] However, the reform would provoke other problems as city councilmen demanded that participants dress in expensive costumes to meet the thematic and ostentatious rigor appropriate to these displays. For example, in the towns of San Angel, Xochimilco, Tacuba, Azcapulzalco, and Tanepantla, individuals decried the excessive cost of having to dress as Roman centurions and stand vigil all night on the Saturday before Easter.[55]

Although it appears that a policy designed in response to concerns in Spain was partially responsible for changes in Mexico, the potential connection between festivals and revolt had been recognized long before the Bourbon reformers. Hapsburg authorities had also recognized that festivals were by their very nature volatile assemblies that attracted large numbers of visitors, occurred on holidays, and were accompanied by significant alcohol consumption.

Certainly some rebels viewed festival times as ideal moments to initiate a revolt since government officials were distracted by the festivities. For example, in 1612, black slaves in the capital planned an uprising for Holy Week because officials would be preoccupied with processions and other religious activities.[56] Corpus Christi was also associated with subversion. As a result, the city council had repeatedly prohibited the wearing of masks to the festival from 1529 to 1556.[57] The largest popular rebellion in the capital before the independence movement of 1810, the corn riot of 1692, occurred during Corpus Christi.[58]

Whether merely motivated by Enlightenment notions of proper political behavior or by a desire to follow the mandates of Madrid or local history, viceregal officials viewed festivals as seeds of subversion and believed that installing a new morality would ensure stability.[59] Since Corpus Christi historically had been associated with revolt and it was the largest annual religious festival in the capital, it fell right into the line of Bourbon fire. What better celebration was there, showcasing as it did the city itself, to "teach" the populace modern behavior?

Reform efforts began with the dances presented during the procession and at the cathedral. Dance troupes now had to acquire authorization and approval from both the city council and the ecclesiastical authorities, who reviewed the content and quality of any potential performance. Any performance that might be labeled as "indecoroso" (unseemly) was prohibited. But by 1744, the city council stopped contracting for dancers and these performances completely disappeared from the procession. Other regulations outlawed food stalls and vendors from the processional route, banned drinking from the festival, and prohibited poorly dressed individuals from attending the festivities.[60]

The manner in which the population dressed was quite a concern with reformers. For example, author Hipólito Villarroel stated that

> nothing disavows and defaces these events like the permissive-ness and tolerance of, under the title of confraternity, a crowd of drunken, semiclothed Indians, filled with misery, wrapped in blankets.[61]

Their dress was also a sore point with the reigning viceroy, the second count of Revillagigedo. He believed it was his duty "to exile for always the shameful voluntary nudity that is seen among many segments of the plebe in th[e] capital and the filthy and indecent rags with which, without shame, they present themselves everywhere and even in the very churches." He prohibited (although it is doubtful that he could have had much success in this endeavor) anyone from entering the city who was not wearing a shirt, short jacket or vest, pants, stockings, and shoes. Natives could wear their traditional clothing "but with the precise understanding that if they do wear it, they do not disfigure it with tattered cloth or other similar rags."[62] Thus festival attendees were to be well dressed and reverential. To underscore these dramatic changes to Corpus, it is sufficient to note that in 1777, based on the instructions of José de Galvez, municipal expenditures for Corpus were limited to 223 pesos, only 6 percent of the Corpus budget of 1618.[63]

Another Bourbon goal was do away with the *enramada*, or thatch arbor, that covered the processional route. As early as 1721, a number of royal decrees also attempted to limit the number of Indians enter-ing the city to build the enramada. Apparently, indigenous groups from as far away as sixty miles had commonly traveled to the capital to build the arbor and participate in the festivities. In 1728, officials reiterated that only villages fourteen leagues or closer to the capital could participate. Nevertheless, in 1777, Indians from distant villages still continued to sojourn to the capital for the festival. In that same year, municipal authorities claimed that having so many Natives, "People so Miserable [impoverished]," enter the city harmed the reputation of the capital.[64] The aldermen felt that the Corpus festi-val had merely served as an excuse to further exploit the indigenous population, an exploitation perpetrated by the Native American elite rather than by the Spanish officials. They stated that

> everything can be believed of the Indians because it is public and notorious how much abuse there is among them, and the tyranny with which their leaders oppress and squeeze them under the pretext of festivals of the Church, confraternity processions, Corpus, Easter and others [festivals], making profit from the sweat and blood of the poor.[65]

According to the city fathers, the Indians viewed the enramada as forced labor.[66]

In 1769, Bourbon officials sought to abolish completely the thatch arbor, claiming that they only had the best interests of the Natives at heart and that they were merely responding to Native demands. Some village leaders had formally complained about the organization of the arbor construction and, specifically, the corrupt actions of the Royal Interpreter.[67] The Royal Interpreter handled the financial aspects of the arbor construction and apparently overcharged the city for his services, skimming funds that were originally intended for indigenous workers. In addition, he received gifts, known as suchil (usually in the form of chickens), from each Native village participating in the enramada construction. Although some of the hens were cooked for the banquets that took place to celebrate Corpus, many were sold, the profit pocketed by the interpreter. However, the Native leaders who filed the protest had only wished to receive the funding that was designated for the workers. It had not been their intention to eliminate the enramada or the celebratory banquets that were a valued part of the tradition.

Claiming that they acted on behalf of Native Americans, the city council instituted a series of measures to reform the enramada tradition. The financial activities of the interpreter would be strictly limited, and the suchil was banned. Authorities prohibited the indigenous banquets, calling them "*pulque* bashes."[68] Only visiting village workers were allowed to come and had to leave their families at home.[69] Native inhabitants of the city could participate in the arbor construction but were specially selected. All castas were banned from assisting the Native workers.

The Native Americans of the capital and nearby villages fought to protect what they perceived to be their right—the construction of the Corpus Christi enramada. Natives maintained an "aesthetic preference" for the magnificently ephemeral, not merely in large civic spectacle but also in smaller, local ritual productions. This may account for their willingness to expend large quantities of labor and funds for these temporary arches (enramadas) decorated with costly flowers. Such tireless devotion to the task spoke to the importance of such rituals and the appreciation or pleasure in the collective enterprise of these endeavors.[70] Furthermore, in the case of Corpus, Natives prepared the way for the sacred (the saints and the Host) and building the arbor was most likely imbued with deep religious significance. This explains why Natives fought with royal authorities for over twenty years to continue this tradition.

In general, Native Americans responded to the Bourbon reform of their religious traditions with legal suits and public disputes with local parish priests. Such reforms were perceived as assaults on community identity and as jeopardizing time-honored practices of accessing the divine in a society in which religion defined the social values of a community and formed part of all institutions.[71] Changes in religious devotion and practice, such as the prohibition of certain dances or a decrease in the sumptuousness of a saint's feast, had the potential to upset the social and political fabric of a community. More importantly, such changes jeopardized the relationship of the community to the supernatural, a precarious position to be in for any agriculturally based society that could be devastated by flood or drought.

The governors of San Juan Tenochtitlan and Santiago Tlatelolco did not outright refuse to comply with viceregal decrees but stated instead that it was impossible to attempt to limit indigenous and casta participation in the enramada construction because the workers "say that some come to the festival for pleasure, and others in order to expedite more quickly the work." Native inhabitants of the city stated that their attendance at the festival was a "privilege inherited from their ancestors." Villagers who came to assist in the arbor construction had not merely perceived their enramada activity as a work duty but also as a family outing or sojourn. Apparently an entire system of selection had been created to determine who would travel to the capital and attend Corpus. Consequently, they reacted very strongly to laws that forbade families from accompanying the workers. They wrote

> that it is not possible to limit the number of Indians that come because it is such a pleasure with which they view it [the festival duty] that they say they are coming to celebrate the great festival and as recreation and joy they bring their wives and children, so that their coming is an honor, that far from esteeming it a bother, they become offended when an attempt is made to exclude them from their corresponding turn [to come].

Responding to city council charges that Natives viewed Corpus participation as forced labor, indigenous leaders claimed that it was the only public obligation "well received."[72]

Officials found regulating the number of individuals entering the city and participating in the arbor construction very difficult. Fiestas and banquets continued to occur but no longer were supported with public funds. The failure of these reforms finally led the viceroy, the second count of Revillagigedo, to ban the enramada entirely, claiming it was "a very indecent thing for the Most Divine Holy Eucharist to pass under." On his instructions, the city council commissioned a large cloth canopy depicting white clouds on a sky blue background.[73] Although indigenous inhabitants continued to participate within the confines of their confraternities and parishes, an important component of the Native Corpus tradition was destroyed.

During that same year, the viceroy also issued a decree permanently banning the giants, big-headed dancers, devils, and the dragon from Corpus Christi. No doubt, he shared the view of Bishop Lorenzana, who claimed that such elements "were the product of barbarism and the ignorance of other times, [that] they counter the gravity and seriousness of the divine worship and distract the attention of the devout from their only object, the Eucharist." With this action, officials disfigured the meaning of the festival.[74] The dancers, giants, devils, and dragon were all related to sin, to the carnivalesque; they symbolically prepared the spectators for the joyous coming of the body of Christ, the truly virtuous one. By banishing sin from the procession, authorities cut the central dramatic and thematic thread of the event. In Spain, officials from the count of Aranda to Archbishop

Lorenzana to Spanish author and policy maker Gaspar Melchor de Jovellanos all counseled that reform of popular traditions and festivals (or their abolition) should occur at a gradual pace. To do otherwise could delegitimize the Church's teachings or lead to discontent with the government. Officials did tone down reforms in Madrid if complaints were numerous and vocal or if they felt the changes would diminish the image of the monarch.[75] Officials in Mexico City appeared to follow similar counsel in the case of Corpus Christi. The fact that it took twenty years to abolish the enramada also attests to the perseverance of the Native leadership.

While Bourbon reformers altered religious festivals such as Corpus Christi, they banned some festivals outright. These were festivals such as carnival that historically had lain outside the purview of the authorities. The prohibition of carnival began with Philip V, who questioned allowing all spontaneous masked dances and parades that lacked official review and approval.[76] In Mexico City, the viceroy issued a order that no one could wear costumes and masks. The archbishop that same year (1722) banned Indian costumes from the traza (the Spanish center, or downtown, of the city), claiming that they were "diabolical." By 1731, Native Americans were actually banned from downtown during carnival and a viceregal order reiterated previous bans on costumes and on men dressing as women. Infractions now carried a penalty of 200 lashes and a stint working at a presidio or a factory. Carnival, as a result, became a much more subdued affair, although individuals did continue to throw candies and eggs. By midcentury, officials sought to encourage a new carnival tradition—Sunday strolls in parks (Alameda) or along major canals (Ixtalcalco). However, such locations were patrolled by police and alcohol was prohibited (in 1780). By 1797, carnival was completely prohibited in the capital and candy makers were ordered to neither make nor sell their wares during this time.[77] However, officials did allow masked revelers to attend special carnival performances at the Coliseo, once an admission fee was paid. In addition, costumes were de rigueur at private elite balls. In Madrid, similar government-organized events were apparently models of "urbanidad." There carnival had been institutionalized to such an extent that officials published a manual titled "Instructions for Attendance at Masked Balls during Carnival."[78]

Conclusion

The Bourbon jura redefined the concept of the perfect vassal, who was now seen as an educated professional such as a physician, a highly skilled wealthy artisan such as a silversmith, or a member of the ruling elite. Perfect vassals were those who reflected the new Enlightenment preferences for science, public health, and urban renewal and were therefore almost exclusively Spanish. With the withdrawal of the guilds, the castas disappeared from the festival as political performers. Natives continued to participate in the ceremony in the main square, but after midcentury they did not perform or contribute to the celebration other than by their presence on the royal stage. Instead, non-Native guildsmen donned Indian costumes and pretended to be Natives showing their homage to the king. Natives appeared in paintings on ephemeral architecture, but here they were no longer the perfect vassal, their virtues no longer evident but only acquired through instruction by the imperial government.

These changes in ritual reflected real differences in ruling philosophies that were not lost on spectators and nonelite participants. The Spanish elite who controlled and constituted the government, including the city council, had always believed in their own inherent superiority over the heterogeneous plebe with whom they shared the capital. However, with Hapsburg rituals and largesse, officials demonstrated that they recognized that they were in the service of the citizenry and could thereby legitimize their claim that they deserved to rule. No such sentiment pervaded Bourbon festivals because vassals were not only ordered to participate but were also held to a high standard of ostentation that was beyond the financial reach of most. To refuse to participate or to complain about the cost placed their status as loyal vassals under suspicion. In the final analysis, vassals were told to be loyal and pay up or else face the consequences.

Popular festivals and activities, especially religious events, were purified of the profane, of superstition, and of disorder in a civil effort to create external orthodoxy. Festivals were no longer needed as integrating, acculturative forces. The Bourbon concept of good governance did not rest on festival patronage but on education programs, public works projects, and services such as street lighting and garbage collection. The city council shared and benefited from the reform of festivals in concrete terms as the elite shielded and separated themselves from the popular traditions they sought to change.

The city councilmen were criollos and as such remained connected to the local cultural nexus and therefore experienced Bourbon economic reforms much as other propertied criollos. Although the reforms opened new opportunities for some colonists, they negatively affected others; the very top echelon of criollos with diverse financial holdings may have actually fared well by taking advantage of some of the reforms. However, the most clearly visible beneficiaries of the economic reforms were a small, extremely wealthy group of newcomer peninsulares.[79] Furthermore, the royal government was suspicious of criollos and of their abilities to govern and, more importantly, of their loyalty. It did not trust them to implement unpopular reform measures. Consequently, the Crown gave preferential treatment to peninsulares, who were more likely to disparage the cause of tradition and custom in legal cases and almost always followed royal decrees, and appointed them to positions on the high court and as intendants.[80] Although little of the growing tension between criollos and peninsulares was directly played out in the oath rituals, it existed nonetheless. For example, in the 1760 description of the archiepiscopal arch, the author beseeched the king to consider and utilize criollo talent in government. He also asked the king to aid the general population, steeped in poverty in the midst of a silver boom. He wished that "if it only could, among the echoes of this joy [the oath festivities], reach the ears of government and good intentions of the Crown, some word of what the People need."[81]

At the end of the eighteenth century, the general population, suffering under inflation, economic stagnation, increased taxes, and limited job opportunities, was deprived of the traditional retinue of festivities to soften the burden of life in the capital. Those that did occur were solemn in nature and watched carefully by authorities. But it was also an era of increasing conspiracies and revolts calling for independence. In the end, many colonists (criollos, castas, and Natives) came to believe that it was not they the vassals who needed instruction in the "civil virtues" but the monarch himself. In the final analysis, celebrating Apollo simply carried too high a price.

Chapter 6

Ritual, Satire, and the Coming of Independence

In honor of Louis I, university students hosted a satirical parade (*máscara ridícula*) through the streets of Mexico City in 1724. Four students dressed respectively as a pig, goat, donkey, and calf serenaded the crowd with screeches and howls and "grabbed the attention of the very cobblestones [in the street]." The outside of the cart was decorated with painted bears, horses, tigers, lions, and other animals. The theme of the float postulated that even the beasts sang in honor of the new king.

Behind this float of beasts marched another squadron of students costumed as soldiers in ragged uniforms. Some of the soldiers wore only one shoe, while others wore no stockings. Many carried broken weapons such as a gun with a missing barrel. All their weapons, however, had been constructed so that they could fire water at the spectators along the route. On top of the cart, the students had constructed a castle at the center of which was a large tub of water that served to replenish the ammunition of the students as they drenched the onlookers. Their satirical coat of arms was mounted on the back of the float and depicted a Turk fleeing on all fours. The message was that even a strangely dressed and poorly equipped squadron of Spaniards could be victorious when their hearts were filled with joy for their new monarch.

Students dressed as cats riding on horseback signaled the arrival of the next float in the parade. Alternately meowing and then menacing with their claws, these "felines" accompanied the second float, which featured an extremely obese cook surrounded by pots filled with pork. On the float, a group of students dressed as howling cats clamored for the cooks' attention, intent on gaining a few scraps of food. As the float passed by, the cook threw pieces of roasted meat to the crowd. The author describing the event stated that "so many pieces were thrown to the crowd that it was unbelievable." The float supposedly represented the love and generosity that the king had for his subjects.

Just behind the felines came a fighting brigade of students dressed as old hags, so battle worn that some appeared to be "newly risen from the grave." Each "woman" appeared to carry a baby that was actually a piece of old dry tree trunk, treating it as though it were an actual human child. In the center of the float that they accompanied was a large bed occupied by an old woman who pretended to have just given birth. The midwife (godmother) and the new father, both made of gunpowder, literally "exploded" with joy. As the students passed they wished the king a long and fruitful life, just as long and as fruitful as that of the comical new mother.

Next came twenty students dressed as a squadron of soldiers from Alexander the Great's army, followed by another group of students masquerading as ancient Greek gods. For the crowd's benefit, this group wore the recognizable attire and accouterments of each god. Thus, for example, Jupiter carried his signature lightning rods in his hand. This float, the focal point of the entire parade, was pulled by six men dressed as lions. Four guards watched over the float, at the center of which was a thirteen-foot helicon (mountain covered in flowers and beautiful foliage). At the top of the helicon stood a wood-and-cloth Pegasus, the winged horse, who by the operation of a lever was made to hit a rock and release a thick white liquid, representing the colony's silver production. A student acting the part of Spain's King Louis appeared as Apollo. He and the other students celebrated the flowing silver as it covered the entire helicon. This meant that Apollo (the Spanish king) had caused Nature to bring forth its precious minerals for the benefit of all. Then all of the performers accompanying the cart paid homage to Apollo/Louis.[1]

All future parades of this nature were banned by royal decree. Bourbon officials were quite aware that satire (in this case a humorous parade), with its use of extreme exaggeration, was a slippery cultural form that could be easily used to condemn institutions, prominent persons, and even societal and religious values. After all, they had issued one decree after another in order to ban carnival. Satirical rituals and poetry became media to express increasing dissatisfaction with the Bourbon colonial regime in Mexico. These acerbic social commentaries did not reject per se the values presented in government-sponsored ritual but rather questioned whether peninsular officials, the king, and official policies best represented those values. Officials in turn tried to ban parades and poems with only limited success. However, eventually the discontent and political tension that lay behind these parodies would no longer be limited to festivals and literature but would escalate to all-out rebellion.

Satire in Colonial Mexico City

Popular satire had a ubiquitous place in colonial Mexico's popular culture. During the seventeenth century, it was common for masked groups to take over sections of the city at night, close off streets, and perform lampoons and parodies of colonial officials and clergymen.[2] Hapsburg officials allowed satirical parades (especially by university students), and these lampoons were a standard part of nearly all major public events before they were banned by the Bourbon authorities. In addition to satirical parades, puppet shows, famous for their satirical content, were performed until the wee hours of the morning on Calle Arsinas.[3] Taverns and pulquerías were also common focal points for composing and performing popular satire.

Poetry in general was a highly valued part of popular culture. Plays with scripts in verse, songs, even rhyming sermons, and political poetic *pasquinades* (lampoons posted in public places) were part of daily experience. Furthermore, a witty turn of phrase appears to have been culturally prized by Spanish, African, and Native American societies. Poetry was an important cultural art, and poetry contests were frequent and well attended as a recognized part of most important events. In addition, tavern culture lent itself to extemporaneous poetry born of group endeavor. Individuals, often drunk, joined to compose witty rhyming lines and create what in essence was an ongoing draft poem. Some of the over 200 poems confiscated by the Inquisition during the seventeenth and eighteenth centuries were probably generated from this tavern culture. Other confiscated poems demonstrate highly developed aesthetic and literary sensibilities that indicate a well-read author. Rarely did the Inquisitors investigate to ascertain an author's identity or residency.[4] Given that literacy rates during the colonial period were very low, authors of these satirical verses were most likely disgruntled criollos and penin-sulares rather than commoners. Although occasional edicts banned certain satires, the majority continued to be performed and shared among better-off criollos and plebeians, finding their way into the popular music and dance forms of the day.[5] Thus satire was part and parcel of the popular culture of the capital.

Anonymous satire, often overlooked by historians, was frequently employed as a form of political communication, even an act of defiance, by those marginal to the power structure or those disgusted with it. As festivals were so clearly linked to politics, it was both logi-cal and inevitable that colonial satirists would turn to ritual (the satir-ical parade) as a means and as a metaphor to mock the government. Satire in all its forms (from parades, to songs, to hastily written ditties) could become a vehicle of expression that challenged the official dis-course of the colonial elite by referring to ideas of good governance and by providing a countervailing or, in the satirists' eyes, more authen-tic humorous interpretation.[6] Satire juxtaposed the idealized version of good governance espoused by the government with a satirical alter-native. The satirist's goal was to unravel the "official" ideology by deflating imagery, allegory, and metaphor to a literal interpretation. The result of successful satire was to deny the validity of the govern-ment's propaganda and the official published festival accounts by chal-lenging their authority and reliability.

The satirist, usually in the guise of a fool, guided his reader/spec-tator through a judicious reading of events, rituals, and character analyses, forcing the viewer/reader to evaluate and interpret significant values, all the while claiming to tell the truth and to be nonpartisan.[7] Popular satirists claimed authority from their status as "perfect vassal," the loyal subject so wronged by the government. Whereas officials sought to represent a pious, orderly, and stable society, a testament to Spain's ability to rule its colony well, satirists emphasized the impiety, disorder, and fragility, even focusing on the incompetence of the officials who ruled the colony. They inverted official representations by creating a parody, in which officials, including the king, were defined by self-interest, avarice, hypocrisy, cruelty, arrogance, and sheer stupidity.

This is what doomed the parade of students in 1724. Although the lampoon claimed to laud the monarch, in actuality it was a stinging social critique. The first float (the beasts) parodied the recent guild parade of the jura ceremony depicting screeching animals as loyal vassals. The second float presented the sorriest excuse for an army that students could apparently invent. Although they were supposedly victorious, such a portrayal of soldiers referenced the actual qualities of the colonial militia. This was a force largely recruited by use of drunkenness and vagrancy laws. Colonial officials commonly raided taverns and then sentenced criminals to army service. For the average soldier, a stint in the army was marked by low pay, harsh discipline, and little prospect of advancement.[8] The parody of the students was obvious to all. The float accompanied by students dressed as felines had presented the king as a corpulent cook who threw scraps from his abundant pot to the students/cats on the float and to the watching crowd. The meaning was clear. The wealthy king threw scraps from his table to the impoverished rather than generate a more long-lasting prosperity. The maternity float, although its intentions were purportedly to laud the new king and wish him well, compared Spain and the Spanish Crown to battle-worn hags. The final float, apparently intended to be more serious, celebrated the silver boom but emphasized that the proceeds of the mineral bonanza should be accessible to all, not just to the monarch.

Although students could no longer perform in satirical parades, officials patronized other events in an effort to replace the student parade with a more appropriate celebration. For example, in 1790, the city council gave permission to the young men of the Santa Veracruz neighborhood to reproduce an oath ceremony as part of the official festivities for Charles IV. The events included "an especially constructed platform, in front of which passed well-dressed young men on horseback, who threw coins made of tin, to the loud acclaim [of the crowd]." Officials were overwhelmingly pleased with the presentation, but it was noted that university students from the sidelines mocked the performers.[9]

Officials also tried to encourage humorous celebrations that would entertain the crowd without including potentially dangerous social commentary. Such events included the *jura mojiganga*, a combination of mock battle and funny parade. *Mojiganga* was a word utilized in seventeenth-century Spain to describe satirical or humorous masked parades originally associated with carnival. In Mexico, mojigangas became a standard variation on the mock battle performed for the oath to the king not only in the capital but in other areas of New Spain as well. For example, three mojigangas accompanied the jura to Charles III in Tamaulipas.[10]

The mojiganga in honor of the ascension of Ferdinand VI in Mexico City during 1747 serves as a fine example of such mock water battles. In this case, forty local notables accompanied by their assistants and the *alférez real* (royal ensign) carrying the royal banner paraded through the streets of the capital and maintained a headquarters on Monserrat Street for the entire month of the jura festivities. From this location, they kept a watchful eye on the inhabitants and maintained night patrols. The mojiganga wore masks and uniforms made of straw trimmed with wide bands of red sheepskin. For weapons they carried sausage stuffers; their ammunition was water. At the end of their month of comical patrol duty, they staged a large water battle in the zócalo.

Although authorities banned outright or sought alternatives to these satirical rituals, anonymous poets could not be stopped as easily. Satire was not unusual during the seventeenth century, but these forms of protest increased in frequency as the eighteenth century progressed, perhaps because satirists had more reasons to put ink to paper. Mocking verses pinpointed the human frailty and folly of the viceroys. A common target were those qualities highlighted on triumphal arches of the entry. In satire, the viceroy no longer was honorable, pious, charitable, wise and prudent, and motivated solely by the people's welfare. He was quite the opposite.

For example, in 1701, Viceroy Juan Ortega de Montáñez was accused of manifesting greed and other vices rather than the virtues of a good ruler: "Gold is his pastime, as well as pearls and jeweled baubles."[11] According to the author, the viceroy was less a Christian prince than a Turkish ruler, a Moor who took a perverted interest in nuns, visiting their convents regularly as though visiting his personal harem. Furthermore, the satirist alleged that the viceroy did not have the qualities to rule, having in fact stolen his position. He was an illegitimate ruler in the eyes of the people because he was not virtuous. As a matter of fact, the author claimed that he was a "glutinous spineless pig who received flattery, gifts, and ceremonies." However, warned the author, the viceroy should be wary because pork is the dish that makes weddings and festivals so special. In this case, the pork stew will have a sauce of crimson red (a reference to the robes of office and to blood, alluding to rebellion).[12] Thus in this satire, the viceroy, the guest and host of the entry ceremony, became the main meal to be consumed by an irate and betrayed populace.

Eighteenth-century satire also attacked Bourbon officials' concept of enlightened piety and their religious reform measures. Corpus Christi in particular had been a focus for reformers. Their goal had been to order into being a reverent and solemn religious experience for both participants and spectators. They replaced the Native enramada with a cloth canopy, banned the dances and the dragon that had traditionally led the procession, and ordered everyone to dress properly. In the process, they provided satirists with a unique forum from which to attack the policies and the piety of the reformers.

In "Relación verífica de la Procesión del Corpus de la Ciudad de Puebla" (confiscated in 1794), Don Hepicurio Almanancer Calancha y Santander (a pseudonym) wrote one of the most detailed anonymous satires utilizing the Corpus Christi procession as his inspiration. Although it depicts a Corpus Christi procession in the city of Puebla, the poem was apparently very popular in the capital.[13]

Calancha first attacked the canopy constructed to shade the participants from the bright sun along the processional route and serve as an honorific cover for the Holy Eucharist. The official cloth canopy had so many holes that "God would be able to scrutinize their every action." He intimated that they had much to hide and that they were not as pious as they believed themselves to be. Paramount among their sins was greed, a clearly defined lack of generosity to the citizenry. He used a clever play on the words *arcos* and *arcas* in order to condemn the elite for their lack of Christian charity. He stated: "The land was so poor; it was a shame that the coffers [arcas] were not as wide open as the holes in the arch (arcos)."

After discussing the canopy, Calancha commented on the participants, each in turn, in the procession. He lamented the poverty of the Native Americans, stating that "being last in all things in New Spain, in Corpus, they finally got to be first [in the procession]." Although they were poor, the author claimed that Natives were the only ones to process "correctly," that is, with real devotion, whereas the other (non-Native) participants had no such devotion. These more advantaged groups only appeared to be devout because they were concerned only with appearances. Here Calancha pointed out the irony of Bourbon decrees on proper dress during the procession because the poorest and most poorly dressed were in fact the most devout.

However, according to Calancha, when non-Natives were equally shabbily attired, their poor dress reflected their lack of piety. For example, he claimed that the religious Third Orders were infected with lice and covered in wax (from the candles that they carried). He alleged that they even had wax for brains. In his eyes, the regular clergy looked like poor ragamuffins and the university professors (also priests) were "all half dressed and half drunk." Quite shocking for the era was Calancha's description of the bishop in the procession. According to the poem, the prelate had almost missed the procession because he preferred to drink spiked chocolate and eat frijoles rather than participate. Calancha claimed that the bishop ran to his place in line just before the procession ended but had no time to dress in his episcopal garments and was forced to grab a purple rug and an Indian sash to wear in the procession. Calancha stated that all the citizens believed this outfit was official episcopal garb because so rarely did people actually see the bishop. He could have worn just about anything.

Finally, Calancha attacked the city council, the sponsors of the procession. He stated that they were not wealthy local notables as they claimed to be but rather simple guildsmen putting on airs. The alcaldes were the only participants in the procession who looked good because they had stolen the shirts right off the backs of Indians in order to dress well for the procession. Ironically, the officials who were the most impious were dressed in the finest garments. Here was a powerful critique of the *reparto de mercancías* (the forced sale of unwanted goods at exorbitant prices to Native communities) and the increase in tribute collection. Calancha painted local government as corrupt, larcenous, and false and encouraged citizens to demand justice of their own accord because it was not forthcoming from the authorities.[14]

Pauperism, sacrilege, corruption, vice, hypocrisy, false devotion, and tawdriness all characterized the procession and religious and civil authorities. The idealized city envisioned by Bourbon reformers was held up to the satirist's exaggerated light of day and found lacking.

The Host was still sacred, but the participants and the spectators apparently had not truly found Christ through their decrees mandating dress and solemn behavior. They were hypocrites who could not live up to their own standards of enlightened piety.

As we have seen for Calancha, anonymous satire gave a satirist the opportunity to critique the government while protecting his identity. However, satire was not merely the weapon of the weak or politically marginalized. More overt resistance to the new piety and religious reforms decreed by Bourbon ecclesiastical and civil reformers did occur, as was the case with Native Americans and the Corpus enramada tradition. Different groups in the capital attempted to mitigate the implementation of these reforms, and satire played a role in their endeavor. The satire in defense of San Gonzalo demonstrates that defenders of religious traditions were found well placed, even within the Church hierarchy.

In 1816, in the midst of the chaos of the wars of independence, a prominent member of the elite, the marquis of Ciria, came before the Inquisition to denounce the goings-on at the Church of Santo Domingo (just across the street from the Holy Office) in connection to San Gonzalo. San Gonzalo was born in 1189 and died in about 1259 near the town of Amarante, Portugal. While serving as a prebendary in Braga, he left his pastoral duties behind and went on a pilgrimage to the Holy Land. On his return, he joined the Dominican order. Once a member of this order, he lived as a hermit near Amarante, where he received many alms and was praised for his virtuous lifestyle. With the donations he received from the faithful, he funded the construction of a bridge over the Tamega River where, in the past, many people had drowned attempting to cross the raging waters.

Dancing to the saint had a long tradition, the origins of which are buried in local folklore. Regardless of the origins, the devout believed that San Gonzalo was pleased by these dances and that he intervened on their behalf with God. In Mexico City, commoners, mostly women, danced before the statue of the saint in an effort to remedy illnesses such as convulsions, migraines, crippled limbs, and the chills. Those who were too ill to travel arranged for the statue to visit their homes, where they and their families danced to him in private. The devotion required no specific type of dance, and therefore supplicants performed what they knew best—popular dances such as the *jarabe*, the *indita,* and the *tinga,* all of which could include sexually suggestive movements. Such devotional dancing to San Gonzalo attracted quite a bit of public attention, including commonly a host of onlookers. Viewers typically were either amused or scandalized by the performances, although some apparently served as an informal chorus. Similar devotions occurred in all Dominican churches, especially those in Portugal, Spain, and Brazil. In New Spain, San Gonzalo appeared to be most popular in Querétaro, Cuautla, and Mexico City.

The Inquisitors (Dominicans themselves) asked experts in theology to investigate the dances at Santo Domingo and file their opinions. In the end, these investigators could not reach agreement on a course of action. Therefore the Inquisitors turned to the learned scholar, reformer, and dean of the cathedral, Father José Mariano Beristáin, to voice his opinion on the subject. Both proponents and opponents of the dances weighed in with their opinions in what was to become a very heated discussion.

Opponents claimed that the dance was superstition and a prostitution of the devotion to the saints. They demanded that the dances be banned permanently. They also believed that if any dancing were to be performed before a saint, it would certainly not be the type and style of dancing performed at Santo Domingo, which had in effect turned the church into a popular dance hall.

The Dominicans defended their devotion by pointing to the long-standing tradition of dancing to San Gonzalo in Portugal, Spain, and Mexico. Neither Iberian nation prohibited the dance or thought it unseemly or superstitious. Dance proponents also sought to defend the entire notion of dancing as a form of legitimate worship by stating that it had been a tradition since "time immemorial and was an essential part of Mexican Catholicism." They noted it had only been altered with the prohibitions of Archbishop Lorenzana in 1769 and even then was only restricted to Corpus and Easter. But ever aware of the official attitude toward such popular religious displays, the Dominicans promised reform and closer scrutiny of the dances within their church.

The promises of reform fell on deaf ears, whereupon the Dominicans sought to publish a treatise in defense of their tradition, titled "No One Is Deceived, nor Suffers Rejection, If He Dances with Faith." The apparently anonymous author had himself danced to the saint and was cured of "mortal fevers that were extinguishing his breathing."

The author denounced those who claimed that the dance was superstitious, stating that such individuals were "tavern and playhouse theologians" who hung out in locales "where there was nary a volume of Saint Thomas's *Suma,* nor a treatise on morality." With one simple scandalous analogy, the author attacked the moral integrity and the intellectual expertise of prominent theologians in the capital who supported the new era's sanitized piety.

The author marshaled biblical evidence in support of the dancing devotion. For example, he pointed out that Mary and David had danced when Moses delivered the Hebrews from Egypt and received the Arc of the Covenant and that even angels in heaven danced. However, most of his argument was grounded in more popular (mundane) analogies. At one point in the treatise, he asked scholar and reformer Beristáin to imagine that he had a younger sister who on Mardi Gras sang the tinga (a popular song and dance style) that satirized and blasphemed the dance of San Gonzalo and then the following day (Ash Wednesday), with complete rectitude, she was found in church singing praises to God. Thus "this person could both sin by singing and sing her devotion to God." After all, the Church did not ban singing because it had both profane and sacred uses. This analogy illustrated one of his main arguments, namely that whether a dance was virtuous or sinful depended on the reasons someone danced and the way they danced. In the end, evoking a local refrain, he asked, "If dancing doesn't offend God and doesn't hurt anyone, what harm does it cause?"

The author even included poems dedicated to the saint, calling on the devout to dance to their heart's content. He was quite proud of his ditty, assuring his reader that it was not composed by "some acrostic-elliptical poet, like those who hang around the Pegasus [the equestrian statue of Charles IV] in the main plaza." This was an attack on the prominent literati, who were usually commissioned to design and then write jura descriptions, and their sophisticated style of verse. It also displayed a certain amount of disrespect for Charles IV by referring to his statue by the horse rather than the monarch.

In the final analysis, the author decided that the question of the dancing devotion had nothing whatsoever to do with piety. In his opinion, the problem with the dance was not the participants but the prejudices of elite spectators who came to criticize how poor people danced for the saint. He accused his opponents of banning the devotion because it was popular with the plebe, pointing out that the authorities were not about to prohibit or dismiss as sinful the fancy balls of the elite.

Such a highly sarcastic, accusative, and angry work was poorly crafted to persuade Beristáin to alter his opinion on the dance. In a letter, in which his anger was only thinly veiled, Beristáin reiterated his position that the dance should be banned permanently and categorically stated that the treatise should never be published. More specifically, he claimed that the "Defense" was full of "sarcasm, satire, jokes, and [popular] refrains" that the author surely did not learn in theology class. He was especially appalled that the author wanted all to believe that a "vague bunch of ignorant women and beasts fond of the latest fad could get all stirred up with spiritual joy." For that to be true, it "was necessary for the dancers to have confessed, received communion, to be fervent penitents, prepared for the holy dance by preceding prayers, lessons, and meditation on the divine truths." But in reality, "the women came running from the their kitchens to the church and the men just from the taverns to the temple, and then begins the hubbub, the uproar, the dance, the laughter, and profanation of the House of God." In addition, Beristáin took umbrage with the comparison between the San Gonzalo dances and that of David and Mary after the escape from Egypt. In his view, the two Hebrews danced alone in a profane location and their motivation for doing so was sincere and disinterested, "a pure gift," while in Mexico City a multitude danced on sacred ground motivated by vile self-interest, namely improved health, increased wealth, or some other temporal gain.

Beristáin, however, did not merely denigrate the author of the "Defense" or the dances but went further and pointed an accusing finger at the Dominican order itself. He in essence declared that this religious order made tremendous sums of money from the supplicants and therefore had a financial interest in maintaining the dance-devotion. It was clear to him that there was "a lot of scum mixed into the matter" of the dances at the Church of Santo Domingo. This last statement alone ensured an angry response from the prior of the

Dominican convent. What had once been an allegation of superstition now became a matter of honor on both sides. Father Juan García defended his order and demanded a detailed investigation of the devotion as a means to reinstate the dances. Furthermore, he questioned whether Beristáin was even qualified to give an opinion on the subject because he (like other opponents of the devotion) had never even witnessed the dances. Satire had turned to direct confrontation. Beristáin found García's tone to be unsuitable and baited him to take judicial action, reminding him that until some higher authority settled the matter, the dances remained prohibited.[15] To the satirist, the banning of the dance was not about religious devotion but about public propriety, and that was unjust and unwarranted. To him, the scandalized authorities and elite were not really pious but hypocrites who used religion to demonstrate their disdain for commoners, in direct disregard for the true teachings of Christ.

Popular satirists such as the proponent of the dance to San Gonzalo and Corpus Christi's Calancha did not articulate a coherent political program as an alternative to the viceregal system. Instead they described the hypocrisy of the royal governors and reforming clergymen, pointing to the disparity between the actions of real officials and policy makers and the utopian ideas presented in government-sponsored festivals. In this respect, the poems and treatises were in essence conservative. They did not directly advocate the dismantling of the system but rather that officials govern in a manner that benefited the colony, seeking to remind both the authorities and the colony's inhabitants of the professed obligation of colonial officials to the citizenry. It is true that we cannot accurately gauge the level of discontent based on the frequency or nature of these confiscated poems. Humor was commonly employed to mitigate personal and societal hardship. However, popular satire certainly had a spirited candor, and it was a deliberate attempt to appeal to the public on political matters.

Some poems, though, were passionately anti-Spanish and had within them the implied threat of rebellion as a way to reestablish the concept of good governance. These poems began to raise rather bluntly the question of Spain's right to rule the colony. For example, in 1768, the Mexican Inquisitors discovered a poetic diatribe against Charles III, the architect of so many of the Bourbon reforms. In this poem, a woman claimed to be Mexico, who on her deathbed was preparing to meet her maker. The cause of her death was the abuse and neglect that she had received from her husband, none other than the "illustrious Mr. Charles III." Addressing the monarch, she reminded him that he should deign to attend her funeral because she had been a loving and loyal wife. She had done her wifely duty always, following all of his "wishes, orders, precepts, and decrees." She placed him in charge of some of their children (she literally returned them to him) who were presented as abusive royal officials (peninsulares). She also pointed out that "these officials with each decree ma[d]e traitors of loyal hearts." Furthermore, she questioned why the king had sent so many soldiers to Mexico and warned him that his Mexican children (criollos) would disown him if he refused to trust them. He had effectively suffocated her heart with his suspicion, jealousy, and lack of confidence. She claimed that her epitaph would state that she "was not oppressed by barbarians/or some strange enemy,/but by a fierce three-headed monster [the fleur-de-lis, symbol of the Bourbon dynasty]/ . . . who sucked her dry to get her silver and gold."[16]

One of the most common types of anti-government satire confiscated by the Inquisitors were Lord's Prayers in which the petitioner asked God to protect and save colonial inhabitants from the poor government inflicted on them by peninsular Spaniards. These satirical prayers were widely circulated in the capital and had almost infinite variations. In general, the verses always ended with a line from the Lord's Prayer, punctuated with an *amen*. In a version from 1776, the author claimed that the Spaniards had failed in their own country, then decided to come to the Indies and refused to leave. They did whatever they wanted once in Mexico and never thought that they were committing a sin by taking the wealth of the region. The poet begged God to respond to his criollo complaints and to liberate the kingdom from the *gachupines* (the derogatory name for peninsulares), who he claimed were an infernal plague. They were the evil from which God was to deliver them.[17]

Both the Lord's Prayers and the "obituary" poem, like so much of popular satire, focused on the injustice of Bourbon economic reforms that were created to generate income for the Spanish Crown. Some colonists clearly felt that such policies not only had a negative impact on the viceroyalty but were motivated by greed and selfishness. In their minds, the king, his officials, and peninsulares resident in the colony cared little for Mexico and its future. The anger and feelings of betrayal of these colonists reflected the breech between criollos and peninsulares that was ever widening.

Ritual and the Coming of Independence

After 1790, as the full impact of the economic reforms became evident, dissatisfaction with the Crown appeared to increase, as did the volume of popular satire. Feelings of discontent expanded further in Mexico City as the Crown instituted its last (ecclesiastical) reform in 1804. Royal officials ordered the confiscation of Church real estate and liquid assets. The Crown claimed that these funds were a loan of sorts and pledged to pay a 5 percent annual interest rate on the principal of the amount confiscated. As a major financial lender, the Church was forced to call in loans given to hundreds of ranchers, farmers, and corporate entities (such as Native towns) in order to satisfy the Crown. From 1805 to 1809, the government collected some 12 million pesos. Although the application of the decree was not necessarily uniform across the colony, many hacienda owners, businessmen, and Native communities were forced to come up with the funds to pay the Church so it could, in turn, pay the royal government. And as if to add insult to injury, the annual interest pledged by the decree was rarely paid in full.[18]

Three attempts to procure independence occurred during this time period. In 1794, the appointment of the marquis of Branciforte as viceroy led to pasquinades proclaiming the ideals of the French Revolution being placed on the walls of buildings. At the same time, conspirators sought to liberate prisoners from the city jail, Native Americans from tribute, and Mexico from the Spanish Crown. Five years later, some criollos in the capital planned to revolt in the name of independence in the Machete Conspiracy (so called because the participants lacked any weapons other than machetes). And in 1801 Native Americans plotted to declare Mexico free of Spain. Officials discovered all three rebel plots, arresting those involved. Some held in prison died. Others were released. Either way, the royal government feared that executing the ringleaders might produce martyrs for the cause of independence.

In 1808, Napoleon Bonaparte invaded Spain and forced Charles IV to abdicate his throne to his son, Ferdinand VII. However, Ferdinand also became a prisoner of Napoleon, who actually selected his brother Joseph Bonaparte to rule Spain. This series of events gave anti-Spanish forces in the colony the perfect opportunity to seek Mexico's independence from the mother country. One popular satirist of the period called for "criollos to throw off the Spanish yoke or face a future filled with misery [under Ferdinand]."[19] At this time, Mexico City's councilmen were composed of prominent criollos and peninsulares whose political and economic ties were to the local Mexican nexus. They believed that Joseph Bonaparte was an illegitimate ruler of Spain and therefore had no authority over New Spain. In the councilmen's opinion, actual authority should naturally reside in the hand of the colony's elite until Ferdinand VII could regain the throne. Thus the councilmen recommended that a provisional government ruling in the king's name be established in Mexico City. The viceroy, José de Iturrigaray, maintaining a cautious attitude, appeared to welcome the councilmen's input and advice on the crisis. Wealthy peninsulares, on the other hand, feared, perhaps justly, that a policy that allowed a provisional government would inevitably lead to independence.

Tensions began to escalate as the city prepared to celebrate Ferdinand's (theoretical) ascension to the throne. The viceroy and his wife distributed money to the crowds during the jura in an effort to garner additional support among the populace, perhaps for the city councilmen's concept of provisional self-government (home rule). During the ceremony, commoners pelted peninsular elites with rocks as they rode by in their carriages. The royal government's stage was decorated, as was the custom, with paintings depicting the monarch as Apollo. A highly visible poetic diatribe against Napoleon was placed on the stage as well. The poem warned Napoleon that his days of ruling Spain and her colonies were short-lived and attacked his character as a ruler. The poet asked whether Napoleon deserved to rule Spain and answered in the negative, pointing out that loyal Spaniards would defeat him. But as if in response to questions raised by the poem, rioting citizens tore down a goodly portion of this stage.[20] Their answer was not that Bonaparte should be destroyed in order that Ferdinand rule but rather that Mexicans should rule themselves, needing neither Ferdinand nor Napoleon. In this fashion, the question of the loyalty of the king's subjects, such a central theme of Bourbon-era juras, finally left the world of paintings, poems, and fanfare with disturbing force.

The significance of these events during the oath and the attempts to call a congress to consider home rule were not lost on the peninsular royalists in the city. They responded by purchasing all the arms and ammunition available in the capital. Their actions were quite conspicuous to everyone. A month after the oath ceremony, wealthy Spanish merchant and *hacendado* (ranch owner) Gabriel de Yermo, with the complete support of the archbishop, Audiencia judges, and prominent citizens, all peninsulares, successfully deposed Viceroy Iturrigaray. Yermo had feared a revolt of commoners in league with the "rebel" city councilmen. This preventive coup had the effect of halting the city council's plan to establish a provisional government. Additionally, it intensified animosity toward the peninsulares, who immediately placed "their" viceroy, Pedro Garibay, in office. In the opinion of many average citizens and the city councilmen, now an illegitimate Spanish government controlled the viceroyalty. The net effect of Yermo's actions was to strengthen the resolve of those who sought an immediate end to Spanish rule in Mexico.[21]

In September 1810, the Cortes at Cádiz (a legislative body leading the effort to expel Napoleon's forces from Spain and attempting to rule in Ferdinand's stead) appointed a new viceroy, Francisco Xavier Venegas, to rule the colony. Royal officials sought to utilize the image of the Virgin of Remedies to consolidate popular and Native support for Ferdinand VII, who was Napoleon's prisoner. One publication, supposedly written by an indigenous author, attempted to duplicate popular speech. This ostensibly Native author consoled Spaniards and assured them that the Virgin, who had performed so many miracles for the Natives, would no doubt protect Mexico. In addition, he claimed that the Indians were ready to die for her, the symbol of the royal government.[22]

The 1810 procession sought the Virgin of Remedies' aid against Napoleon; however, the focal point of the festival was the relationship between the king and the Indians. The author, Luis José Montaña, describing the event, claimed that the altars along the processional route did not include the customary statues of saints and

Mary; rather, inhabitants decorated everything, even their houses, with tapestries and statues of Ferdinand. The procession organizers presented a float showing a Native American awaiting the defeat of Napoleon through the intervention of the Virgin. Alongside the Indian was an angel standing on the defeated Bonaparte. An accompanying banner proclaimed: Indian Loyalty Without Rival. Large numbers of Natives dressed in pre-Columbian costumes escorted the cart; some carried representations of Juan de Tovar, the early–sixteenth-century Native leader before whom the Virgin first appeared.[23] Just as Montaña was about to publish his description of the procession, Father Miguel Hidalgo y Costilla led an army of Native Americans, castas, and some criollos on a march toward the capital, taking town after town for the independence cause.

The royal propaganda machine, in control of newspapers and printing presses, attempted to frighten city inhabitants and discourage their support of the Hidalgo revolt. These government tracts emphasized the violent and destructive nature of Hidalgo´s army. Such royal propaganda painted the revolt as an Indian rebellion rather than as a patriotic movement.

The Crown now further emphasized the Virgin of Remedies' role as the Conquest Virgin. New apparition histories and political tracts were published in which the events of the Noche Triste were reiterated. She was again called upon to fight against Native Americans, the majority of the participants in Hidalgo's army. Poetry and broadsides intended for Natives lauded the benefits of Spanish empire and claimed that without the Conquest, the Virgin of Remedies would never have come to Mexico. Other authors described sixteenth-century mural paintings at the Virgin's shrine that depicted the Virgin fighting alongside the conquerors and injuring the Aztec warriors as they attempted to remove her statue from the high altar in the Templo Mayor. Such documents conveniently failed to mention all the other murals (the majority) that had presented the Virgin as protectress of individual Indians, Africans, and Spaniards. There was even a movement among royal officials to move her feast day to August 13, thereby combining it with the Festival of the Royal Banner, which commemorated the fall of Tenochtitlan to Cortés in 1521.[24]

Furthermore, royal officials renamed the Virgin of Remedies. She became the Generala (the General), the symbolic head of the royalist troops in the field against Mexican patriots. The nuns of San Jerónimo even dressed the statue in military garb.[25] Author Agustín Fernández de San Salvador wrote that the Virgin, now at the cathedral, had brought clouds and a great wind to the city. Lightning struck near her shrine, a sign that she did not wish to leave the capital but rather wanted to protect the city's citizens from Hidalgo, who sought "to vomit all the calamities of civil war onto New Spain." The procession and novena of February 24, 1811, took place to show royalist gratitude to the Virgin of Remedies for the impending defeat of the rebels.[26]

Hidalgo's partisans attempted to counter the royalist rhetoric with their own pamphlets and pasquinades and with their own image of Mary, namely the Virgin of Guadalupe. But government propaganda was at least partially successful as the urban masses did not rise up to join Hidalgo's army when it encircled the city. Citizens most likely believed the government propaganda and feared the destruction that would be wrought in the city by Hidalgo's army. Nonetheless, sympathy for independence appeared to be extremely strong in Mexico City. Royalists crushed at least two conspiracies that sought to kidnap Viceroy Venegas and deliver him to the rebels. Secret societies such as the Guadalupes were created by patriots to aid rebels in the countryside and coordinate pro-independence activity in the capital.

However, with Spanish military forces strengthened by mandatory conscription and royalist garrisons housed in the university buildings situated in the center of the city, Viceroy Venegas had the upper hand in Mexico City. He redesigned the Junta of Police and Public Security and created a passport system that limited the mobility of citizens and tracked their comings and goings. The combined effects of these changes helped limit rebel infiltration of the city. However, these measures aggravated the already strained relations in the capital between Venegas and a populace inflamed by constant reports of arrests of those supposedly plotting against the royal government.

Hidalgo was arrested and executed some six months after the revolt had begun, and the Virgin of Remedies was believed responsible for the successes of royal forces during the rebellion. Government pamphletist Fernández de San Salvador claimed that this was a lesson to be learned by all those who sought to insult the Virgin with impunity. In his eyes, the Generala had protected the people from the "demonical fanaticism" that threatened both religion and the Crown.[27] Thus at the end of the colonial period, the Virgin of Remedies, who for centuries had represented the Madonna, the patroness of all Mexicans regardless of ethnicity, had come full circle. Now in the guise of the Conquest Virgin, the ally of Cortés, she fought against any who would question the right to rule of the Spanish king. Mary became an essential tool of despotism. However, José Maria Morelos y Pavón, another priest, picked up the banner of Guadalupe and continued the independence fight.

In this atmosphere, the Constitution of Cádiz was promulgated (1812) by the Cortes in Spain. The constitution was a progressive document that called for a constitutional monarchy with Ferdinand at its head, and it granted more rights to the colonies, such as limited freedom of the press and local elections. In Mexico City, an enthusiastic city council sought to implement the reforms of the constitution. Although Venegas stalled repeatedly on the implementation of freedom of the press, he was eventually forced to allow elections for municipal government. These elections handed an overwhelming victory to criollos, who favored autonomy from Spain and now controlled the city council with the support of the masses. Large segments of the general population had participated, casting their votes against the monarch. After the balloting, the city celebrated for two entire days. Viceroy Venegas quickly annulled the election results. Pressure to respect the results continued from local patriots, and Venegas's successor, Viceroy Félix María Calleja del Rey, was in essence forced to hold a second election. Again criollo patriots won the city council seats. This time they actually took office. However, Calleja and the royalist Audiencia frustrated all efforts of the newly elected city council to institute the other reforms, such as freedom of the press, of the Constitution of Cádiz.

That same year the royalists in the city sought to celebrate the Royal Banner Festival in an effort to honor the king. Royal officials increased the stipend to host the official banquet to 1,400 pesos, a record in the history of the celebration. The increase in funds was part of an effort to entice the independence-leaning city councilmen to put on a fine public show for the king.[28] But the celebration never took place because it was abolished by Spain's Cortes of Cádiz. The Cortes wished to promote a new equality among the different provinces (colony or metropolis) of the realm. Consequently, the Cortes abolished the raising of the Royal Banner celebration because the "monuments of the old system of conquest and colonies ought to disappear before the majestic idea of the perfect equality of reciprocal love and the union of interests" between the colonies and Spain.[29]

When Ferdinand VII regained his throne in 1814, his first act was to abolish this liberal constitution. Mexico City's elected councilmen's last act, under this constitution, was to plan the jura to celebrate the Spanish monarch's restoration to power. Once the jura was over, the overjoyed royalists in Mexico City turned on the councilmen elected under the 1812 constitution and accused them of treason, arresting several of them on trumped-up charges. With the return of the monarch to power, royal officials in Mexico re-instituted the Royal Banner Festival. The viceroy informed the reconstituted city council, dominated by royalists, that the parade would take place in carriages. Councilmen participating in the event would simply hang the royal banner outside the window of their coach.[30] Although the festival was designed to "inspire in the hearts of American vassals the sentiments that toward the king they ought to possess,"[31] the king received letters informing him that the festival staged in Mexico City was a laughable sight.[32] But even the royalist city councilmen believed that government funds were better spent on fighting against the insurgents.[33]

By 1815, Morelos, leader of the independence rebels, had been captured and executed. The royalists then moved against the secret Guadalupes in Mexico City who had supplied arms, money, and political support to insurgents like Morelos. As a fine show of absolutism, the king wanted a raising of the royal banner festival and he wanted it done properly. In 1816, he resurrected the parade on horseback. The viceroy again granted the 1,400-peso stipend, and in a letter sent to the viceroy, the councilmen stated: "Such an August ceremony always was solemnized in an extraordinary manner corresponding to the magnitude of its purpose, being able to assure that in nothing did it cede to the [now] in ruins Roman triumphs." In their opinion, the parade of carriages had been a travesty that attracted no audience from the general populace. They likened the coach retinue to a funeral procession that produced "gossip among the People, even those at the lowest level." The councilmen believed that given the recent rebellion, the festival had to be celebrated with dignity.[34]

However, in Spain during 1820, the Riego Revolt, a major insurrection of the Spanish army against Ferdinand, led to a liberal victory and the re-institution of the Constitution of Cádiz. The city council in Mexico City hosted a 15,985-peso celebration to honor the constitution. However, Ferdinand had no intention of allowing a constitutional monarchy to take permanent hold in Spain. Criollos and allied peninsulares feared, and rightly so, that Ferdinand would take the first opportunity to abolish the constitution again and control the government completely. Consequently, Mexican patriots decided to join Agustín de Iturbide's independence movement. In so doing, they rejected Ferdinand as their monarch but retained the Constitution of Cádiz. In 1821, Mexican-born Iturbide, a general in the royalist army who switched sides, and his army of the Three Guarantees entered the city to the effusive acclamations of the inhabitants, passing through a triumphal arch erected by pro-independence officials.

That same year (1821) the Festival of the Royal Banner was eliminated from the city's festival calendar. José Joaquín Fernández de Lizardi, famed author, journalist, political satirist, and patriot, wrote an epitaph for the old colonial celebration titled "Life and Death of Sir Royal Banner by His Friend the Thinker." Years later, the church of Saint Hippolytus was rededicated to Saint Jude. All that is left of the ill-fated Roman martyr selected to represent the Spanish victory in 1521 is a small statue at the side of that church. In the end, the conquest fiesta had become, in effect, a festival of the royal demise in Mexico. The Virgin of Remedies was still used in processions in response to epidemics during the early nineteenth century. Today she is all but forgotten except for a small number of the devout who reside near her shrine, which is now a parish church.

Conclusion

Throughout the entire pre-independence period, royal officials and many of the peninsular elite, especially Viceroys Venegas and Calleja, consistently violated established political traditions in the capital, openly disobeyed the law, and acted in a tyrannical fashion from the perspective of much of the population. For example, Viceroy Calleja was so hated that it became common for rebels to hold nightly dances in which his likenesses were cut to pieces.[35] The viceroys, firmly entrenched in a system of absolutism, chose to govern by force rather than allow the limited reforms of the Constitution of Cádiz, an act that might have staved off independence. The viceroys by their actions and King Ferdinand by his refusal to accept the constitution had subverted the models of the ideal ruling prince that had earlier sustained the monarchs. Coupled with the impact of the Bourbon reforms, the economic hardship of the period, and the general spirit of independence that pervaded the colony, their actions delegitimized the Crown. The government did not act in the people's welfare; the social contract had been broken, and, to a significant percentage of the population in the city, it was beyond repair. The royal government itself, as opposed to an ineffectual or corrupt individual viceroy, had become bad government.

Although the ruling system was discredited throughout Mexico, the legacy of the Bourbon ruling mythology about the person of the king was still evident in manifestly interesting ways. After all, the royal government had made it a point to demand that every cabecera town celebrate an oath to the king; thus the mythology of the king as the ideal prince was evident in those towns as well as in the capital. The ruling mythology struck a particularly poignant nerve in these provincial areas that resonated even among patriots. For example, some Native insurgents claimed that the Spanish king was supporting their cause. In the case of some in Hidalgo's army, they even alleged that the king was actually in New Spain. According to these stories, he supposedly witnessed battles, commanded troops, and cheered on and rewarded the rebel forces. He appeared wearing a silver mask and dark clothes and traveled about by carriage. Some claimed to have seen him accompanying Hidalgo himself. This emphasis on a rebel king represented the insurgents' "messianic hopes" that a mythical, semidivine, and just king would rightly side with their cause.[36] This clearly played on the long established tradition of rituals such as the oath to the king and official discourse that emphasized the role of the king as final arbiter in disputes and champion of justice. In this fashion, the monarch maintained his prestige, but he did so by liberating his oppressed subjects from his own officials and the burdensome imperial system of which he was the head. By fighting on the patriot side during independence, his already sacred stature was reconceptualized, strengthened, and adjusted to the circumstances at hand.[37]

In effect, the Natives under Hidalgo's command lacked a well-for-mulated political program or alternative to the colonial system and postulated a revised version of "long live the king, down with bad gov-ernment" that had frequently been the battle cry for many local revolts. The king as rebel, so central to this particular popular politi-cal vision, only emphasized the impact of a long cultivated vision of the monarch as symbol rather than concrete individual. Insurgents could come to see the king as a non-Spaniard at the same time that they violently attacked local gachupines. The officials and those who benefited from unjust Bourbon policies were made to suffer rather than the monarch. The king-as-savior metaphor was not connected to the rebel cause in Mexico City, where he had lost his mythic stature and had become more accountable in both ritual and real life for the policies of the imperial state. Those policies were especially tangible and recognizable in the capital, the home of Bourbon abso-lutism in the colony. In the end, the king was held responsible for his own tyrannical actions and those of his impious viceroys.

Chapter 7

Concluding Thoughts

It must be considered that there is nothing more difficult to carry out, nor more doubtful to success, nor more dangerous to handle, than to initiate a new order of things.[1]

No doubt this was a sentiment shared by the early Spanish friars and administrators intent on maintaining an empire and fostering the creation of a society that took into account the complexity of relations among Europeans, Amerindians, and Africans. A number of factors aided Spanish control in the central valley of Mexico. Among the most important were the highly complex and stratified nature of pre-Columbian society and government that served as the foundation for Spanish policies; for example, the already existing indigenous institutions such as tribute and labor duty. The Native American elite also accepted European religious and governmental structures, at least publicly. The corporate and very public forms of religious devotion of both societies facilitated the nominal acceptance of Catholicism. The demographic disaster of the sixteenth century created cultural spaces for Spanish religious and political traditions. The evangelization process, though not as uniform or comprehensive as initially desired, did seek to create a Christian society based on the finest of Hispanic values and customs. As part of that process, European religious festivals, an essential component of Spanish Catholicism, crossed the Atlantic and became an integral part of worship and daily life. The government also introduced modest festive traditions to honor the new political system and the distant king.

The vision of a separate Spanish and Indian world that early religious and civil officials envisioned began to lose validity almost as soon as it was formulated. By the late sixteenth century, life in the capital was characterized by tremendous ethnic diversity that resulted from both racial mixing and cultural exchange that unsettled the ordered world originally conceptualized by Spanish authorities. Maintaining control and stability became even more of a concern in the wake of further demographic change, natural disasters, and economic dislocations and stagnation. Unable to alter such powerful trends, officials sought to maintain control by recourse to a number of policies, most striking among them the creation of the caste system. Large government-sponsored celebrations also became an integral part of their policy.

Large-scale public spectacles gave the authorities an opportunity to organize and orchestrate music, dance, mock jousts and battles, parades, processions, fireworks, lighting, painting, poetry, and monumental (ephemeral) architecture in an effort to put forth political and social concepts. More specifically, it gave them the means to articulate the rationale for their continued control and privileged position in colonial society. Through these celebrations of the senses, officials sought to persuade inhabitants to accept their definition of good governance. They also wished to provide colonial ritual structures and language to encourage identification with a local environment composed of Natives, Africans, and Spaniards. Officials wished to control both the message and the medium to foster an acculturation that benefited their continued rule.

The cornerstone festival for the articulation of good governance was the viceregal entry, where officials created a vision of the magnificence, power, and generosity of the government. On these occasions, the viceroy appeared as a savior, a deliverer, who, endowed with all the classic virtues, was capable of re-instituting the golden age of Saturn. Consequently, he was presented publicly there, in the midst of the assembled people, to be acclaimed, almost worshiped. The festival placed an ideal government on display in order to impress onlookers, to instill hope in the possibility of change and renewed prosperity, and to garner popular support for the government.

The Hapsburg jura ceremony presented the Spanish monarch to the multitudes of Mexico City. He was presented by festival patrons as a semidivine figure. Thus the oath paid homage to a mythic personage as the ceremony celebrated the individual on whom rested the entire monarchical system. The ceremony lauded the authority and the successes of the Spanish empire, in this case the conquest of the Aztec empire. The allegiance ritual also showcased the official vision of a world divided into Spanish and Native American spheres. Spaniards and Natives separately pledged their fidelity and, as a result, were joined by their obedience to one monarch; in this sense, the entire meaning of the festival was ritualized submission. Each part of society necessary for successful governing gave a public pledge to honor the monarch and, in so doing, formed a symbolic bond.

Hapsburg officials eagerly patronized and attended religious festivals in an effort to express their own faith, engage in a type of public charity, and incarnate, though their actions, the image of the "pious ruler" deserving of authority and worthy of imitation. The processions of Corpus Christi and the Virgin of Remedies were festivals that encouraged the status quo as each group participated in rank and order. Those wielding power and socioeconomic advantage held the most prestigious locations near the Host or near the statue of the Madonna. This placement implied that political and moral authority were joined again as they were in the entrance ceremony. Yet at the same time, the government joined celebrations in which it humbled itself before higher divine authorities. The viceroy was subservient before the Eucharist and Mary and devout before his subjects and, in so doing, fulfilled the most important characteristic espoused on the triumphal arches of the entry. As all were joined by allegiance to the monarch, so they were also joined by their love of God.

The city councilmen, the festival organizers, and allied viceroys all believed that government sponsorship of festivals was in and of itself a virtue. They were concerned about positive public opinion, and a "happy," entertained populace was less likely to rebel, less likely to question their right to rule and the existing social order. They not only believed that it was a good idea to entertain the populace, especially Native Americans, but also that it was a central characteristic of a good government. The festival sponsored by the government served as a "gift" whereby merriment, the momentary forgetting of the problems of daily life, helped promote the image of a generous government and thereby courted allegiance. A decrease in festival ostentation was considered detrimental to not only the government's well-being but that of the populace.

The entry ceremony in particular ritualized a social contract in which the governor swore to defend the city and govern well and appeared to accept the qualifications of the ideal governor put forth by the local authorities and intellectuals—integrity, industriousness, generosity, and compassion for one's subjects. The oaths themselves and the symbolic message of the arches gave voice to the aspirations of the local leadership (on behalf of the populace) and provided a common idiom for the responsibility of the colonial government to the people.

Popular participation was designed to complement this image of the government. It was not sufficient to merely allow spectators to bear witness to the greatness of the government and the inherent virtues of its ministers. It would simply have too boldly shown the festivals as the self-serving propaganda that they were. Spectacle had been designed to incorporate popular participation because without it the meaning of the festivals would have been incomplete and one-dimensional. Corpus Christi, the viceregal entry, Remedios, and the allegiance ceremony all attempted to celebrate, in some form, a multiethnic society, to serve as both integrative and hegemonic tools. In the midst of a fast-growing heterogeneous population, the ideal colonial Christian prince could not exist without his counterpart, the perfect vassal, who performed publicly as a representative of his/her ethnic group.

In this fashion, the propaganda of good governance posited the concept of hierarchical unity, that an effective, caring government, motivated by religious zeal and Christian virtue, sought to serve the people in an effort to forge a better society and that the creation of such a society included a role, both in theory and in actual ritual participation, for every citizen, whether Native, African, or Spaniard, always in their appropriate place according to a hierarchical system that gave preference to wealthy Spaniards. In exchange for acceptance of Spanish imperial rule (the prerequisite for achieving the golden age), this perfect vassal received increased income through state largesse, prestige, political favors, and even freedom from slavery.

The festivals also reflected the political reality of the capital because city councilmen, by and large wealthy criollos, were in charge of the organization and funding of Hapsburg festivals. They recognized that not only popular opinion but also popular participation was essential to large-scale spectacle in the capital. And popular participation in Mexico City festivals was much larger than that in similar events in Spain. Spaniards in Mexico constituted a minority that precariously ruled a society composed of diverse groups who, if they joined, held the potential to easily depose them from power. In addition, the councilmen, identifying with their capital, emphasized local concerns and pressed those concerns onto the message of the festivals. They also prioritized festivals in the capital, giving preference to the entry, which was far more elaborate and expensive (and remained such for over 100 years) compared to the oath to the king. The entry honored the power of the imperial government, where it was most immediate, most accessible, most tangible—in the person of the viceroy.

Although at first glance the festivals appear to have focused on the viceroy, the councilmen also showcased city inhabitants and themselves as civic leaders. They and their fellow citizens were the perfect vassals; thus the true star of the entry was none other than the city itself. The aldermen showed the viceroy and his entourage that the capital would not be outdone by other cities, that it was equal to or perhaps even superior to its European counterparts. They also educated the viceroy about the power and wealth of the local social network and, in so doing, performed not only the power of the imperial government but that of their local class.

Eighteenth-century authorities valued rituals as political tools but evaluated Hapsburg festival statecraft just as they reviewed all other aspects of their predecessors' rule in the colonies. Bourbon officials made use of Hapsburg traditions and festive style but reshaped them to a different political philosophy. The Bourbon governing concept placed emphasis on the Crown, and as an obvious consequence, the ceremony of the oath to the king received the majority of the attention, funding, and organizational expertise of colonial officials in Mexico City. Royal officials also appropriated the ritual devotion to the Virgin of Remedies in an attempt to redirect popular support toward the Crown and its goals. Royal officials even resurrected the Festival of the Royal Banner and reconfigured it in order to provide a medium through which the monarch could be celebrated on a more regular basis, thereby "rectifying" local prioritization of imperial rituals under the Hapsburgs.

New ostentation fortified the significance of the allegiance festival, and the king, presented as the sun god, Apollo, was posited as a wise, just, and virtuous ruler who deserved the homage and respect of his vassals. He became the ideal Christian prince, a representation closer to what had always been the case in European festivals. He was cast in virtuous terms, linked to visions of utopia, and popular participation was marshaled, mandated, and orchestrated to showcase colonial residents as model citizens. In this respect the Bourbon oath festival was similar to the Hapsburg entry ceremony. The Bourbon jura made consistent references to the duties of vassals, including undying loyalty and personal sacrifice for the king. Unheroic or disloyal acts would be punished severely, as each jura included direct warnings about popular uprisings and the questioning of government legitimacy.

Bourbon authorities scaled down the festival dedicated to the king's minister while celebrating the monarch, the focus of their political philosophy. As the Crown created the intendancy system in an effort to diminish the overriding authority of the viceroy in the colony, so it attacked the festival that lauded the viceroy's power, the entry ceremony. Funding for the entrance immediately decreased dramatically. Popular participation in the entry also was eliminated. The only public entertainment associated with the festival that survived was the bullfight, where an admission price was charged. The viceroy was still the highest royal official in the land, but the festival that attempted to impress the populace with his power and authority lost meaning in the eyes of his subjects. Strikingly, government officials still realized the power of the king's minister and therefore continued to impress the new viceroy with gifts, dinners, dances, and theatrical performances, but all this took place in private. The triumphal arch and related activities that had articulated the symbolic social contract no longer formed part of the ceremony, and even when they did, the new minister was no longer viewed as a virtuous hero but as an efficient bureaucrat who served the king.

While Hapsburg officials appeared to take every opportunity to promote their role as festival sponsors and were willing on many occasions to fund popular performances, Bourbon administrators felt very strongly that it was the colonial subject's duty to celebrate the distant king (the government). They expected and attempted to mandate compliance and were suspicious of those vassals who claimed a lack of resources that prevented elaborate displays of homage. As time progressed, only wealthy Spanish vassals resident in Mexico City participated, and they came to represent the idealized perfect subjects of the king. The only "gift" the Bourbon government offered the people was the hope of superior monarchical government influenced by certain aspects of the Enlightenment.

The Bourbon ruling philosophy, similar to its seventeenth-century Hapsburg counterpart, also viewed the colony's increasing number of castas with concern, as a destabilizing factor. Increasingly authorities saw the potentially subversive nature of the city's multitudes as a source of moral ills. Thus Bourbon social reforms sought to modernize and morally fortify the populace, attempting as it did so to institute a new behavioral code. In contrast to the Hapsburgs, who created vehicles to channel and influence popular opinion, the Bourbons issued decrees that stifled popular participation and traditional festive exuberance in those instances when the festive environment was viewed as too volatile. This perceived volatility was usually connected, as it was in Corpus Christi, with all that was genuinely popular. What the Hapsburgs had encouraged or tolerated in the name of security and legitimacy, the Bourbons generally found unacceptable for exactly the same reasons. Bourbon authorities, for a variety of motives, from fiscal conservatism to a fear of popular revolt, established a hierarchy of festivals and popular pastimes and emphasized those they believed benefited and uplifted society. At the same time, they reformed or banned those that were seen as dangerous, too exuberant, or too connected to Indian or African cultural traditions.

In many respects, Bourbon festival policy was about difference and exclusion as opposed to the Hapsburg emphasis on difference and inclusion. The perfect vassals were wealthy Spaniards, and Natives and castas disappeared from state festivals and suffered from these reforms of popular celebrations. With the two religious festivals that were state sponsored the concept of exclusivity was particularly manifest. With both the celebrations of the Royal Banner and the Virgin of Remedies, officials resurrected images of the Conquest, the brutality and superiority of the victorious Spanish. The Crown imposed its will on Native peoples in the sixteenth century by force of arms and would seek to do the same with a refashioned symbolic image of the Conquest to counter patriotic sentiment in the eighteenth century.

Independence was brought about by a myriad of factors, including the destabilizing effects of the Bourbon economic reforms; however, essential to the momentum toward independence was a growing perception among significant sectors of New Spanish society, particularly the criollos, that the royal government was consumed by its own self-interest. Although criollo city councilmen considered themselves to be enlightened men who shared the zeal of Bourbon reformers on many issues, in the end their allegiance was with the local culture and society, and their identity was Mexican. Furthermore, the constant emphasis on the king and his connection to prosperity in the realm in the jura led spectators to attribute the distance between utopia and the harsh realities directly to the monarch and not to an unjust or incompetent minister. At a time when Bourbon administration of the realm was increasingly called into question, the king was made accountable for his actions in the most important celebration of the late colonial period. This fact was acknowledged during the jura itself: the arch of the physicians guild in the 1747 oath ceremony claimed that unpopular decrees were necessary for the general welfare, regardless of how colonists may have felt.[2]

Control and legitimacy were at the center of both Hapsburg and Bourbon rituals, and those festivals became politically effective forms of communication that was indicative of real political, social, and economic issues. The government used its power and the symbolic power of ritual to persuade the masses and represent idealized power relations that justified Spanish domination and control. However, although it consistently posited the superiority of the Spanish governing system, these rituals placed citizens, whether participants or spectators, in the essential position of judging the effectiveness of that system.

Different groups no doubt viewed the festivals in different ways. Native American elites appeared to have valued participation in the jura as a way to enhance their own prestige within both Spanish and Native hierarchies and social structures. The construction of the thatch arbor for Corpus apparently was viewed as a festive duty and an honor, one they would "fight" to retain. Incorporation of European ritual elements such as emblems, triumphal arches, and accompanying poetic recitals, arches, and mock battles was indicative of an acculturation of meaning as well as of form. Rituals and symbols were refashioned and interpreted to demonstrate and encourage community and group pride and identity.

In many respects, we can claim that the citizenry did accept the values of the festivals and came to esteem the qualities of good governance more than many government officials. Good governance was defined using broad moralistic terms that were understood by all. The government's propaganda was a useful and powerful political weapon. The ubiquitous place of festivals and their use as a tool to represent and instill a certain set of values and moral behavior created a language about rituals and rituals that was then codified in commissioned public descriptions. This official discourse, however, created, in essence, a template of symbols that could be manipulated and reinterpreted. It provided social critics with the means, the symbolic subject matter, and the ritual terminology to discuss and judge their leaders and their society. Authors/performers maneuvered within this preestablished discourse, acknowledging principles of leadership and all the while holding governmental officials accountable to the high standard of the entry. All the authors implicitly addressed questions about how the colonial leadership might forfeit the loyalty of the people, and they provided the answer: when those officials wantonly disregarded their oaths and placed their personal ambitions and fortunes above the needs of the people. There was no effort to completely vilify the government, or the office of the viceroy, or the values associated with the ceremonies. Authors pointed to individual failures to live up to the expectations outlined in the great festivals. Therefore the authors/performers did not discard the utopian aspirations of these festivals but put forth alternative or authentic utopias that were linked to specific Mexican experiences and aspirations.

As Mexico moved toward the nineteenth century, the nature of the discourse and the relationship between rulers and vassals in regard to good governance began to change from dialogue to contestation as Bourbon policies attempted to alter established socioeconomic and cultural patterns. Colonial authors, especially anonymous satirists, began to develop a more Mexican political language to forcefully counter the regime and advocate a rejection of the Spanish system of governing. The disparity between good governance and actual governance became too great. In many colonies, an anti-colonial nationalism with its own domain of sovereignty was created right within colonial society, before overt struggles for independence began.[3] Similarly, the discourse of rulership surrounding government festivals served as the foundation for a later political discourse that, along with armed struggle, brought about Mexican independence. The Bourbon plan—"concerted, formulated with much forethought, carried out with great certainty"—failed,[4] and in the end, festivals could no longer deflect or contain the societal tensions, long present, that finally burst onto the political stage.

Appendix

Spanish Monarchs and Years of Oath Ceremonies in Mexico City

Philip II	1557
Philip III	1599
Philip IV	1621
Charles II	1666/76
Philip V	1701
Louis Ferdinand I	1724
Ferdinand VI	1747
Charles III	1760
Charles IV	1789
Ferdinand VII	1808–14

List of Viceroys and Years of Reign in New Spain

Antonio de Mendoza	1535–50
Luis de Velasco	1550–64
Marquis de Falces	1566–68
Martin Enríquez de Almanza	1568–80
Count of Coruña	1580–83
Archbishop Pedro Moya de Contreras	1584–85
Marquis of Villamanrique	1585–90
Marquis de Salinas (Velasco II)	1590–95
Count of Monterey	1595–1603
Marquis of Montesclaros	1603–07
Marquis of Salinas	1607–11
Bishop García Guerra	1611–12
Marquis of Guadalcázar	1612–21
Marquis of Gelves	1621–24

Marquis of Cerralvo	1624–35
Marquis of Caderyta	1635–40
Count of Villena	1640–42
Bishop Juan Palafax y Mendoza	1642
Count of Salvatierra	1642–48
Bishop Marcos Torres y Rueda	1648–49
Count of Alva de Aliste	1650–53
Duke of Alburquerque	1653–60
Count of Baños	1660–64
Bishop Diego Osorio de Escobar	1664
Marquis of Mancera	1664–73
Duke of Veragua	1673
Archbishop Payo Enríquez de Rivera	1673–80
Marquis of la Laguna	1680–86
Count of la Monclova	1686–88
Count of Galve	1686–96
Archbishop Juan de Ortega y Montanés	1696
Count of Moctezuma y Tula	1696–1701
Archbishop Juan de Ortega y Montánes	1701–2
Duque de Alburquerque	1702–11
Duque de Linares	1711–16
Marquis de Valero	1716–22
Marquis de Casafuerte	1722–34
Archbishop Juan Antonio de Vizarrón	1734–40
Duke of la Conquista y Marquis de Gracia Real	1740–41
Count of Fuenclara	1742–46
1st Count of Revillagigedo, Fco. Guemes y Horcasitas	1746–55
Marquis of las Amarillas	1755–60
Fco. Cajigal de la Vega	1760
Marquis of Cruillas	1760–66
Marquis of la Croix	1766–71

Antonio Maria de Bucareli	1771–79
Martín de Mayorga	1779–83
Matias de Galvez	1783–84
Count of Galvez, Bernardo de Galvez	1785–86
Archbishop Alonso Núñez de	
Haro y Peralta	1787
Manuel Antonio Flores	1787–89
2nd Count of Revillagigedo	1789–94
Marquis de Branciforte	1794–98
Miguel José de Azanza	1798–1800
Félix Berenguer de Marquina	1800–3
José de Iturrigaray	1803–8
Pedro Garibay	1808–9
Archbishop Fco. Javier de	
Lizana y Beaumont	1809–10
Fco. Xavier Venegas	1810–13
Félix Ma. Calleja del Rey	1813–16
Juan Ruíz de Apodaca	1816–21
Juan O'Donoju	1821

Notes

Chapter One: Introduction

1. For details on the revolt of 1624, see Richard Boyer, "Absolutism," 475–627; Feijoo, "El tumulto de 1624," 42–70; and Stove, "Tumulto of 1624." Eventually the king sent a *visitador*, Martín de Carillo, to investigate the riot. After reviewing the case, he suggested that the Crown grant a general pardon.

2. *Actas*, Libro 25, 184, 210, 229, and Libro 26, 34.

3. Sebastián Gutiérrez provides a description of the cathedral arch in his *Arco triunfal*.

4. *Actas*, Libro 26, 186, 187.

5. For the theory of cultural hegemony, see Gramsci, *Prison Notebooks*.

6. Geertz, "Centers, Kings, and Charisma," 15–16, 30.

7. For Mexico´s African population, see Palmer, *Slaves*; Aguirre Beltrán, *La población negra*; and Carroll, *Blacks in Colonial Veracruz*. The literature on mestizaje is quite large. A finely conceived recent study on the caste system in the capital is Cope, *The Limits*.

8. As quoted in Lira and Muro, "Siglo de la integración," 105. Nahua chronicler Chamalpahin, writing some sixty years later, also documented mestizo cruelty toward the Natives and their unwillingness to acknowledge their Indian blood. They concentrated on passing themselves off as Spaniards. See Chamalpahin's passage in Lockhart, *The Nahuas*, 385.

9. *Instrucciones y memorias*, 184.

10. For the revolt of 1612, see Vetancurt, *Teatro mexicano*, 217. Antonio Morga led the investigation on the rumored African revolt of 1612; as a result thirty-six blacks judged guilty of conspiracy against the Crown were hanged in the main plaza. Uprisings outside the city that caused concern included the great rebellion of the Natives of Durango in 1604; the 1658 disturbance of King Yanga and his runaway slave band; the great revolt of 1661 in Oaxaca, so severe in scope that troops were sent from the capital; and the 1693 revolt in nearby Tlaxcala, which followed on the heels of the 1692 uprising in Mexico City. Guijo also mentions uprisings in Tehuantepec (1660) and the bishopric of

Guadina on the Chichimec frontier (1652). See his *Diario*, vol. 2, 133, vol. 1, 195. Another maroon (runaway slave) rebellion occurred on the Gulf Coast during 1617–18, and in 1646 violence broke out between Spanish and mulato sections of the Spanish garrison at Veracruz (see Robles, Diario, vol. 3, 41). For more details on some of the riots and rebellions during this period, see Israel, *Race*; Guthrie, "Riots," 245–58; Davidson, "Negro Slave Control," 235–53; Leonard, *Alboroto*; and Cope, *The Limits*, chap. 7. For the quotes on the 1624 revolt, see Gutiérrez, *Arco triunfal*, 24, and *Actas*, Libro 26, 188.

11. Seed, *To Love, Honor, and Obey*.

12. Viqueira Albán, in *Relajados*, provides one of the most comprehensive descriptions of popular pastimes in the capital and the impact of Bourbon social reforms.

13. Connerton, *How Societies Remember*.

14. See John and Jean Comaroff, *Ethnography and the Historical Imagination*, 258, for their idea of "colonization of consciousness." For a similar idea on the conquest of the imaginaire (imagination, worldview, or consciousness), see Gruzinski, *Conquest of Mexico*, chap. 1.

15. Turner, in *Dramas, Fields, and Metaphors*, believed that rituals attempted to create inclusive values, the lack of which would lead to conflict, a belief apparently shared by the criollo city councilmen in the late sixteenth and seventeenth centuries.

16. See Maravall, *The Culture of the Baroque*, 75–77, on the role of public opinion in the seventeenth-century political culture. He also lists a series of moralists who studied and wrote on the manner and consequences of affecting the individual and by extension the general public.

17. For a discussion of the concept of good governance as a dialectical relationship between vassals and rulers, see Agovi, "A King Is Not Above Insult," 57–59. For persuasion and typification in order to rule, see Furniss, "Power of Words," 137.

18. Nancy Fee, in "La Entrada Angelopolitana: Ritual and Myth in the Viceregal Entry in Puebla de lost Angeles," 283–320, points out that Native Americans and castas had little to no participation in similar government-sponsored festivals in Puebla.

19. Stanley Brandes, in *Power and Persuasion: Fiestas and Social Control in Rural Mexico*, 5, makes a similar point about contemporary festivals in Mexico.

20. Louisa Schell Hoberman, in *Mexico's Merchant Elite, 1590–1660: Silver, State and Society*, chap. 1, points out that in 1620, the capital had

more architectural monuments per capita than any other city in New Spain and that it had a more sophisticated and consuming public.

21. One of the most dramatic and moving examples of local pride and its connection to festival patronage is found in de Mendieta Rebollo, *Suntuoso festivo*, 6–7.

22. For further elaboration of this general idea of urban centers as cultural landscape, see Carrasco, *City of Sacrifice*, 8.

23. For a discussion of the demographic disaster, see Cook and Borah, *The Indian Population of Central Mexico*, 1531–1610; Dobyns, "Estimating the Aboriginal American Population," 395–435; and Denevan, *The Native Population of the Americas in 1492*.

24. For agricultural hardship that produced grain shortages and for data on epidemics, see Gibson in *The Aztecs*, appendix 5, 453–56, and appendix 4, 449–50, and Guijo, *Diario*, vol. 2, 169. On the floods of the 1620s and 1630s, see *Actas*, Libro 23, 183; *Actas*, Libro 26, 248; *Actas*, Libro 27, 144; Lira and Muro, "El siglo de la integración," 93; Israel, *Race*, 30; Hoberman, "Bureaucracy and Disaster," 211–30; and Boyer, *La gran inundación*.

25. Woodrow Borah believed that the demographic disaster and resultant labor shortage affected silver mining, thus explaining what appeared to have been an economic depression during the seventeenth century. See his study *New Spain's Century of Depression*. Chevalier demonstrated that a reduction in demand for products connected to the mining centers caused the haciendas to produce for personal consumption, affirming Borah's thesis. See his *Land and Society in Colonial Mexico: The Great Hacienda*, 277–88, 311, and also Gibson, *The Aztecs*, 242, 533. Earl J. Hamilton in *American Treasure and the Price Revolution in Spain 1510–1650* and Pierre and Huguette Chaunu in *Seville et l'Atlantique (1504–1650)* showed a marked decline in silver being sent to Spain. However, more recent studies claim that there was no century-long depression in the mining industry although total silver production did decline from 1641–50 and 1671–80, amounting to a decrease of 21 percent. See Hoberman, *Mexico's Merchant Elite*, 14. For international and regional trade, see Florescano and Gil Sanchez, "La epoca," vol. 2, 188; Schurz, *The Manila Galleon*, 90, 350, 355; Tepaske, "New World Silver, Castile and the Far East (1590–1750)," 444–45; Atwell, "International Bullion Flows and the Chinese Economy circa 1530–1650," 86–90; Boyer, "Mexico in the Seventeenth Century: Transition of a Colonial Society," 455–78; MacLeod, *Spanish Central America: A Socioeconomic History*, 1520–1720, 358; and McAlister, *Spain and Portugal*, 375–81. For

the confines of the debate on the depression, see Tepaske and Klein, "Seventeenth Century Crisis in the Spanish Empire: Myth or Reality?" 116–35. For an up-to-date review of the seventeenth-century decline and the literature on the period, see the introduction to Hoberman, *Mexico's Merchant Elite*, chap. 1.

26. On the issue of trade and its impact, see Fisher, "Imperial 'Free Trade' and the Hispanic Economy, 1778–1796," 21–56, and Hamnett, *Politics and Trade in Southern Mexico, 1750–1821*. For an analysis of the mining industry and the boom, see the now classic study of David A. Brading, *Miners and Merchants in Bourbon Mexico, 1763–1810*.

27. See Garner, "Prices and Wages in Eighteenth-Century Mexico," 73–108; Van Young, "The Age of Paradox,"64–90; and Haslip-Viera, *Crime*, 21.

28. For general descriptions of colonial Mexico City, see Leonard, *Baroque Times in Old Mexico*, chap. 1; Vázquez Mellado, *La ciudad de los palacios*; Cope, *The Limits*, chap. 1; and Haslip-Viera, *Crime*, chap. 1.

29. *Actas*, Libro 21, 245.

30. For the 1640 quote, see *Actas*, Libro 32, 77. For the 1651 epidemic, see Guijo, *Diario*, vol. 1, 179–80. For the painting of the count of Salvatierra, see de Medina, *Espejo de príncipes católicos y governadores políticos*, C.

31. For more information about the councilmen, see Nwasike, "Mexico City Town Government, 1590–1650"; Alvardo Morales, "El Cabildo y regimento de la ciudad de México en el siglo SVII," 489–514; and Flores Olea, "Los regidores de la ciudad de México," 149–72.

32. The details of the ruling mythology are best accessed through the hundreds of publications that were printed in order to describe the festivals in detail. These documents formed a cohesive corpus—the literary genre of festival description. Publication of festival descriptions was not a novelty exclusive to New Spain, but was a literary tradition, complete with its own formulaics, inherited from Europe. The authors of the descriptions were the same literati selected by the city councilmen and the cathedral chapter to design important facets of the festival, especially the themes on the triumphal arches. The published descriptions were written, not only as official descriptions of a festival, but also as souvenirs, eyewitness accounts for those absent from the festivities, literary evidence of civic pride, exaltations of the festival sponsors, and, more important, as historical records for future ceremonies. Nonetheless, the published descriptions are reconstructed written accounts of events and have within them

all of the challenges of such mediated historical documents. Authors selected and edited events for inclusion according to their own standards of worthiness. The authors were officially charged with the meticulous and eloquent articulation of their patrons' concept of good governance, and this theme defines all of the descriptions with great uniformity over time. Once the draft description was completed, the manuscript went through another round of editing as the sponsors reviewed and approved the descriptions before publication. Thus there remains the question: how great a disjuncture existed between what spectators actually saw and what was described in a published account? Extant drawings of the arches and archival materials do complement and verify the descriptions. It appears that authors sought to give a relatively accurate picture of the iconography displayed on ephemeral architecture, the activities of the festival participants, and importantly the goals of their patrons, the festival sponsors. However, descriptions of other performances and certainly nonofficial popular performances were rarely included in a published description, although some, as we will see, can be accessed through archival records.

33. The 1700s under the Bourbons were plagued by constant warfare that crippled international trade and depleted the royal coffers. The War of Spanish Succession (1700–48) was quickly followed by the War of Jenkins' Ear (1739–48) with Britain, which was primarily played out in the Caribbean. The Seven Years' War (1756–63) was particularly devastating because the British took and held the major port of Havana, Cuba. After 1789, wars among the European powers occurred constantly. The new ruling authorities were also concerned about contraband trade between colonists and other European nations such as the French and the English and were worried about the French on New Spain's northern frontier (modern Louisiana and Florida).

34. The literature on the Bourbon reforms is extensive. See Florescano and Gil Sanchez, "La época," vol. 2, 185–301, for an overview of all the reforms. See Burkholder and Chandler, *From Impotence to Authority: The Spanish Crown and the American Audiencias 1787–1808*, for their impact on the high court. For military reform, see Archer, *The Army in Bourbon Mexico*, 1760–1810, and McAlister, *Fuero Militar*. See Ladd, *The Mexican Nobility at Independence*, 1780–1826, for the overall impact of the reforms on the colonial elite.

35. For an overview and details of the Bourbon ecclesiastical reforms, see Taylor, *Magistrates of the Sacred*, and Farriss, *Crown and Clergy in Colonial Mexico 1759–1821*.

36. Scholars such as Gayatri Spivak in "Can the Subaltern Speak?" believe that subaltern voices cannot be truly recovered and that scholars in essence speak on their behalf. For a detailed discussion defining the subaltern and scholars' efforts to represent their voice, see Beverley, *Subalternity and Representation,* chaps. 4 and 5.

37. See, for example, James Scott's *Domination and the Arts of Resistance* for the notion that people can manifest acts of resistance while appearing to accept established power relations. For the promotion of social solidarity through symbols holding diverse cultural interpretations, see Fernandez, "The Performance of Ritual Metaphors," 100–31.

38. For the idea that festivals never resolve social tension and conflict but merely present schemes by which the solutions to those conflicts are deferred, see Bell, *Ritual Theory, Ritual Practice.*

39. Vetancurt, *Teatro Mexicano,* vol. 2, 193.

Chapter 2: The Ideal Prince

1. The following description is based on Gutiérrez de Medina´s *Viaje por mar y tierra del virrey Marqués de Villena.*

2. This small palace fell into ruin during the early eighteenth century and no longer exists today. The present-day traveler to Chapultepec Park encounters a large palace at the top of the hill that houses Mexico´s National History Museum. Authorities began construction of this structure in 1785, but it was not completed until after 1821.

3. This was the standard parade lineup for all entries; for a specific example, see *Actas,* Libro 32, 84.

4. For a detailed description of the viceroy´s saddle and mount, see *Actas,* Libro 9, 80.

5. Gundersheimer, *Ferrara,* 267.

6. Veyne, *Bread and Circuses,* 463.

7. This concept was emphasized by Niccolo Machiavelli in *The Prince,* 65–67. See also the discussion in Strong, *Art and Power,* 39–40.

8. Díaz del Castillo, *La historia verdadera,* 186.

9. Records demonstrate that three arches were built in 1531 and 1535, but unfortunately, the documents provide no details about where they were in the city, why three arches were constructed, and which groups or organizations might have patronized them. Lawrence M. Bryant, in *The King and the City in the Parisian Royal Entry Ceremony,* mentions that there were three decorated gates or arches in the Parisian entry

ceremony during the Renaissance, one of which was the responsibility of the guilds. Perhaps during this early period in Mexico, the guilds, religious orders, and the city each erected an arch. See as an example *Actas*, Libro 4, 240.

10. For entry descriptions and itemizations of costs, see for 1566, *Actas*, Libro 7, 295–96, 301, 304–5, 320; for 1568, Libro 7, 417–18, 452; and for 1580, Libro 8, 449, 452, 461–62, 486, 535. See also *Actas*, Libro 12, 244, and Libro 9, 72. For a description of a flag performance from 1595, see *Actas*, Libro 12, 223.

11. In 1595, the councilmen stated that the entry usually cost 24,000 pesos (see *Actas*, Libro 12, 211). Estimated total costs for available years generally coincide with that statement. Expenditures found in the *Actas* are as follows: 1565, 15–20,000 pesos (Libro 9, 6, 71, 72, 76, 79, 180, 119; not all expenditures listed; parts of the estimate based on descriptions of items); 1595, 24–25,000 pesos (Libro 12, 214, 221, 225, 230, 271, 326, and Libro 13, 340); 1603, 36,800 pesos (Libro 15, 196, and Libro 18, 377); 1607, 25,000 pesos (Libro 17, 53, 54, 56, 72, 80, 83, 84, and Libro 16, 32); 1611, 21,849 pesos (Libro 18, 94, 104–5); 1612, 18,000 pesos (Libro 18, 401, 419); 1621, 5,000 pesos (Libro 24, 139, 137, 144, 164, 172, 179); 1624, 20,000 pesos (Libro 25, 184, 210, 229, and Libro 26, 34); 1635, 15,000 pesos (Libro 30, 33, 34, 35, 52, 53, 63, 80); 1640, 40,000 pesos (Libro 32, 82); 1642, 30,000 pesos (Libro 33, 370, 373, 375, 377, 379). The annual income of the city in 1620 was listed as 16,500 pesos (*Actas*, Libro 23, 170), 6,800 pesos less than the average entry. Even if revenue to the city improved considerably as the seventeenth century progressed, the city would still have expended almost the entire annual budget on one festival alone. Neither does this take into account that during some entry years, such as 1603 and 1640, the city council spent considerably more money than the average 23,300 pesos.

12. *Actas*, Libro 15, 222, and Libro 18, 377. This sum is taken from records of the entry of Montesclaros in 1603 and is an unusually expensive entry even for the period. However, descriptions of the councilmen's festival wear for other entries are the same, leading me to believe that 18,000 pesos may have been close to the standard costs for the gowns of office. During attempts to limit spending on the entry, the city councilmen only applied cost-saving measures to their attire as a last resort.

13. *Actas*, Libro 24, 139.

14. Dimensions of the arches for particular years are as follows: 1624 (cathedral arch), 25 (h), 14? (l); 1640 (city arch), 90 feet (h), 70? feet (l),

7? feet (w); 1642 (city arch), 28 (h), 16 (l); 1650 (city arch), 35 (h), 19 (l), 5 (w); 1650 (cathedral arch), 27 (h), 16 (l); 1653 (city arch), 28 (h), 16 (l); 1653 (cathedral arch), 27 (h), 16 (l); 1660 (cathedral arch), 27 (h), 16 (l); 1664 (city arch), 30 (h), 16 (l); 1673 (cathedral arch), 30 (h), 16 (l); 1680 (city arch), 90 feet (h), 50 feet (l), 12 feet (w); 1680 (cathedral arch), 30 (h), 16 (l); and 1688 (city arch), 30 (h), 16 (l). Unless indicated, all measurements are in varas. For purposes of this study one vara equals .84 meter. The average height was twenty-eight varas. City council *Actas* show the following prices for the arch in the indicated entry years: 1580, 62 pesos (Libro 8, 468); 1585, 500 pesos (Libro 9, 66, 71); 1603, 2,000 pesos (Libro 15, 210); 1611, 1,415 pesos (Libro 18, 102, 109, 255–56); 1621, 2,200 pesos (Libro 24, 164, 172, 179); 1624, 2,100 pesos (Libro 25, 180); 1642, 2,288 pesos (Libro 33, 375); and 1650, 2,000 pesos (Guijo, *Diario*, vol. 1, 108).

15. In *Art and Ceremony in Late Antiquity*, 9, Sabine G. MacCormak analyzes the Roman entry ceremony and points out the particular importance of the welcoming speech in that celebration. It is unclear whether the speeches of the various officials were recorded in some fashion during the Hapsburg period. Unfortunately, none have been found to date. For an example of an eighteenth-century speech, see Cuevas Aguirre, *Arenga*.

16. For the lure of pictures during the period, see Praz, *Studies in Seventeenth-Century Imagery*, 169.

17. Veláquez de León, *Ilustración*, 14.

18. Orgel and Strong, *Inigo Jones*, and Bergeron, *English Civic Pageantry*, 2.

19. De la Cruz, "Neptuno," vol. 21, 930. For a discussion of emblems in colonial Mexico, see the essays by José Pascual Buxó, Santiago Sebastián, and Jaime Cuadriello in *Juegos de ingenio y agudeza*, 30–116.

20. Díaz del Castillo, *La historia verdadera*, 504. The theme of the ruler as deliverer was highly developed in the entry at Binche, directed to Philip in the Low Countries, and was repeated again and again all over Europe in the late sixteenth century. See Strong, *Art and Power*, 93.

21. Gutiérrez de Medina, *Viaje*, 84.

22. The viceroys and their mythological counterparts were as follows: (1624) Cerralvo—Caesar Octavio (cathedral arch); (1640) Villena—Mercury (city); (1642) Salvatierra—Joseph (cathedral) and Prometheus (city); (1650) Alba de Liste—Perseus (city) and Hercules (cathedral); (1653) Alburquerque—Ulysses (city) and Mars (cathedral); (1660) Baños—Jupiter (cathedral); (1664) Mancera—Aeneas (city); (1663)

Veragua—Perseus (cathedral); (1680) Paredes—Aztec emperors (city) and Neptune (cathedral); (1688) Galve—Cadmo (cathedral) and Paris (city); and (1696) Montezuma—Hercules (city). For a detailed analysis of the arches constructed by Siguenza y Góngora and Sor Juana, see Fernández, "The Representation of National Identity in Mexican Architecture"; von Kugelgen, "Carlos de Siguenza y Góngora" 151–61; and my "Sor Juana Inés de la Cruz."

23. See Gutiérrez's *Arco triunfal*, 20. For other entries, see *Descripción y explicación de la fábrica y empresas del suntuoso arco que la Ilustrísima*, 2, 3; Bocanegra, *Teatro*, 2; Alonso de Medina, *Espejo*, A2; *Portada alegórica*, 1; Salazar y Torres, *Elogio panegírico*, 1; *Marte católico*, 1; Ramírez de Vargas, *Elogio*, 2; and de la Cruz, "Neptuno," 927–28.

24. Azevedo, *Silva*, 20–21. For similar descriptions for other entries, see *Descripción y explicación* (1640), 5; Bocanegra, *Teatro*, 1; Medina, *Espejo*, A4; Alavés Pinelo, *Astro mitológico*, 51; and Ramírez de Vargas, *Elogio*, 8.

25. Paintings showing the prowess of the governor on the battlefield were present in the following arches and descriptions: Gutiérrez, *Arco triunfal*, 23, 32; Bocanegra, *Teatro*, 12–13; Salazar y Torres, *Elogio*, 2, 8, 10–11; *Marte católico*, 3, 4; Ramírez de Vargas, *Elogio*, 11; and Azevedo, *Silva*, 16. In some cases more than one painting on the arch presented this theme; thus the citation of several pages. Noble lineages of both the viceroy and his wife were included on almost all the arches; see Gutiérrez, *Arco triunfal*, 32, 33; *Descripción y explicación*, 7, 10; Bocanegra, *Teatro*, 7; Medina, *Espejo*, B3; Alavés Pinelo, *Astro*, 17–18; *Portada alegórica*, 5; Salazar y Torres, *Elogio*, 4–6; *Marte católico*, 8; Fernández Osorio, *Júpiter benévolo*, 5; Pérez Quintanilla and Ribera, *Histórica imagén*, 5; and de la Cruz, "Neptuno," 946, 947.

26. *Descripción y explicación*, 8, and Fernández Osorio, *Júpiter*, 5 and (for the quote) 9.

27. Alavés Pinelo, *Astro*, 29.

28. De la Cruz, "Neptuno," 945. See also Siguenza y Góngora, *Teatro*, 62–65.

29. Ramírez de Vargas, *Elogio*, 10.

30. For a systematic listing of all the virtues attributed to viceroys, see Alavés Pinelo, *Astro*, 41; Gutiérrez, *Arco triunfal*, 43; Ramírez de Vargas, *Elogio*, 15, 16; and Azevedo, *Silva*, 18–19, 22–23.

31. De la Cruz, "Neptuno," 926. The same theme of wisdom and prudence as the real crown of princes was repeated in the city arch of 1688

(see Azevedo, *Silva*, 21) and 1680 (see Siguenza y Góngora, *Teatro*, 59–60). For wisdom as a general virtue, see *Descripción y explicación* (1640), 14; *Portada alegórica*, 8; Fernández Osorio, *Júpiter*, 7. For the relationship between wisdom, prudence, and justice, see also Pérez Quintanilla and Ribera, *Histórica imágen*, 6, 8, 10.

32. Salazar y Torres, *Elogio*, 7.

33. Gutiérrez, *Arco triunfal*, 22, 47.

34. *Descripción y explicación*, 12; Bocanegra, *Teatro*, 13, 14; Fernández Osorio, *Júpiter*, 8; Ramírez de Vargas, *Elogio*, 13; Azevedo, *Silva*, 19; *Portada alegórica*, 8, 9; Bocanegra, *Teatro*, 11, 12; and *Marte católica*, 9.

35. Azevedo, *Silva*, 19.

36. Bocanegra, *Teatro*, 8; Medina, *Espejo*, B2; *Portada alegórica*, 6; Fernández Osorio, *Júpiter*, 4; de la Cruz, "Neptuno," 933; and Azevedo, *Silva*, 16. In the 1680 cathedral arch designed by Sor Juana, a large painting crowned the arch, pleading with the viceroy to promote the completion of the cathedral; see p. 942. For more on the desagüe, see Cooper, *Epidemic Disease*, 9, 10–11.

37. Medina, *Espejo*, C1; Ramírez de Vargas, *Elogio*, 4, 16; and de la Cruz, "Neptuno," 934.

38. Salazar y Torres, *Elogio*, 12.

39. Alavés Pinelo, *Astro*, 44, 45; Medina, *Espejo*, A2; Pérez Quintanilla and Ribera, *Histórica imagén*, 14, 15; and Siguenza y Góngora, *Teatro*, 55, 76, 80, 82.

40. Fernández Osorio, *Júpiter*, 6.

41. Gutiérrez, *Arco triunfal*, 25. See also Salazar y Torres, *Elogio*, 16.

42. Azevedo, *Silva*, 14.

43. Bocanegra, *Teatro*, 8, and Alavés Pinelo, *Astro*, 34.

44. Fernández Osorio, *Júpiter*, 7–8, and Azevedo, *Silva*, 23.

45. For more information, see my "Giants and Gypsies: Corpus Christi in Colonial Mexico City," 1–26.

46. Walsh, *Cuadro poético*, 63.

47. *Actas*, Libro 25, 125. Although not as common, the king did occasionally participate in the Corpus procession in Madrid. See, for example, Anonymous, "Fiestas del Corpus in Madrid," in José Simón Díaz, *Relaciones breves*, 213–14.

48. Marmalejo, *Loa sacramental*.

49. For more information, see my "Native Icon to City Protectress to Royal Patroness: Ritual, Political Symbolism and the Virgin of Remedies," 367–91.

50. For descriptions of Easter, see Robles, *Diario*, vol. 1, 198, 207, 260, vol. 2, 39, and vol. 3, 15; Vetancurt, *Teatro* Mexicano, vol. 3, 114–15; and Gemelli Carreri, *Viaje*, 73–75.

51. For the staging of the autos-de-fé, see Cañeque, "Theater of Power," 321–44.

52. For examples of other religious festivals that were patronized by the authorities, see *Actas*, dated October 19 and 20, 1588, March 6 and 25, 1597; Libro 7, 511, 512; Libro 22, 88–89, 139–40, 194–98; and Libro 27, 39, 40, 43.

53. A number of royal festivals are mentioned or described in "Gacetas de Mexico,"; Guijo, *Diario*; Robles, *Diario*; and in the almost three centuries of the city council minutes. In some cases, the city councilmen commissioned official descriptions of royal festivals. See, for example, Fernández de Castro, *Relación ajustada*. The death of the monarch was also cause for public display and mourning, lasting for at least one month. Government officials wore demure, officially sanctioned garments of black. Information on the *honras fúnebres* of the king were also the subject of a number of published descriptions, the most famous being that of Cervantes de Salazar, *Túmulo imperial*, which documents the public mourning for Charles V.

54. For the jura of 1531, see *Actas*, Libro 2, 86. For the 1557 oath, see *Actas*, Libro 6, 290–93. The cost was 900 pesos. The financial data for this oath are limited. Allocations of resources for entry and Corpus Christi ceremonies are only sporadically cited and consist of small, isolated expenditures. The cost of this jura is the single largest amount listed in the *Actas* for one individual festival during this early period. For the 1599 oath, see *Actas*, Libro 13, 298–300, or AHA, vol. 2282, exp. 1, f.s.n. For later oath ceremonies, see Villalobos, "Obediencia," 297, and Valdés, "Compendium de historia del descubrimiento y conquista de Nueva España," vol. 2, 184. The specific streets taken by the banner carrier were not listed in seventeenth-century descriptions; however, they can be found for the year 1701 in AHA, vol. 2282, exp. 2, f.s.n.

55. The exception was the 1676 oath to Charles II, which included an evening parade with floats sponsored by certain guilds. See *Actas*, Libro 13, 296, and Libro 24, 129. City council records show that the oath to Philip II served as the model for the oath to his son. In 1599, the city council borrowed 4,000 pesos from the desagüe funds. The oath to Philip IV, however, included a number of additional festive items not presented in the oath to his father. Therefore one can safely assume that the cost

of the ceremony to Philip III would have been somewhat less than the 4,000 pesos spent on the oath to Philip IV. See AHA, vol. 2282, exp. 1, f.s.n. Expenditures for the festivities to Charles II were burned in the fire of 1692; however, the oath to the first Bourbon monarch, Philip V, in 1701 cost approximately 5,000 pesos. See AHA, vol. 2282, exp. 2, f.s.n. More than likely the seventeenth-century jura cost between 4,000 and 5,000 pesos. The cost of Corpus Christi is based on the 1620 review of finances, listing 3,500 pesos as the traditional annual Corpus expenditures (*Actas*, Libro 23, 177).

56. Brown and Elliott, *Palace*, chap. 1; Elliott, "La corte de los Hapsburgos españales," chap. 7, and in the same volume, "Poder y propaganda en la España de Felipe IV," chap. 8, especially p. 211. Many published descriptions of the sixteenth and seventeenth centuries document royal travels, the pomp and circumstance of the royal entrances, and the monarch's participation in certain public festivals in Madrid. See Díaz, *Relaciones* and *Fuentes para la historia de Madrid* and Alenda y Mira, *Relaciones*.

57. See McAlister, "Royal Government in the Indies," 203–7, and Elliott, "Spain and America in the Sixteenth and Seventeenth Centuries," vol. 1, 287–340, especially the section titled "Colonial Realities," 310–19. A glaring exception to this rule was the thwarted conspiracy of 1562, led by Martín Cortés (son of the conqueror) and Alonso de Avila in response to royal decrees stipulating that *encomienda* could no longer be inherited.

58. By the mid-seventeenth century, the city council had spent 141,181 pesos. Years and amounts borrowed are as follows: 1595, 20,000 pesos (*Actas*, Libro 12, 211, 221); 1603, 26,188 pesos (Libro 15, 196); 1611, 14,000 pesos (Libro 18, 94); 1612, 16,000 (Libro 18, 401, 450–54); 1624, 10,000 pesos (Libro 25, 182, 184, 187–89, 196); 1640, 40,000 pesos (Libro 32, 82); and 1642, 15,000 pesos (Libro 33, 377). The 206,000 total was listed in a 1690 royal decree sent by Charles II as part of an effort to tone down the festival. See AGN, Correspondencia de los Virreyes, vol. 282, ser. 1a., ff. 46v–47. The city councilmen also sought to procure more funding in a variety of ways. For the sale of rental income, see *Actas*, Libro 9, 66; Libro 18, 104–5; for the use of cheaper cloth for costumes, see Libro 12, 211, Libro 17, 84; for rental of items for viceregal living quarters, see Libro 12, 211; and for rental of bleachers in the main plaza, see Libro 17, 72. In 1612, the city council refused to pay a city employee his three-years' back salary because they needed this extra money to help fund the entry of

Guadalcazar. That same year, they put out a general plea to all, asking for a loan of 10,000 pesos. See *Actas*, Libro 18, 385, 422–23.

59. The Audiencia issued an auto (decree), admonishing the city councilmen. See *Actas*, Libro 12, 320.

60. *Actas*, Libro 17, 53–54, 56, 60, and Libro 18, 92.

61. *Actas*, Libro 18, 394–85.

62. *Actas*, Libro 23, 232–34.

63. *Actas*, Libro 24, 161.

64. *Actas*, Libro 24, 159–60.

65. *Actas*, Libro 24, 159.

66. AGN, Correspondencia de los Virreyes, vol. 282, 1a. ser., ff. 43, 44–45.

67. Guijo, *Diario*, vol. 3, 243, and AGN, Correspondencia de los Virreyes, vol. 282, 1a. ser., ff. 46v–47, 48–48v, 51.

68. AGN, Correspondencia de los Virreyes, vol. 282, 1a. ser., f. 92v.

69. *Actas*, Libro 23, 237–38.

70. Israel in *Race* goes into great depth on the problems and less than satisfactory administrations for a number of seventeenth-century viceroys; for his discussion of Baños see 260–66.

71. For more details on Baños, see Robles, *Diario*, vol. 1, 28–30, and Guijo, *Diario*, vol. 2, 233.

72. Guijo, *Diario*, vol. 2, 119.

Chapter 3: The Perfect Vassal

1. Carrasco, "Sacrifice," 39.

2. See Zorita's *Historia de la Nueva España*, 408.

3. Durán, *Aztecs*, 188.

4. *Actas*, Libro 2, 130. For the entrance of Antonio de Mendoza, see *Actas*, Libro 3, 122.

5. For a specific description of the coronation ceremony of Montezuma II, see Durán, *Aztecs*, 220–25.

6. Sahagún, *Florentine Codex*, book 6. Although the Florentine Codex provides some of the most detailed information about the Aztec prior to the arrival of the Spanish, that information was compiled after the Conquest by indigenous scholars and intellectuals (all bilingual and bicultural) who assisted Sahagún in his efforts to document pre-Columbian life. Therefore it is unclear how much post-Conquest influence affected the presentation of information. Other accounts of

the Aztec, such as Duran's work, appear to corroborate the Florentine Codex in the case of Mexica festival statecraft. Given all that we know about Aztec statecraft and the role of the ruler in that society, the descriptions given here seem appropriate and not necessarily a European construct imposed on pre-Columbian traditions. However, if they are a result of European influence, they perhaps demonstrate that indigenous intellectuals and rulers understood well the new role of festivals in the post-Conquest political environment.

7. Ibid., chap. 17, 51, 54.

8. *Instrucciones y memorias*, vol. 1, 177.

9. Sahagún, *Florentine Codex*, book 6, chap. 11, 57–58.

10. Ibid., chap. 10, 55, 58.

11. *Actas*, Libro 18, 103; Libro 21, 245; and Libro 32, 77. José de Acosta, SJ, in *Historia natural y moral de las Indias*, 37, also stated that good government and festival patronage were linked.

12. See *Actas*, Libro 26, 125, for the viceroy's importance to the Corpus Christi procession.

13. For the quote, carvings at Chapultepec, and the festival to Quetzalcoatl, see Durán, *Book of the Gods and Rites*, 459, 439, and 134–35, respectively. For complete details on the feasts to Tlaloc and Xochiquetzalli mentioned below, see Durán, ibid., 156–65.

14. For examples, see *Actas*, Libro 12, 209, and Libro 9, 371. In 1539, such a forest re-creation included a mock battle between two types of Natives and African Americans. Unfortunately, subsequent records on the forest neither mention whether mock battles were part of this event nor provide other details on the participants except that they were Native Americans. For a very brief description of the 1539 forest battle, see Díaz del Castillo, *Historia*, 399–400. For discussions of the significance of this performance, see Lopes Don, "Carnivals, Triumphs, and Rain Gods in the New World," 17–40, and Harris, *Aztecs, Moors, and Christians*, 123–31.

15. For a further discussion of this process and how it is evident in sixteenth-century writings on Mexica history, see Gillespie, *Aztec Kings*, introduction, especially pp. xxvii–xxxiv.

16. For discussions of Native acculturation, see Florescano, *Memory*, 111, Klor de Alva, "Religious Rationalization and the Conversions of the Nahuas," 237–38; Lockhart, *The Nahuas*; and Kellogg, *Law and the Transformation of Aztec Culture*, 1500–1700 68–69, 144–45.

17. Although their citizens were also reduced due to epidemic disease, neighboring city-states engaged in a more natural evolution because

their cities remained intact as well as their (modified) vision of the image of those cities. It is unclear whether Natives in Mexico City took note of this difference, but old rivalries among *altepetl* (sovereign indigenous states) did not disappear due to Spanish control.

18. For a very brief description of events, see the second part of the *Codex Aubin* reproduced in *Tlatelolco*, 293. For the 1636 entry of the marquis of Caderyta, see "Anales de Juan Miguel" in the same volume (p. 259). For the 1611 entry of García Guerra, see *Actas*, Libro 18, 101, and AGN, General de Parte, vol. 2, exp. 1014, f. 222v.

19. Native ephemeral architecture was not unusual in the capital. For example, in 1578 Natives erected two triumphal arches to celebrate the arrival of holy relics sent by Pope Gregory XIII to the capital. See Rojas Garcidueñas, "Fiestas en México en 1578," 39–40. In the *Códice Tlatelolco*, the image for 1565 depicts an image of a Spanish arch, the royal coat of arms, and a skeleton archer. Scholars have posited that it represents either the funeral pyre of Charles V or that of Viceroy Luis de Velasco (I). However, the architectural design is that of the standard triumphal arch utilized during the period for the viceregal entry. Thus the image may be both referring to the death of Velasco in 1564 (the skeleton archer) and to the impending arrival (the arch) of his successor, the marquis of Falces, in 1566. In 1593, no doubt with the agreement of Franciscan friars, Indians at the chapel of Saint Joseph depicted the Mexica eagle on a cactus being ridden by Saint Francis. The following year, chapel decoration included a cloth panel with pre-Conquest battle scenes and the ancient rulers of Tenochtitlan. In the center of the panel was the same image of Saint Francis astride the eagle on the cactus. As described by Chimalpahin in Lockhart, *The Nahuas*, 236.

20. Villalobos, "México en 1623," 308.

21. According to historian Charles Gibson, Valeriano represented fully this new hispanized Indian culture that was coming into being. Gibson, *The Aztecs*, 168–70.

22. *Actas*, Libro 12, 223; AGN, General de Parte, vol. 11, exp. 398, f. 356. In 1640, 400 Natives wearing fancy *tilmas* (capes) danced. See Gutiérrez de Medina, *Viaje*, 78–79.

23. *Actas*, Libro 12, 223.

24. Although generally the Native entry occurred on the same day as the city entry, in some instances, such as 1624, when the revolt deposed Gelves, the viceroy remained at Tlatelolco for the entire day, thereby delaying the Spanish entry. Gutiérrez, *Arco triunfal*, 28.

25. For quotes and a description of the 1621 oath, see Villalobos, "México en 1623," 295–309.

26. Florescano makes the same claim for the primordial titles. Primordial titles were documents generated in indigenous communities purporting to establish a community's rights to land. They also included historical information, some of which was more legend than fact. See his *Memory*, 118.

27. Gutiérrez de Medina, *Viaje*, 52–53. The viceroy listened to the counsel of Native American leaders and promised to come to their aid.

28. I am indebted to Susan Schroeder for a copy of this journal entry. See Chimalpahin Quauhtlehuanitzin, *Codex Chimalpahin*.

29. Lockhart, *The Nahuas*, 378, 391.

30. For example, the indigenous governor of Puebla, Juan Bentura Ximénez, desired reappointment to his office for an additional year outside of the proper sequence mandated in his community. It is unclear whether he was reappointed, but he described in detail his patronage of an oath ceremony in his community to the viceroy as a means of demonstrating his loyalty, effectiveness, and worthiness as Native governor. AGN, Historia, vol. 478, exp. 4, f. 1–1v. For another eighteenth-century example, see AGN, Historia, vol. 437, exp. s.n., f. 2.

31. Bordering neighborhoods of San Juan Tenochtitlan and Tlatelolco maintained a rivalry that included (mock?) battles on an annual basis. See Gibson, *The Aztecs*, 383.

32. Gibson, *The Aztecs*, 179.

33. Ibid., 191.

34. Native nobility and prominent intellectuals were actively engaged in a process of reclaiming, naming, and recording their own pre-Columbian and colonial histories. See, for an example, Schroeder, *Chimalpahin and the Kingdoms of Chalco*.

35. Aztec song and dance had been used to convey sacred knowledge. It was fundamental to rituals connected to kingship and theology, and musicians had been considered an elite professional caste of individuals. During the colonial period, musicians, with some success, sought to keep that privileged position, some even holding noble titles. See Schroeder, "Marginal Intellectuals: Nahua Musicians and the Church."

36. Unfortunately, I have not yet located seventeenth-century paintings of Natives performing in the entry or the jura. Eighteenth-century images, such as on the cover of this book, show a high degree of acculturation in terms of ritual attire.

37. A comparable analysis is made by Carolyn Dean for Peru in *Inka Bodies and the Body of Christ*, 164–66.

38. Exact amounts are difficult to ascertain because city councilmen lumped together expenditures for entertainments. Nonetheless, in 1535, the aldermen paid Natives 60 pesos for their participation; see *Actas*, Libro 3, 122. In 1580, they paid for the decorations in Native neighborhoods at the cost of 112 pesos of gold; see AGN, General de Parte, vol. 2, exp. 1014, f. 222v. In 1595, they paid for the forest re-creation but did not list the exact amount expended (see *Actas*, Libro 12, 209, 211), and in 1664, they paid for Native dances (AGN, General de Parte, vol. 11, exp. 392, f. 356).

39. This was the average cost for the entry in Tlaxcala, which included similar rituals and entertainment to that presented at Tlatelolco. For two detailed descriptions of the Tlaxcalan entry, see Ciudad Real, *Tratado de curioso y docto de las grandezas de la Nueva España*, vol. I, 104, and Gutiérrez de Medina, *Viaje*, 70. Native elite in Huejotzingo and Tlaxcala also hired Native artists. See AGN, Inquisición, vol. 721, exp. 32, f. 462–70v.

40. With each location along the route, the entry allowed the royal government to reaffirm its legitimacy as well as emphasize the unity of the realm under a Spanish sovereign. For a similar analysis, see Geertz, "Centers, Kings, and Charisma," 153, 163.

41. For financial data, see AGN, Indios, vol. 12, exp. 160, f. 269–70; Correspondencia de Virreyes, vol. 282, 1a. ser., f. 66–67v; and Ayuntamientos, vol. 216, exp. 2, fsn. See also Instituto Nacional de Antropología e Histora, Sección de Microfilm (henceforth INAH, Secc. Micro), Tlaxcala, Rollo 10, no. 30, f. 2v–4v; Rollo 11, no. 9, f. 2–2v. The issue of how to fund the entrance in Tlaxcala continued well into the eighteenth century (1771). Huejotzingo was either exempted from paying tribute or had an embargo lifted on accounts so that tribute monies could fund the entry. See AGN, Indios, vol. 19, exp. 191, f. 140v, and vol. 24, exp. 457, f. 332v–33v.

42. For the case of San Martin, see "Anales coloniales de Tlatelolco," *Tlatelolco*, 252–53. For a general discussion of governors and their responsibilities in regard to tribute payments, see Gibson, *The Aztecs*, 392. For the Native stage, see *Actas*, Libro, 24, 123–24.

43. *Actas*, July 23, 1543, Libro 1, 349.

44. Argüello, *Sermon moral al Real Acuerdo de Mexico*, 27. The friar had some renown in the capital as an accomplished and inventive orator

and scholar and was a professor of theology at the Colegio de San Buena Ventura, the Franciscan seminar in the Native barrio of Tlalteloco.

45. Ibid., 13.

46. The illnesses were based on the porticoes at the Bethesda pool and Psalms 87, verse 10 (fever), 145, verse 8 (blindness), 17, verse 46 (limp), and 111, verse 4 (dryness/drought). The fifth was a unique invention of the friar.

47. Ibid., 17.

48. Ibid., 18–21, 23–26.

49. Ibid., f. 28.

50. Ibid., 5–6, 8, 10.

51. Ibid., 8.

52. Ibid., 2, 5, 7, 8. His sermon was not actually delivered before the general public but rather in the Royal Chapel within the viceregal palace during the ritual of the Real Acuerdo. This was a private elite function wherein the seal was broken on the royal orders conferring power on the viceroy. The attending authorities pledged their allegiance, and a sermon and banquet followed the ceremony. This would not be the only time that Argüello's sermons got him into trouble. In 1703, Jesuit qualifiers of the Holy Office took umbrage with a sermon that he delivered in the city of Puebla. Argüello submitted the sermon to the Inquisitors themselves and after a few recommended changes received permission to publish that sermon. See AGN, Inquisición, vol. 722, exp. 32, ff. 474–81. Two years later, another sermon delivered in Puebla led to a whole series of attacks and counterattacks by anonymous individuals. However, Argüello's sermon was not considered heretical by the Holy Office. See AGN, Inquisición, vol. 722, exp. 32, ff. 476–77, exp. 40, ff. 568–604v. Though a controversial figure at times, it appears that his expertise as a theologian was undisputed, as he was named an official qualifier of texts for the Inquisition. See his opinion on some satirical poems in AGN, Inquisición, vol. 722, exp. 28, ff. 457–58.

53. For African participation in a 1539 celebration, see Díaz del Castillo, *Historia*, 545–48.

54. In the 1583 Corpus procession, the Cabildo even awarded a prize (24 pesos), in addition to an already set fee, to the dance team led by a morena named Simona Aranda (see *Actas*, Libro 8, 643). See *Actas*, Libro 10, 170 for the 1592 dance. In 1623, black men complained to the Council of the Indies because the city officials in Havana tried to force married black women to dance in Corpus and other festivals. It was customary for single black women to participate. The Crown sided

with the offended husbands, stating that married black women did not have to dance. The royal decree further added that the colonial authorities could not force any woman, single or married, to dance if she did not wish to do so. See Konetzke, *Colección*, 278. The two most popular dances of the era, the *chacona* and the *zarabanda*, had their origins among people of color in New Spain. For the impact of African musical forms in colonial Mexico, see Ramos Smith, *La danza*, 36. In addition, women of color were active participants in private religious devotions that included dancing, feasting, and honoring patron saints. See my "Rosa de Escalante's Private Party," 254–69.

55. For the descriptions of paintings and performers that follow, see *Festín hecho por las morenas criollas*.

56. See as examples Córdoba, *Jardín de nobles doncellas*; Talavera, "De como se ha de ordenar el tiempo para que sea bien expendido," 93–103; Vives, *Instrucciones de la mujer cristiana*; and León, *La perfecta casada*.

57. For further discussion of the erotization of slave women, see Bush, *Slave Women in Caribbean Society*, 11–22.

58. See Konetzke, *Colección*, 135, 182, 183.

59. Gage, *Thomas Gage's Travels*, 64–65, 68–70, 73.

60. For more details, see Flinchpaugh, "Economic Aspects of the Viceregal Entrance in Mexico City," 345–66.

61. For a similar discussion of Tenochtitlan as a ceremonial city, see Carrasco, *City of Sacrifice*, chap. 1, especially pp. 6–12.

Chapter 4: Celebrating Apollo

1. The detailed account of the oath is found in Abarca y Valda, *El sol*. For the platforms and the archiepiscopal arch, see 93, 96–97, 111, 129, 135, 151–56, 160; for the lace and thread makers and painters, 305, 176–78; for Native American participation, 67–68; for city council fireworks, 80; for the teachers' guild and children, 300; for the confectioner, candle makers, and dye masters, 258–62; for the guild parade, 208–58; and for bullfights, games, and shields, 266–67, 270, 273–76. For the contributions of the physicians' guild, see Campos y Martínez, *El iris, diadema inmortal*, 41, and *La corona sin término*. For university participation, see Rodríguez de Arizpe, *Coloso elocuente*.

2. Mendieta Rebollo, *Suntuoso festivo*, 7. See also AHA, vol. 376A, f.s.n., and Robles, *Diario*, vol. 3, 146–47. The Bourbon oath also inaugurated

the use of specially minted coins engraved with the likeness of the sovereign. The coins, always limited in number (for example, 500), varied in terms of their worth. In 1789, medallions were sent to the king, the cardinal patriarch of the Indies, the governors of the Council of the Indies, Audiencia members in Guadalajara, all the bishops of New Spain, the city councils of all major cities in the viceroyalty, and the heads of the major militia garrisons. In 1621, during the jura ceremonies in Madrid, the city council threw minted coins with the profile of the monarch to the crowd. See Anonymous, "Verdadera relación en la qual se da cuenta de como en la Corte se levantó el Estandarte Real de Castilla, por su magestad el Rey Don Felipe Quarto nuestro Señor . . . 1621," in Díaz, *Fuentes para la historia de Madrid y su provincia*, 125. For the 1701 medallions minted for the Mexico City oath, see Mendieta Rebollo, *Suntuoso festivo*, 46–48. For the 1747 oath, see Abarca y Valda, *El sol*, 72. For 1789 medallions, see AHA, vol. 2282, exp. 20, f. 183–90.

3. *Explicación de el Arco*, 2, 3.

4. *Explicación de el Arco*, 15.

5. For detailed descriptions of illumination as part of the oath ceremony, see *Explicación de el Arco*, 78, and AHA, vol. 2282, exp. 4, f.s.n., and exp. 28, f.s.n. For the city office illumination in 1808, see AHA, vol. 2282, exp. 31. For the Inquisitors and their participation, see AGN, Inquisición, vol. 1224, exp. 4, f. 163v and 160; vol. 810, exp. 6, f. 477; vol. 810, exp. 6, f.; and vol. 886, exp. 12, f. 127v and 132v. For guilds and their use of illumination, see Abarca y Valda, El sol, 223, 236, 238, and Salcedo y Somodevilla, *Breve relación*, 13–14, 17. For fireworks descriptions, see AHA, vol. 2282, exp. 2; AHA, vol. 376A, f. 78; *Gazetas*, vol. 4, 4–5; and AHA, vol. 4300, exp. 23, f.s.n.

6. *Gazetas*, vol. 6, 440. Abarca y Valda, *El sol*, 270. In 1762, 1783, 1785, and 1787, officials ordered citizens to illuminate the streets at their own expense, a policy that failed due to the unwillingness of the inhabitants to fund the project. In 1790, 1,000 oil lamps were installed and maintained by the city government, so ordered by the count of Revillagigedo. See Viqueira Albán, *Relajados*, 237. See also Lemoine Villicaña, "El alumbrado público," 783–818.

7. See *Descripción y explicación*, 5. In Spain, the count-duke Olivares developed a sun king mythology around Philip IV. See Brown and Elliott, *Palace*, chap. 6; Orso, *Art and Death at the Spanish Hapsburg Court*; and Lisón Tolosana, *La imagen del rey*. Charles II was also acclaimed as the sun king in the 1676 festival in Seville; see "Heroyco

aplauso, célebres júbilos de lustrosas demostraciones, assi de festines, como de lúcido aparato de las Reales Fiestas de toros, y cañas, que el invicto Cabildo de la Muy Noble siempre, Y Muy Leal Ciudad de Sevilla, ha hecho, y su popular aclamación . . . de aver cumplido los catorze años de su edad el invictíssimo y católico . . . D. Carlos Segundo," in Alenda y Mira, *Relaciones*, 395. The sun theme was also evident in the Madrid jura in 1789. Apollo/Charles IV was said to have been presented on the facade of the royal palace, on the silversmith arch, and on the arch erected by the marquis of Valmediano in Descripción de los ornatos, 1, 3.

8. Velázquez de León, *Explicación breve*, 83–84, 110–11; Castillo and Campos Martínez, *El Salomón*, 6–7; Mendieta Rebollo, *Suntuoso festivo*, 10; Ruíz Guerra y Morales, *Letras, Ceremonial*, 100; and Salcedo y Somodevilla, *Breve relación*, 3.

9. Larrañaga, *Colección*, 6, 8, 16, 18.

10. *Explicación de el Arco*, 6; Velázquez de Leon, *Explicación breve*, 104, 106; and *Ceremonial*, 99. Once again, in 1789, the empire became the central theme on the platforms. Utilizing various paintings, the city council joined Spain and America and all of the capitals and major cities of the two worlds. All paid homage to Charles IV; see BNM, ms. 1389, f. 316.

11. Abarca y Valda, *El sol*, 199–205, 216, 220–22.

12. Castillo and Campos Martínez, *El salomon*, 18.

13. Velázquez de León, *Explicación breve*, 85, 90, 93, 96, 100; BNM, ms. 1389, f. 315; Abarca y Valda, *El sol*, 117, 210; Campos Martínez, *El iris*, 51; and Castillo and Campos Martínez, *El Salomon*, 11, 16.

14. Campos Martínez, *El iris*, 15, and Abarca y Valda, *El sol*, 103. In *Descripción de los ornatos*, the jura in Madrid presented many of the same themes showcased in the Mexican oath ceremony. The Madrid oath festivities concentrated on presenting the virtues of the king (pp. 21, 31, 44) and emphasizing prosperity, abundance, commerce, and the arts and sciences (pp. 11, 27, 31, 48). The king was connected to Hercules and the imperial lion (pp. 6, 31, 39). The arch erected by the duke of Alba presented the eight provinces of Spain, Europe, Asia, Africa, and America, all ruled by Charles IV (p. 24).

15. Abarca y Valda, *El sol*, 278–79.

16. Ruíz Guerra y Morales, *Letras*, 19–20; Abarca y Valda, *El sol*, 208–9, 212, 243, 278–79; Campos Martínez, *El iris*, 59; and Castillo and Campos Martínez, *El Salomón*, 8–10.

17. AHA, vol. 376a, f.s.n.

18. For the 1760 oath bullfights, see *Ceremonial*, 94–98. For the corrida and other entertainments for the festival to Charles III, see AHH, vol. 251, exp. 8, f.s.n. For the bullfights for Ferdinand VII, see AHA, vol. 4300, exp. 23, f.s.n., and AHH, vol. 252, exp. s.n., f.s.n.

19. For the remate for Charles III, see AHH, vol. 250, exp. 1, f. 34v, 43, 43v, and AHA, vol. 2282, exp. 9, f. 125, 127. For Ferndinand VII's remate, see AHH, vol. 252, exp. s.n., f. suelto, and AHA, vol. 4300, exp. 23, f.s.n.

20. The expenditure amounts can be found in the following: Philip V—AHA, vol. 2282, exp. 2, f. 20, 26, 28, 36; Louis I—AHA, vol. 376a, fsn.; Charles III—AHH, vol. 251, exp. 8, f.s.n., vol. 250, exp. 1, f. 34v, 43v, AHA, vol. 2282, exp. 9, f. 125, 127; Charles IV—AHH, vol. 251, exp. 8, f.s.n., vol. 250, exp. 21, no. 14, AHA, vol. 2282, exp. 28, f. 255; Ferdinand VII(1808)— AHA, vol. 2282, exp. 31, f. 263, 264, exp. 28; and (1814)—AHH, vol. 252, exp. s.n., f. s.n., and AHA, vol. 2277, exp. 28, f. 38.

21. AHH, vol. 250, exp. 21, no. 14.

22. Much of the information presented on the Virgin of Remedies during the Bourbon period can also be found in my "Native Icon." The *venidas* (processions) were as follows: 1702: fleet and drought (AHA, vol. 372A, June 2, 1702); 1704: drought (AHA, vol. 372A, April 18, 1704, possibly at the shrine); 1705: drought (AHA, vol. 372A, May 8, 1705, possibly at the shrine); 1705: drought (AHA, vol. 372A, May 8, 1705, possibly at the shrine); 1706: for the monarchy (*Actas*, Libro 43–47, 55–56); 1708: birth of an heir to the throne (*Actas*, Libro, 43–47, 103); 1710: unclear why she was brought to the cathedral (*Actas*, Libro 43–47, 34); 1711: drought and sickness (*Actas*, Libro 43–47, 86); 1712: birth of an heir to the throne (*Actas*, Libro 43–47, 181–83); 1713: drought (*Actas*, Libro 43–47, 196); 1716: fleet (*Actas*, Libro 48–50, vol. 2, 162); 1717: drought and ex-viceroy's health (*Actas*, Libro 48–50, vol. 2, 39); 1719: the monarch (*Actas*, Libro 48–50, vol. 2, 188); 1732: fleet (AHA, vol. 59A, vol. 1, f. 31–38); 1734: fleet (AHA, vol. 59A, vol. 1, f.s.n.); 1735: drought (AHA, vol. 60A, f. 43–44); 1761: fleet and drought (AHA, vol. 82A, May and June, 1761); 1762: wars in Europe (AHA, vol. 83A, July 22, 1762); 1766: fleet (AHA, vol. 86A, f. 68); 1784: epidemic (*Gazetas*, vol. 1, 150); 1785: drought (*Gazetas*, vol. 1, 308); 1786: epidemic (*Gazetas*, vol. II, 106); 1790: drought (*Gazetas*, vol. IV, 122); 1793: wars against France (*Gazetas*, vol. 5, 380–81); 1794 (twice): drought and war with France (*Gazetas*, vol. 6, 323, 707, respectively); 1797: drought (*Gazetas*, vol. 8, 279); 1789: drought (*Gazetas*, vol. 9, 37); 1799: drought and sickness (AHA, vol. 3895, exp. 2, f.s.n.); 1800:

drought and general happiness (Gazeta, vol. 9, 37); 1802 (twice): health of monarch, Charles IV, and drought (*Gazetas*, vol. 11, 5, 85, respectively); 1808 (twice): epidemic and drought (*Gazetas*, vol. 12, 59, 111, respectively); 1808: epidemic and drought (*Gazetas*, vol. 15, 416); and 1810: drought and general happiness (AHA, vol. 3895, exp. 2, f.s.n.).

23. For the sermon, see Pulgar, *Sermón que en acción de gracias ofrecido a Dios*, 1–3. The Virgin had been asked in a formal petition to protect the queen; see González de Valdeosera, *Gentheliaco elogio*. The floats are described in *Actas*, Libro 43–47, 103.

24. *Actas*, Libro 48–50, 188, 220.

25. AHA, vol. 3895, exp. 2, f.s.n.; vol. 372A, September 13, 1700; and *Actas*, Libro 48–50, 12, 176.

26. *Actas*, Libro 48–50, vol. 2, 118; AHA, vol. 376A, January 25, 1724, and vol. 3898, exp. 8, f.s.n.; for Jesuit involvement, see *Actas*, Libro 51–53, 53. For the city council's apology, see *Actas*, Libro 51–53, 83. In 1733, the Native festival was once again canceled because the viceroy would not allow the image to return to the shrine. See AHA, vol. 3898, exp. 8, f.s.n. For the royal decree of 1750, see AHA, vol. 3895, exp. 2, f.s.n.

27. Curcio-Nagy, "Native Icon," 367–77.

28. For the case of 1754, see AHA, vol. 386, exp. 21, f. 1. For 1789, see AHA, vol. 3895, exp. 2, f.s.n.

29. Taylor, "The Virgin of Guadalupe in New Spain," 14, and Poole, *Our Lady of Guadalupe*, 175–76, 181.

30. I am currently writing a detailed analysis of the Hapsburg conquest festival titled "The Festival That Failed: Representing the Conquest in Sixteenth- and Seventeenth-Century Mexico City."

31. AHA, vol. 2277, exp. 5, f. 10, 15–18.

32. AHA, vol. 2277, exp. 5, f. 1.

33. *Actas*, Libro 53, 188–89, and AHA, vol. 2277, exp. 5, f. 28, 29. The aldermen initially chose to host the *cañas* (joust) because that what was apropos of 100-year anniversary celebrations. See AHA, vol. 2277, exp. 5, f. 8. For Native Americans in the parade and at the cathedral, see *Actas*, Libro 52, 86; *Actas*, Libro 53, 188; and AHA, vol. 2277, exp. 5, f. 29–30.

34. AHA, vol. 372A, f.s.n. For 1710, see AHA, vol. 43–47, 32. For 1716, see AHA, vols. 48–50, 191.

35. AHA, vol. 53, f. 354. Special bleachers constructed for bullfights in the Plaza del Volador alone cost 6,000 pesos. See AHA, vol. 4300, exp. 1, f.s.n. A letter of June 26, 1728, suggests that the Cabildo actually spent 16,000 pesos (8,000 at San Cristóbal and 8,000 in Mexico City); however,

the city councilmen adamantly claimed that they had only spent 2,000 at Guadalupe/San Cristóbal and another 4,000 in Mexico City. See AGN, Correspondencia de los Virreyes, v. 282, 1a ser., f. 88v. Other records show that the aldermen spent 7,408 pesos in Mexico City alone. See INAH, *Fondo Lira*, v. 78, f. 4–5.

36. AHA, vol. 62A, f.s.n. AGN, Correspondencia de Virreyes, vol. 282, 1a. ser., f. 89v.

37. AHA, vol. 65A, f.s.n.

38. Robles, *Diario*, vol. III, 243.

39. City council records do not list the horse and saddle as expenditures as early as the 1722 Casa Fuerte entrance. By 1766, the entrance on horseback was definitely a thing of the past. A painting shows the marquis of la Croix entering the city in a beautiful carriage.

40. In 1716, Indian musicians at Chapultepec did receive fancy new costumes, but dances and Native American participation declined in frequency. See AHA, vol. 48–50, f. 190. Once Chapultepec was eliminated from the itinerary, Native public performances there ceased. Although an indigenous group did perform for the count of Galvez in 1785, the dance took place inside the palace (*Gazetas*, vol. 6, 473). Nor did costume parades take place with the same sort of frequency as in the previous century, although records show that in 1702 the university students performed a costume parade (Robles, *Diario*, vol. 3, 245). The free public mock jousts and the artillery shows of the previous century also vanished after 1722. The author reached this conclusion based on the fact that after this date, that of the entrance of the marquis of Casa Fuerte, no mentions of uniforms, prizes, and preparation of the plaza were made in connection with viceregal entries except when they constituted the intermission entertainment during the bullfights. Only those spectators who paid the admission price could attend.

41. AHA, vol. 4300, exp. 2, f.s.n., and AHA, vol. 65A (1740), f.s.n. For discussions of the changing architectural style and tastes from the baroque to the neoclassical in Mexico, see Charlot, *Mexican Art and the Academy of San Carlos*, and Toussaint, *Arte colonial*, 213–51.

42. In 1722, the Cabildo spent 1,250 pesos on the arch and claimed that it had been an extraordinary expenditure, implying that the usual cost of the arch during that time was considerably less. See AHA, vol. 4300, exp. 2, f.s.n. An exception was the 3,800 pesos spent on the arch of the marquis of Valero in 1716. See INAH, Fondo Lira, vol. 78, f. 4–5.

43. (1716) Valero—Belerofont (cathedral) and Scipion (city), (1722)

Casa Fuerte—Augustus Caesar (city) and Prometheus (cathedral), (1743) Fuenclara—Julius Maximinius (city) and Ulysses (cathedral), (1746) Horcasitas—Atlas (city), (1756) Amarillas—Aeneas (city) and eyes (cathedral), (1761) Cruillas—Hercules and other allegories (city), (1771) Bucareli—Ulysses and other allegories (city), and (1783) Galvez—Vespa family and other allegories (city).

44. For example, in 1722, the king riding in the chariot of the sun breathed resplendent light that ignited the scepter of the viceroy/ Prometheus. See *Arco triunfal*, A2. Paintings with similar situations were described in the *Simulacro y alegórica*, 1; *Julio Maximinio*, 6, 9; and Rodríguez de Arizpe, *Representación*, 4.

45. For references to noble lineage and experience on the battlefield, see *Descripción métrica*, 2, 3 (lineage) and 4 (battle experience); *Julio Maximinio*, 4, 5; Rodríguez de Arizpe, *Alegórico simulacro*, 1, 2; Urrutia de Vergara y Estrada, *Loa*, 4 (lineage) and 6 (battle experience); Velázquez de León, *Ilustración*, 34–37 (lineage) and 23 (battle experience); and Rodríguez de Arizpe, *Alegórico simulacro*, 2, 5 (battle experience). *Lisonja* (flattery) and work were discussed only in 1743 and 1761. See *Descripción métrica*, 3; *Métrico Indicio*, 3, 4 (flattery) and 5–6, 8 (work); *Julio Maximinio*, 7; and Velázquez de León, *Ilustración*, 33 (flattery) and 26 (work).

46. *Alegórico simulacro*, 6 (prudence) and 3 (public welfare); *Descripción métrica*, 2 (integrity) and 1, 2 (justice and compassion); *Triunfal pompa*, B2 (dedication/*ánimo* [will or dedication to accomplish a task] and forgiveness); *Arco triunfal . . .* , A2 (prudence); *Métrico indicio*, 3 (viceroy as an example to the people) and 7 (prudence); *Julio Maximinio*, 3, 8 (generosity); Rodríguez de Arizpe, *Representación*, 5, 6 (public welfare and integrity); Abarca y Valda, *Ojo político*, 23 (love); Urrutia de Vergara y Estrada, *Loa*, 5 (prudence); and Velázquez de León, *Ilustración*, 28 (justice).

47. Velázquez de León, *Explicación*, 5, 11.

48. Velázquez de León, *La estirpe vespasiana*, 155, 156–58.

49. All subsequent eyewitness accounts and Cabildo records do not mention the arch at all. No published descriptions exist after 1783.

50. The celebration for the Bernardo de Galvez (the count of Galvez) in 1785 amounted to 55,593, and the entry for José de Iturrigaray in 1803 totaled 53,921 pesos. The known entry expenditures for fifteen celebrations are as follows: (1716) approximately 10,000 pesos—AGN, Correspondencia de Virreyes, vol. 282, 1a. ser., f. 88v., and INAH, *Fondo*

Lira, vol. 78, f. 4, 5; (1722) 12,000 pesos—AGN, Correspondencia de Virreyes, 1a. ser., vol. 282, f. 89–90v, and INAH, Fondo Lira, vol. 78, f. 150, 152v; (1760) at least 6,000 pesos—AHH, vol. 250, exp. 1, f. 44; (1766) 12,392 pesos— AGN, Correspondencia de Virreyes, 1a. ser., vol. 283, f.s.n; (1773) 11,918 pesos—AGN, Correspondencia de Virreyes, la. ser., vol. 283, f.s.n.; (1779) 14,949 pesos, AGN, Correspondencia de Virreyes, 1a. ser., vol. 282, f. 2–6; (1783) 60,350 pesos—AGN, Correspondencia de Virreyes, vol. 282, f. 7–16v, and AHH, vol. 250, exp. 11, f.s.n; (1785) 55,593 pesos—AGN, Correspondencia de Virreyes, 1a. ser., vol. 283, f.s.n., and vol. 282, f. 29–36; (1787) 16,749 pesos—AGN, Correspondencia de Virreyes, 1a. ser., vol. 283, f. 11–11v; (1789) 14,372 pesos—AGN, Correspondencia de Virreyes, la. ser., vol. 282, f. 4v, 55; (1798) at least 27,000 pesos—AHH, vol. 251, exp. 15, f. 9; (1803) 53,921 pesos—AHH, vol. 252, exp. 1, f.s.n; (1810) 14,448 pesos—AGN, Ayuntamientos, vol. 129, exp. 1, f. 2; (1813) 3,407 pesos—AGN, Correspondencia de Virreyes, 1a. ser., vol. 283, f. 84; and (1816) 8,527 pesos—AGN, Correspondencia de Virreyes, 1a. ser., vol. 283, f. 95–95v.

51. The tradition of auctioning the right to host the bullfights as a means to pay for the entry began in 1724. See AGN, Ayuntamientos, vol. 216, exp. 2, in a royal decree dated July 10, 1724. Documents show that in 1783 and 1803, the city received 73,735 pesos and 51,960 pesos respectively.

52. The accounts listing the total expenditures for the available entries include items such as dinners, refreshments, lodging, and pantry supplies for the palace, plays, musicians, and balls or dances. The only public aspect documented in the accounts was the bullfight that included a sortija, jousts or horse races funded by the aldermen. It was common practice to include bullfights for the entry; however, the data are incomplete and the average is based on the years 1783 and 1785. In the first year, 20,762, or 34 percent, was spent on the corrida out of a total of 60,350; in the second year, 11,076, or 24 percent, of 44,860 was expended. See AHH, vol. 250, exp. 6, f. 45, and AGN, Correspondencia de Virreyes, 1a. ser., vol. 283, f.s.n; AHA, vol. 4300, exp. 7, f.s.n.; and AHA, vol. 86A, f. 45.

53. *Gazetas*, vol. 16, 689.

Chapter 5: His Majesty's Most Loyal and Imperfect Subjects

1. Velázquez de León, *Explicación*, 79–80. See also Ceremonial, 101.
2. Carrera Stampa, *Los gremios*, 100; Valle Arizpe, in *Notas de*

Platería, devotes an entire chapter to silversmith festivals and reproduces the manuscript by Juan Rodríguez de Abril titled *"Duque de T'Serclaes. Verdadera relación de una máscara que los artífices del Gremio de la Platería de México y devotos del doloroso San Isidro el Labrador de Madrid, hicieron en Honra a su gloriosa beatificación."* See also Jiménez Rueda, "El certámen de los plateros en 1618," 343–84.

3. Salcedo y Somodevilla, *Breve relación*, 1, 4–5, 13–14, 16, 17.

4. Ibid., 14.

5. See AHA, vol. 2282, exp. 8, f.s.n.; see also AHH, vol. 251, exp. s.n.

6. The Real Protomedicato was established in 1646 and was charged with maintaining high professional standards within the medical and allied professions. It administered examinations for physicians, surgeons, pharmacists, and philbotanists. It also inspected pharmacies to check licenses and to check if medicines were fresh and counseled the viceroys on public health issues. For more data on the medical profession in New Spain, see Fernández del Castillo, *El tribunal*; García Icazbalceta, "Los médicos de México en el Siglo XVI"; González Ullóa, *La medicina en México*; and Muriel, *Hospitales de la Nueva España*. For their sermon and celebration to Charles IV, see Castillo and Campos Martínez, *El Salomón*.

7. For information on university and other student literary festivities for the three juras mentioned, see Ramírez del Castillo, *Hércules coronado*; Ruíz Guerra y Morales, *Letras*; Beye Cisneros y Quixano, *Amorosa contenida*; Rodríguez de Arizpe, *Augusto iluminado*; and *Cifra feliz*.

8. Platero contributions to the oath in Madrid paled in comparison to those sponsored in Mexico City. For example, in 1760, the silversmith guild in Spain commissioned an arch in front of their building. Although lavish, the structure did not include any silver ornamentation or panels.

9. For an analysis of the mining industry and the boom, see the now classic study of Brading, *Miners and Merchants in Bourbon Mexico 1763–1810*.

10. For a discussion of the economic issues affecting the capital during the eighteenth century, see Haslip-Viera, *Crime*, 20–21, 27; Garner, "Prices and Wages," 73–108; and Van Young, "The Age of Paradox," 64–90.

11. Florescano and Gil Sanchez, "La época," 269.

12. AHA, vol. 2282, exp. 15, f. 195.

13. For Mexico City, see AHA, vol. 2282, exp. 15, f.s.n. For Madrid, see *Descripción de los ornatos*; for the Seville festival, see Gil, *Relación*.

14. See AHA, vol. 2282, exp. 8, for the qualifications of the joust participants and the city's donation of 700 pesos in 1747. See AHH, vol. 251, exp. s.n.

15. During the oath to Philip V in 1701, Native Americans not only presented bird-filled globes as in Hapsburg oath ceremonies but also showcased a large mechanical eagle attached to a great staff decorated with ribbons. At the appropriate moment, by some manipulation of a lever, the eagle moved its head and pierced its heart, releasing hundreds of doves. See Mendieta Rebollo, *Suntuoso festivo*, f. 44. In 1724, Natives also participated in and sponsored dances. See AHA, vol. 2282, exp. 4, f. 102.

16. AHA, vol. 2282, exp. 10, f.s.n. For the Hues Hues (young men dressed as old men who danced about, making fun of the crowd and flirting with young women, an essential part of Native carnival in the capital), see Abarca y Valda, *El sol*, 217.

17. *Ceremonial*, 88–89.

18. *Gazetas*, vol. 4, 3, 4.

19. AGN, Historia, vol. 483, exp. 8., f.s.n. Cheryl English Martin in *Governance and Society in Colonial Mexico: Chihuahua in the Eighteenth Century* points out that Natives, Africans, and women did not appear in festivals in that region during the 1700s. Bourbon officials appeared to make it a policy to exclude popular participation from their official ceremonies.

20. It is noteworthy that guilds in Spain, at least in Madrid, did not provide as much jura entertainment for the crowd as they did in Mexico City. In general, Madrid guilds funded the construction of an ephemeral facade in front of their main office. See *Descripción de los ornatos*, 36, and *Los gremios*.

21. *Ceremonial*, 98–101.

22. AHA, vol. 2282, exp. 15. For whatever reasons, the city fathers thought better of saddling the guilds with yet another expenditure in honor of Charles IV. See AHA, vol. 2282, exp. 28. Guild floats for 1789 are mentioned in BNM, ms. 1389, f. 319. Castro Gutiérrez documents the financial decline of the guilds at the end of the eighteenth century; this, no doubt, accounted for their conspicuous absence in 1808. See his *La extinción de la artesanía gremial*, 40 and the conclusion.

23. Haslip-Viera, *Crime*, 49.

24. AHA, vol. 2282, exp. 11.

25. This figure is based on Abarca y Valda's description in *El sol*, 195–256.

26. For wages for guildsmen, see Carrera Stampa, *Los gremios*, 48, and Gibson, *The Aztecs*, 250, 251.

27. AHA, vol. 381, exp. 7, no. 11, f. 68; see also AHA, vol. 2282, exp. 11, f.s.n.

28. AHA, vol. 381, exp. 7, no. 11, f. 69.

29. AHA, vol. 381, exp. 7, no. 11, f. 64, 70v. The anonymous author of *Ceremonial* (p. 100) claimed that the cereros and confiteros sponsored six "chariots of fire," carts rigged to explode with fireworks, in the 1760 oath to Ferdinand VI.

30. AHA, vol. 2282, exp. 15, f. 195.

31. See the 1780 decree on fireworks in AGN, vol. 2, exp. 63.

32. Salcedo y Somodevilla, *Breve relación*, 2. For Viceroy Francisco de Guemes y Horcacitas's comments on the 1747 jura themes, see AHA, vol. 2282, exp. 7, f. 196.

33. Velázquez de León, *Explicación breve*, 95, 100, 101, 105, 238. Other paintings of loyalty can be found on pp. 90–91, 92, 97–98, 103. See also Salcedo y Somodevilla, *Breve relación*, 4–5, and Larrañaga, *Colección*, 9, 26–27.

34. Abarca y Valda, *El sol*, 179. For the hearts aflame on jousts shields, see 273, 275, 279.

35. Abarca y Valda, *El sol,*, 216, and *Ceremonial*, 98.

36. See Mendieta Rebollo, *Suntuoso festivo*, 44, 211; Larrañaga, *Colección*, 14, 24, 25–26, 191–92; and Velázquez de León, *Explicación breve*, 89, 101.

37. Castillo and Campos Martínez, *El Salomón*, 15.

38. Velázquez de León, *Explicación breve*, 85, 96, 98, 99, 100, 101.

39. Abarca y Valda, *El sol*, 226, 241–45, and BNM, ms. 1389, f. 315.

40. *Explicación de el Arco*, 8, 9.

41. Both parish priests and royal district governors (after 1778) were charged with establishing and maintaining such schools. The decrees appear to have been somewhat successful, albeit for limited periods of time. However, many factors such as inadequate funding, poorly qualified instructors, and parents reluctant to send their children for instruction determined the success of the schools. See Taylor, *Magistrates*, 335–38.

42. Castillo and Campos Martínez, *El Salomón*, 12.

43. Del Río, "Represión," 310.

44. Castillo and Campos Martínez, *El Salomón*, 16. The "garden of delights" was a reference to Italy, where Charles had reigned before assuming the Spanish throne.

45. Taylor, *Magistrates*, chap. 5.

46. Archbishop Lorenzana as quoted in Taylor, *Magistrates*, chap. 7, n. 95, 252.

47. Florescano, *Memory*, 181–82.

48. AGN, Historia, vol. 432, exp. s.n., ff. 1–2v.

49. Del Río, "Represión," 303.

50. Villarroel, *Enfermedades*, 185–86; for the quote see pp. 505–6.

51. Taylor, *Magistrates*, 252.

52. Viqueira Albán, *Relajados*, 154–55.

53. Del Río, "Represión," 311, 313, 316–17.

54. AGN, Historia, vol. 437, exp. 2, f.s.n.

55. AGN, Historia, vol. 437, exp. 7, entire expediente.

56. Israel, *Race*, 69.

57. *Actas*, Libro 3, 172, and Libro 6, 232, respectively.

58. At the time, the capital was experiencing severe shortages of wheat and corn grains and prices were at the highest in a century. Native Americans sought aid from the archbishop and the viceroy, and when those two failed to hear their grievances, the riot ensued. The expectation, so emphasized in the official ritual, was that the viceroy was to act as the good Christian prince and aid the populace. The riot in essence was an explosion of frustration as citizens were left alone to survive the grain crisis because the viceroy (and the archbishop) had abandoned them. Fear of another revolt over grain shortages permeated the procession the following year. See Robles, *Diario*, vol. 3, 154–55, and Cope, *The Limits*, chap. 7. The potential of festivals to occasionally backfire on their ecclesiastical or civil organizers is well documented in studies such as Le Roy Ladurie, *Carnival in Romans*, and Davis, "The Rites of Violence," 51–91.

59. Viqueira Albán, *Relajados*, 31–32.

60. Robles, *Diario*, vol. 3, 154–55. In 1765, food and drink sellers initially were asked to leave the streets once the procession began (AHA, vol. 3712, exp. 6, f. 2). Taverns were also banned from selling liquor during and after the procession (AHA, vol. 1066, exp. 3).

61. Villaroel, *Enfermedades*, 188–89.

62. AHA, vol. 383, exp. 21, f. 61.

63. Sedano, *Noticias*, vol. 1, 96. As a point of comparison, Oaxaca City in 1773 spent 144 pesos on their Corpus procession. See AGN, Ayuntamientos, vol. 142, exp. 2, f. 17v–18. The decline in Mexico City Corpus expenditures began earlier in the century. For example, in 1716 the city council spent 496 pesos on the procession and in 1719 spent 634 pesos. See INAH, Fondo Lira, vol. 78, f. 3, and vol. 81, f. 392–93, respectively.

64. AHA, vol. 3712, exp. 7, f. 1. For the 1721 decree, see AHA, vol. 3712, exp. 3, f. 1. For the discussion on which villages were permitted to participate, see AHA, vol. 3712, exp. 7, f. 7–8.

65. AHA, vol. 3712, exp. 7, f. 2.

66. AHA, vol. 3712, exp. 7, f. 3.

67. AHA, vol. 3712, exp. 7, f. 7.

68. AHA, vol. 3712, exp. 8, f. 15.

69. All reforms are listed in AHA, vol. 3712, exp. 7, f. 9–10.

70. Clenidinnen, "Ways to the Sacred," 115. See also Burkhart, "Pious Performance," 361–81.

71. Florescano, *Memory*, 167, and Taylor, *Magistrates*, chap. 14.

72. For all the quotes, see AHA, vol. 3712, exp. 7, f. 21 and 28.

73. Years earlier, when the dispute first began, municipal authorities contacted the royal architect about the construction of a cloth covering, but they discarded the idea when they learned the proposed cost of the canopy—1,370 pesos. For details, see AHA, vol. 3712, exp. 8, f. 15, exp. 7, f. 11, 21. For the cloth canopy that was finally utilized, see AHA, vol. 3712, exp. 19, f. 1., and *Gazetas*, vol. 4, 122.

74. Del Río, "Represión," 305. Although Bourbon reforms severely altered Corpus, children still continued to wave *tarasquitas* (little paper dragons) during the procession in the nineteenth century. Gómez, "Diario curioso," 341, and González Obregón, *México viejo*, 438. The Bourbon measures against Corpus Christi in Spain took effect ten years earlier, in 1780. See Very, *The Spanish Corpus Christi*, 107. The last citywide Corpus of Mexico City took place in 1866. See García Cubas, *El libro*, 370.

75. Del Río, "Represión," 305, 306, 327, 309.

76. Del Río, "Represión," 310. The Inquisition in 1679, 1700, and again in 1709 issued edicts against dressing as clerics and nuns and demanded that inhabitants not mix the profane and the sacred by such disrespectful costume displays. See AGN, Inquisición, vol. 543, 2a parte, no. 63, f. 476.

77. Viqueira Albán, *Relajados*, 140, 144, 145, 146.

78. Del Río, "Represión," 322.

79. Ladd, *Mexican Nobility*.

80. Taylor, *Magistrates*, 16, and Burkholder and Chandler, *Impotence to Authority*.

81. *Explicación de el Arco*, 16.

Chapter 6: Ritual, Satire, and the Coming of Independence

1. Ruíz Guerra y Morales, *Letras*, 6–11, 18–21, 25–27.

2. Boyer, "Absolutism," 488.

3. Viqueira Albán, *Relajados*, 224.

4. Inquisitors did publish edicts attempting to ban certain poems that came to their attention or to ban satirical poems in general. For an example of the latter, see AGN, Inquisición, 3ra. Parte, exp. 6, f. 558.

5. For examples of popular satire in song lyrics, see Rivera Ayala, "Lewd Songs and Dances," 27–46.

6. Agovi, "King," 47–50.

7. Greer Johnson, *Satire in Colonial Spanish America*, chap. 1.

8. Archer, *The Army in Bourbon Mexico*; McAlister, *Fuero Militar*; and Haslip-Viera, *Crime*, 139.

9. Sedano, *Noticias*, vol. 2, 94.

10. Abarca y Valda, *El sol*, 263. It is believed that *mojiganga* is derived from *boxiganga*, a word applied to rudimentary comic troupes that wore strange costumes during the seventeenth century. During the eighteenth century, mojigangas in Spain also formed part of the entertainment inside playhouses. In Spain, a direct correlation between the mojiganga and water battles does not seem to exist as it apparently did in Mexico City. (The term *mojiganga* was probably connected to *mojarse*, meaning to get wet.) Mojigangas were, on some occasions, highly orchestrated intellectual exercises. In New Spain, evidence suggests that during the 1600s, the term *mojiganga* was not utilized, as most satirical or silly costume parades were referred to as a *máscara ridícula*. The term *mojiganga* is utilized much more frequently in the Bourbon century. For more details on these parades and performances in Spain, see Deleito y Piñuela, *También se divierte el pueblo*, 20, and Mori, *Colección de Entremeses*. For the mojiganga in Tamaulipas, see Escandón, *Informe al virrey de la Nueva España*.

11. "Tres sátiras contra Juan Ortega y Montáñez, Arzo y virrey," AGN, Inquisición, vol. 178, 1a parte, exp. 18, f. 176. This is the first satire, titled "Cuelga al Exmo. Sr. D. Juan de Ortega, Arzobispo en posesión y sin palio."

12. AGN, Inquisición, vol. 178, 1a parte, exp. 18, f. 176v. This is the satire titled "A la posesión del Virrey sin cédula en octava de Difuntos."

13. AGN, Inquisición, vol. 321, exp. 10, ff. 50–50v.

14. AGN, Inquisición, vol. 321, exp. 10; for holes in the canopy-and-coffers analogy, see f. 51v; for Natives in the procession, see ff. 52v–53; for commentary on the bishop, see f. 55v; and for city councilmen and alcaldes, see ff. 56–56v.

15. The original documents are now lost but were reproduced in Jiménez, "Nadie se engaña si con fe baila." For quotes, see 537, 539–40, 550, 555, 556–57, 558–59, 563, 564–65, 568, 577, 581, 584, 581–88.

16. AGN, Inquisición, vol. 1052, exp. 12, f.s.n. For another, similar poem, see the same volume and expediente, ff. 78–79.

17. "Padre Nuestro de los Gachupines por un criollo americano," AGN, Inquisición, vol. 1095, f. 337. For other examples, see the same volume, ff. 307–8v, 321–23, 337–37v, and vol. 1267, ff. 40–40v.

18. Lavrin, "Execution of the Law of Consolidation in New Spain" 27–49, and Hamnett, "Appropriation of Mexican Church Wealth by the Spanish Bourbon Government," 85–113.

19. AGN, Inquisición, vol. 1441, exp. 11, f. 49v.

20. AHA, vol. 2282, exp. 31, f. 263.

21. For the major events leading to independence in the capital, see Anna, *Fall of the Royal Government in Mexico City*, 55–56, 78, 81–83, 94.

22. *Clamor que un indio*, 1.

23. Montaña, *Rasgo épico*, 9, 13, 14.

24. *Deseñgano a los indios haciéndoles*, 11, and AHA, vol. 3903, exp. 65, f. 1, 2.

25. Poole, *Our Lady*, 3.

26. *Mexico a su Generala María Santísima de los Remedios*, 283, 285.

27. Fernández de San Salvador, *Acción de gracias a nuestra Generala María SS*, 2–3, 5.

28. AHA, vol. 2277, exp. 29, f. 14.

29. AHA, vol. 2277, exp. 26, f. 2.

30. AHA, vol. 2277, exp. 28, f. 42.

31. AHA, vol. 2277, exp. 28, f. 36.

32. AGN, Reales Cédulas Originales, vol. 217, exp. 2, f. 1v.

33. AGN, Reales Cédulas Originales, vol. 217, exp. 2, f. 1v. For the aldermen and their position on the stipend and the festival, see AHA, vol. 2277, exp. 28, f. 45.

34. AHA, vol. 2277, exp. 28, ff. 54–56.

35. For an example, see AGN, Infidencias, vol. 18, exp. 5, ff. 12, 13v, and 23v.

36. Van Young, "Who Was That Masked Man, Anyway?, 18–35.
37. Florescano, *Memory*, 312.

Chapter 7: Concluding Thoughts

1. Machiavelli, *The Prince*, 21.
2. Campos Martínez, *El Iris*, 20.
3. For a detailed discussion on this anti-colonial colonial discourse, see Chatterjee, *Nationalist Thought and the Colonial World*.
4. Campos Martínez, *El Iris*, 18.

Bibliography
Manuscript Texts

AGN   Archivo General de la Nación (Mexico City)

AHA   Archivo Histórico del Antiguo Ayuntamiento de la Ciudad de México (Mexico City)

AHH   Archivo Histórico de Hacienda, AGN

BNM   Biblioteca Nacional de México (Mexico City)

INAH   Biblioteca del Instituto Nacional de Antropología e Historia, Museo Nacional de Antropología (Mexico City)

Printed Primary Sources/Festival Descriptions

Abarca y Valda, José Mariano. *El sol en león. Solemnes aplausos con que el rey nuestro señor d. Fernando VI, sol de las Españas, fue celebrado . . . por la Muy Noble, Muy Leal Imperial Ciudad de México.* Mexico: María de Ribera, 1748.

———. *Ojo político, idea cabal y ajustada copia de príncipe, que dio a la luz la santa iglesia metropolitana de México, en el magnífico caro que dedicó amorosa en la entrada que hizo a su gobierno el Excmo. Sr. Don Agustín Ahumada y Villalón, Marqués de las Amarillas, virrey . . .* Mexico: Imprenta Nueva de la Biblioteca Mexicana, 1756.

Acosta, José de, SJ. *Historia natural y moral de las Indias.* Madrid: Historia 16, 1987.

Actas de Cabildo de la ciudad de México. 44 vols. Mexico: Aguilar e Hijos, 1889–1911.

Alavés Pinelo, Alonso de. *Astro mitológico político que en la entrada y recibimiento del Excmo. Sr. Don Luis Enríquez de Guzmán, Marqués de Alba de Liste, virrey . . . consagró la ilustrísima, nobilísima y Muy Leal Ciudad de México . . .* Mexico: Juan Ruíz, 1650.

Alenda y Mira, Jenaro., comp. *Relaciones de solemnidades y fiestas públicas de España.* Madrid: Sucesores de Rivadeneyra, 1903.

Arco triunfal que la insigne iglesia metropolitana de México dibujó en su entrada al Excmo. Sr. Don Antonio Vázquez de Acuña,

Marqués de Casa Fuerte, virrey . . . Mexico: José Bernardo de Hogal, 1722.

Argüello, Manuel de. *Sermon moral al Real Acuerdo de México al tiempo que tomó posesión con pública entrada el Exmo. Señor D. Joseph Sarmiento Valladares, Conde de Moctezuma . . . virrey . . .* Mexico: Juan Joseph Guillena Carrascoso, 1697.

Augusto Alegórico en que la Nobilíssima Ciudad de México, dibuxó en su entrada al Exmo. Sr. D. Juan Antonio Vazquez de Acuña, Marqués de Cassa Fuerte . . . virrey. Mexico: José Bernardo de Hogal, 1722.

Azevedo, Francisco de. *Silva explicativa del arco con que celebró la entrada del Excmo. Sr. Don Gaspar de Sandoval, Conde de Galve, virrey . . . recibiólo por su príncipe la Muy Noble y Muy Leal Ciudad de México, alegorizada en París.* México: Viuda Francisco Rodriguez Lupercio, 1689.

Beye Cisneros y Quixano, Manuel Ignacio. *Amorosa contenida de Francia, Italia, y España sobre la augusta persona de el Señor Don Carlos III, exaltado al trono español . . .* Mexico: Imprenta del Real y mas Antiguo Colegio de San Ildefonso, 1761.

Bocanegra, Matías. *Teatro jerárquico de la luz, pira cristiana política del gobierno que la Ciudad de México erigió en la real portada que dedicó al Excmo. Sr. Don García Sarmiento de Sotomayor, Conde de Salvatierra . . . en su feliz entrada por virrey . . .* Mexico: Matías de Bocanegra, 1642.

Breve Razón del Carro y Loa de los tres gremios de Cereros, Confiteros, y Tintoreros . . . Mexico: José Bernardo de Hogal, 1732.

Campos Martínez, Juan Gregorio de. *El Iris, diadema inmortal. Descripción de los festivos aplausos con que celebró la feliz elevación al trono de Nuestro Rey el Sr. D. Fernando VI . . . el Real Tribunal del Protomedicato de esta Nueva España . . .* Mexico: Viuda de José Bernardo de Hogal, 1748.

Castillo, José del, and Campos Martínez, Juan Gregorio de. *El Salomón de España. Oración panegírica con que el día 1 de mayo de 1761 celebró en la iglesia del Hospital de la Concepción y Jesús Nazareno de la Ciudad de México, la feliz coronación de nuestro rey y señor Don Carlos III . . . el Real Tribunal del Protomedicato . . .* Mexico: Imprenta del Real Colegio de San Ildefonso, 1762.

Castro Santa Ana, José Manuel de. *Diario de sucesos notables escrito por . . . y comprende los años de 1752 a 1754. Vols. VI-VII in Documentos para la historia de México.* Mexico: Imp. de Juan R. Navarro, 1853–54.

Ceremonial de la nobilisima Ciudad de México de lo acaecido en el año 1755. Mexico, 1974.

Cervantes de Salazar, Francisco. *México en 1554 y Túmulo imperial.* Mexico: Editorial Porrúa, 1991.

Chimalpahin Quauhtlehuanitzin, Don Domingo Francisco de San Antón Muñón. Vol. 3, *Codex Chimalpahin: Chimalpahin's Mexico City Journal.* Edited by James Lockhart, Doris Namala, and Susan Schroeder. Norman: University of Oklahoma Press, forthcoming.

Cifra feliz de las dichas imponderables que se promete la monarquía española bajo el suspirado dominio de su augusto soberano el Sr. D. Fernando VI . . . certámen poético conque la humilde lealtad y reconocida gratitud del Real y mas antiguo Colegio de San Ildefonso de México . . . celebró . . . Salamanca: Imprenta de Santa Cruz, 1749.

Ciudad Real, Fray Antonio de. *Tratado curioso y docto de las grandezas de la Nueva España.* Mexico: UNAM, 1993.

Clamor que un indio hizo a nuestra Señora de los Remedios en su santuario la mañana del 11 de agosto de 1810. Mexico, 1810.

Córdoba, Fray Martín de. *Jardin de nobles doncellas.* Madrid, 1953.

La corona sin término. Oración panegyrica con que celebró en la Iglesia de el Hospital de la Concepción, y Jesus Nazareno de la Ciudad de México, la feliz coronación de nuestro Rey, y Señor D. Fernando Sexto . . . el Real Tribunal de el Protomedicato . . . Mexico, 1748.

Cruz, Sor Juana Inés de la. "Neptuno alegórico, océano de colores, simulacro político que erigió la muy esclarecida, sacra y augusta iglesia metropolitana de México en las lúcidas alegóricas ideas de un arco triunfal que consagró obsequiosa y dedicó amante a la feliz entrada del Excmo. Sr. Don Tomás Antonio Lorenzo Manuel de la Cerda, Conde de Paredes, virrey . . . 1680." Vol. 21, *Obras completas,* int. Francisco Monterde. Sepan cuantos . . . , 100. Mexico: Editorial Porrúa, 1969, 919–54.

Cuevas Aguirre, José Angel de. *Arenga que, a nombre de la Muy Noble, Insigne, Muy Leal, Imperial Ciudad de México hizo y dijo don . . . regidor decano de su Ayuntamiento, en la solemne y pública entrada del Excmo. Sr. Don Antonio María de Bucareli y Ursúa, virrey . . .* Mexico: Felipe de Zúñiga y Ontiveros, 1771.

Dávila Padilla, Agustín. *Historia de la fundación y discurso de la provincia de Santiago de México de la Orden de Predicadores . . .* 3rd ed. Mexico: Editorial Academia Literaria, 1955.

Descripción de los ornatos públicos con que la corte de Madrid ha sol-
emnizado la feliz exaltación al trono de los reyes nuestros Señores
Don Carlos IIII y Doña Luísa de Borbón, y la jura del serenísimo
Señor Don Fernando, príncipe de Asturias. Madrid: Imprenta
Real, 1789.

Descripción métrica del triunfal arco que la Imperial México erigió al
Excmo. Sr. Marqués de Valero y Ayamonte, governador y capitán
general de Nueva España. Mexico: n.p., 1716.

Descripción y explicación de la fábrica y empresas del suntuoso arco que
la Ilustísima, Nobilísima y Muy Leal Ciudad de México, cabeza
del occidente imperio, erigió a la feliz entrada y gozoso
recibimiento del Excmo. Sr. Don Diego López Pacheco, Marqués
de Villena, Duque de Escalona . . . virrey. Mexico: Juan Ruíz,
1640.

Descripción y representación panegírica del arco triunfal que a las puer-
tas de su Real Templo erigió al public ingresso del Excmo. Sr. D.
Pedro Cebrián, Y Agustín, Conde de Fuen-Clara . . . la primada
de ella en México, Santa Iglesia Metropolitana . . . Mexico: José
Bernardo de Hogal, 1743.

Desengaño a los indios haciéndoles ver lo mucho que deben a los
Españoles. Conversación que tuvieron en el campamento de esta
ciudad un Dragón con una Tortillera y su marido Pasqual, y la
presención de A.V. Mexico, 1810.

Díaz, José Simón, comp. *Relaciones breves de actos públicos celebrados*
en Madrid de 1541 a 1650. Madrid: Instituto de Estudios
Madrileños, 1982.

———. *Fuentes para la historia de Madrid y su provinica.* Madrid:
Instituto de Estudios Madrileños, 1964.

Díaz del Castillo, Bernal. *La historia verdadera de la conquista de la*
Nueva España. Mexico: Editorial Porrúa, 1970.

Durán, Fray Diego de. *Aztecs: The History of the Indians of New*
Spain. New York: Orion Press, 1964.

———. *Book of the Gods and Rites and the Ancient Calendar.* Norman:
University of Oklahoma Press, 1971.

Escandón, José de. *Informe al virrey de la Nueva España sobre los*
primeros actos culturales en la Provincia de Nuevo Santander.
Mexico: Vargas Rea, 1943.

Explicación de el Arco erigido en la puerta de el Palacio Arzobispal de
México, a la gloria de el Rey N. Señor D. Carlos III, en el día de
su solemne proclamación . . . Mexico: Colegio Real y mas
Antiguo de San Ildefonso, 1790(?).

Fernández de Castro, Gaspar. *Relación ajustada, deseño breve y montea sucinta de los festivos aplausos conque desahogó pequeña parte de los inmensos júbilos de su pecho, en la regocijada nueva del feliz nacimiento de nuestro deseado príncipe Don Felipe Próspero*. Mexico: Juan Ruíz, 1658.

Fernández de San Salvador, Agustín Pomposo. *Acción de gracias a nuestra Generala Maria SS. De los Remedios, Disipiadora de las nubes fulminantes de la ira de Dios* . . . Mexico, 1810.

Fernández Osorio, Pedro. *Júpiter benévolo, astro ético político, idea simbólica de príncipes que en la suntuosa fábrica de un arco triunfal dedicó la santa iglesia de México al Excmo. Sr. Marqués de Leiva, Conde de Baños, virrey* . . . Mexico: n.p., 1660.

Festín hecho por las morenas criollas de la Muy Noble y Muy Leal Ciudad de México al recibimiento y entrada del excmo. Sr. Marqués de Villena, virrey . . . Mexico: n.p., 1640.

"Gacetas de México." Vol. 4, 2nd ser., *Documentos de la historia de México*. Mexico: Imp. F. Escalante y Día, 1954–55.

Gage, Thomas. *Thomas Gage's Travels in the New World*. Norman: University of Oklahoma, 1985.

García Cubas, Antonio. *El libro de mis recuerdos*. Mexico: Arturo García Cubas Hermanos, 1904.

Gemelli Careri, Giovanni Francesco. *Viaje a la Nueva España*. Mexico: UNAM, 1976.

Gil, Manuel. *Relación de la Proclamación del Rey N. Sr. D. Carlos III y Fiestas con que celebró la muy noble y muy leal Ciudad de Sevilla*. Madrid: Imprenta Viuda de Joaquín Ibarra, 1790.

Gómez, José. *Diario curioso de México de* . . . Vol. 3, *Documentos para la historia de México*. Mexico: Imp. de Juan R. Navarro, 1853–54.

Gómez de Cervantes, Gonzalo. *La vida económica y social de la Nueva España al finalizar del siglo XVI*. Mexico, 1944.

González de Valdeosera, Miguel. *Gentheliáco elogio, prognóstico felice, en la expectación del Real Agosto parto* . . . *que venera esta Nueva España con la advocación de los Remedios*. Mexico: Juan Joseph G. Garrascoso, 1701.

Los gremios mayores de Madrid, artífices de la entrada pública en la capital de España de los Reyes Fernando VI y Doña Bárbara de Braganza. Madrid, 1980.

Guevara, Juan de. *Felicísima entrada y recibimiento que esta Muy Noble y Muy Leal Ciudad de México hizo al Excmo. Sr. Don Francisco Fernández de la Cueva, Duque de Alburquerque, virrey* . . . Mexico: Bernardo Calderón, 1653.

Guijo, Gregorio M. de. *Diario 1648–1664.* 2 vols. Mexico: Porrúa, 1952–53.

Gutiérrez, Sebastian. *Arco triunfal y explicación de sus historias, empresas y jeroglifos con que la iglesia catedral metropolitana de la Ciudad de México hizo recibimiento al Excmo. Sr. Don Rodrigo Pacheco Osorio, marqués de Cerralbo, virrey* . . . Mexico: Diego Garrido, 1624.

Gutiérrez de Medina, Cristóbal. *Adición a los festejos que en la Ciudad de México se hicieron al Marqués de Villena, mi señor, con el particular que le dedicó el Colegio de la Compañía de Jesús.* Mexico: Bernardo Calderón, 1640.

———. Viaje por mar y tierra del virrey Marqués de Villena. Aplausos y fiestas en México. Mexico: UNAM, Insituto de Historia, 1947.

Instrucciones y memorias de los virreyes novohispanos. 2 vols. Mexico: Editorial Porrúa, 1991.

Isla, Josef Francisco de. *La mojiganga teológica. Descripción de la fiesta que hicieron los jóvenes teólogos en la ciudad de Salamanca en 1781.* Madrid: Mundo Latino, 1930.

Jovellanos, Gaspar Melchor de. *Espectáculos y diversiones públicas; Informe sobre la ley agraria.* Madrid: Ediciones Cátedra, 1977.

Julio Maximinio Verdadero, bajo cuyos heroícos hechos, y altas prendas symbolizó el estudio las del Excmo. Sr. D. Pedro Cebrián y Agustín, Conde de Fuen-Clara . . . y se expressaron en el Jano Bifronte, y triunfal archo, que a su público ingresso erigió la Capital de estos reynos, Imperial Mexico. Mexico: n.p., 1743.

Kontezke, Richard. Vol. 2, *Colección de documentos para la historia de la formacion social de Hispanoamérica 1493–1810.* Madrid, 1958.

Larrañaga, Bruno Francisco. *Colección de los adornos poéticos distribuídos en los tres tablados que la Noble Ciudad de México erigió y en que solemnizó la proclamación y jura de . . .* Fernando VII. Mexico: Imprenta de Arizpe, 1809.

León, Fray Luis de. *La perfecta casada.* Mexico: Editorial Porrúa, 1970.

Machiavelli, Niccolo. *The Prince and the Discourses.* New York: Modern Library, 1940.

Marmolejo, Pedro de. *Loa sacramental en metáphora de las calles de México. Representada en las fiestas que celebró, en honra del Sanctíssimo Sacramento.* Mexico: Francisco Salbago, 1635.

Marte católico, astro político, planeta de héroes y ascendiente de príncipes que en las lúcidas sombras de una triunfal portada ofrece, representa, dedica, la siempre esclarecida, sacra, augusta

Iglesia metropolitana de México al Excmo. Sr. Don Francisco Fernández de la Cueva, Duque de Alburquerque, virrey . . . Mexico: Vuida de Bernardo Calderón, 1653.

Mendieta Rebollo, Gabriel de. *Suntuoso festivo, real aparato en que explica su lealtad la siempre Noble, Ilustre, Imperial y Regia Ciudad de México, metrópoli de la América y Corte de su Nueva España, en la aclamación del muy alto, muy poderoso, muy soberano príncipe Don Felipe V, su católico dueño, Rey de las Españas . . .* Mexico: Juan Guillen Carrascoso, 1701.

Medina, Alonso de. *Espejo de príncipes católicos y gobernadores políticos. Erigióle en arco triunfal la santa iglesia metropolitana de México a la entrada del Excmo. Sr. Don García de Sotomayor, conde de Salvatierra, virrey . . .* Mexico: Francisco Robredo, 1642.

Métrico indicio y representación pánegyrica del Triumphal arco, que al recibimiento, y feliz ingresso del Excmo. Sr. D. Pedro Cebrián, y Augustín, Conde de Fuenclara . . . le erigió su Capital, Nobilíssima Imperial Ciudad de México . . . Mexico: n.p., 1743.

México a su Generala María Santíssima de los Remedios en la procesión solemne del día 24 de febrero con que concluyó el novenario de acción de gracias por la prosperidad de las armas del Rey contra los rebeldes. Mexico: Arizpe, 1811.

Montana, Luis José. *Rasgo épico. Peregrinación de la sagrada Imagen de la Santísima Virgen María, Nuestra Señora de advocación de los Remedios.* Mexico: Arizpe, 1810.

Mori, Cotarelo. *Colección de entremeses, loas, bailes, jácaras y mojigangas desde los fines del siglo XVI a mediados del XVIII. Vols. 17 and 18, Nueva Biblioteca de Autores Españoles.* Madrid, 1911.

Motolinía (Fray Toribio de Paredes). *Relaciones de los ritos antiguos, idolatrías y sacrificios de los indios de la Nueva España, y de la maravillosa conversión que Dios en ellos ha obrado. Manuscrito de la ciudad de México.* Mexico: Ciudad de México, DDF, 1979.

Narváez y Saavedra, Juan de. *Sermón en la solemnidad que se consagró a Christo Señor Nuestro Sacramentado y a su Santíssma Madre en su Milagrosa Imagen de los Remedios por el feliz suceso de la Flota en el viage de vuelta a España.* Mexico: Herederos de la Viuda de Francisco Rodríguez Lupercio, 1699.

Nuevo Ulysses, delineado según el original del Grande Homero, en las Tablas de Odyssea; y esplendido en el Arco Triumphal, que la Primada Nueva España Santa Iglesia de México erigió en sus puertas al ingresso de Exmo. Sr. D. Pedro Cebrián Agustín, Conde de Fuenclara . . . Mexico, n.p., n.d.

Pérez Quintanilla, Miguel de and Ribera, Diego de. *Histórica imagen de proezas, emblemático ejemplar de virtudes ilustres del original Perseo: prevenido en oráculos mitológicos y descifrado en colores poéticos que a los congratuladores fastos y aparato célebre dispuso para la felice entrada y recibimiento del Excmo. Sr. Don Pedro Colón de Portugal, Duque de Veragua, virrey . . . La santa iglesia catedral metropolitana de México . . .* Mexico: Viuda de Bernardo Calderón, 1673.

Portada alegórica, espejo político, que la augusta, y muy exclarecida yglesia metropolitana de México, dedicó al Excmo. Sr. Don Luís Henrique de Guzmán . . . virrey . . . Mexico: Vuida de Bernardo Calderón, 1650.

Prieto, Guillermo. *Memorias de mis tiempos.* 5th ed. Mexico: Editorial Patria, 1969.

Prometheo Alegórico que la insigne iglesia Metropolitana de México, dispuso a su entrada, al Exmo. Sr. D. Juan Antonio Vásquez de Acuña, Marqués de Cassa Fuerte . . . Mexico: José Bernardo de Hogal, 1722.

Pulgar, Blas de. *Sermón que en acción de gracias ofrecido a Dios . . . en su imagen de los Remedios.por el parto de la Reina . . .* Mexico: Viuda de Miguel de Rivera Calderón, 1708.

Ramírez de Vargas, Alonso. *Elogio panegírico, festivo aplauso, iris político y diseño triunfal de Eneas verdadero, con que la Muy Noble y Leal Ciudad de México recibió al Excmo. Sr. Don Antonio Sebastián de Toledo y Salazar, Marqués de Mancera, . . . virrey.* Mexico: Viuda de Bernardo Calderón, 1664.

———. *Simulacro histórico-político, idea simbólica del héroe Cadmo que en la suntuosa fábrica de un arco triunfal decida festiva y consagra obsequiosa la Ilma. Imperial, Iglesia Metopolitana de México al Excmo. Sr. Don Gaspar de Sandoval, Conde de Galve, virrey . . .* Mexico: Viuda de Francisco Rodríguez Lupercio, 1688.

———. *Zodíaco ilustre de blasones heroicos, girado del sol político, imágen de príncipes que ocultó en su Hércules tebano la sabiduría mitológica, descifrado en poéticas ideas y expresando en colores de la pintura que en el festivo aparato del arco en el más fausto día erigió al Excmo. Sr. don José Sarmiento, Conde de Moctezuma, virrey . . . la santa iglesia metropolitana de México.* Mexico: Juan José Guillena, 1696.

Ramírez del Castillo, Pedro. *Hércules coronado, justa académica, palestra ingeniosa. Parnaso de las musas mexicanas en que se representa alegorizada por métricos pinceles y delineada por bien* sonoras voces. . . . *La Imperial, Pontificia y doctísima Minerva mexicana* . . . Mexico: José Bernardo de Hogal, 1724.

Robles, Antonio de. *Diario de sucesos notables 1665–1703.* 3 vols. Mexico: Editorial Porrúa, 1946.

Rodríguez de Arizpe, Pedro José. *Alegórico simulacro del célebre príncipe Atlante, que en la suntuosa montea de un triunfal arco erigió la sacra, Imperial, Metropolitana Iglesia de esta Corte de México en el solemne feliz ingreso del Excmo. Sr. D. Juan Francisco Guemes de Horcasitas* . . . Mexico: Viuda de José Bernardo de Hogal, 1746.

———. *Augusto iluminado, justa literaria palestra métrica para cuya ingeniosa minerval arena, lucidamente sombreada con los ilustres pinceles de gloriosas preseas en el inmortal volumne de la heroicidad romana, la imperial, Pontíficas, Leal y erudita Palas de México convoca a los adalides canoros y esforzados cisnes del occidental Caistro para aun en dulces, numerosas cadencias, celebren obsequiosos la plausible Cornación de nuestro castólico monarca Fernando VI . . . Real Colegio Seminario de esta Corte.* Mexico: María de Ribera, 1747.

———. *Coloso elocuente que en la solmne aclamación del augusto monarca de las Españas Don Fernando VI erigió sobre brillantes columnas la reconocida lealtad y fidelísima gratitud de la Imperial, Pontificia Universidad mexicana* . . . Mexico: Imprenta del Nuevo Rezado, 1748.

———. *Representación panegírica y métrica descripción del triunfal arco que en la solemne entrada del Excmo. Sr. Don Juan Francisco Guemes y Horcasitas* . . . *virrey, erigió la sacra, imperial, metropolitana iglesia de esta corte de México.* . . . Mexico: Viuda de José Bernardo de Hogal, 1746.

Ruíz Guerra y Morales, Cristóbal. *Letras felizmente laureadas, laurel festivo de letras que con ocasión de la Jura nuestro amado rey y señor Don Luís Fernando I brotó . . . por el celeste suelo de su Real, Pontificia Academia, Atenas de las Indias Occidentales y ofrece en nombre de esta Ilustre y Muy Leal Universidad.* . . . Mexico: José Bernardo de Hogal, 1724.

Sahagún, Fray Bernardino de. *Florentine Codex: General History of the Things of New Spain.* Santa Fe and Salt Lake City: School of American Research and the University of Utah, 1954.

Salazar y Torres, Agustín de. *Elogio panegírico y alcamación festiva, diseño triunfal y pompa laudatoria de Ulises verdadero, consagrada al Excmo. Sr. Don Francisco Fernández de la Cueva,*

Duque de Alburquerque, virrey . . . la Muy Leal y la Muy Ilustre Imperial Ciudad de México. . . . Mexico: Hipólito Rivera, 1653.

Salcedo y Somodevilla, Modesto de. *Breve relación de las funciones que hicieron en los días 31 de enero y 2 y 7 de febrero de 1790 los patronos del noble arte de platería en debida demostración de su amor y lealtad por la exaltación al trono de Carlos IV.* Mexico: Felipe de Zúñiga y Ontiveros, 1790.

Sedano, Francisco. *Noticias de México (Crónicas de los siglos XVI al XVIII).* Mexico: Talleres Gráficas de la Nación, 1974.

Siguenza y Góngora, Carlos. *Teatro de virtudes políticas que constituyen a un príncipe: advertidas en los monarcas antiguos del Mexicano imperio con cuyas figuras se hermoseó el arco triunfal que la Muy Noble, Muy Leal, Imperial Ciudad de México erigió para el digno recibimiento en ella del Excmo. Sr. Virrey Conde de Paredes . . .* Mexico: n.p., 1680.

Simulacro y alegórica idea del príncipe Belerofonte que en la montea suntuosa de un arco triunfal consagra, reverente, y ofrece amorosa la siempre augusta imperial iglesia metropolitana de México al Excmo. Sr. D. Baltasar de Zúñiga, Marqués de Valero, virrey . . . Mexico: n.p., 1716.

Talavera, Fray Hernando de. "De cómo se ha de ordenar el tiemo para que sea bien expendido. Avisación a la . . . muy noble señora Doña María Pacheco, Condesa de Benavente." Vol. 16, *Escritores Místicos Españoles 1, Nueva Biblioteca de Autores Españoles.* Madrid, 1911, 93–103.

Tlatelolco. Fuentes e Histora. Obras de Robert H. Barlow, vol. II. Mexico: INAH, 1989.

Triunfal pompa que la nobilíssima Ciudad de México dispuso a la entrada del Excmo. Sr. Don Juan Antonio Vázquez de Acuña, Marqués de Casa Fuerte, virrey . . . Mexico: José Bernardo de Hogal, 1722.

Urrutia de Vergara y Estrada, Manuel. *Loa y poética explicación del arco que esta Nobilísima, Imperial Ciudad de México erigió, a la pública entrada del Excmo. Sr. D. Augustín de Ahumada y Villalón, Marqués de las Amarillas . . .* Mexico: Imprenta Nueva de la Biblioteca Mexicana, 1756.

Valdés, Manuel Antonio. *Gazetas de México, Compendio de Noticias de Nueva España.* 16 vols. Mexico: Zúñiga y Ontiveros, 1784–1809.

Vázquez de Espinosa, Antonio. *Descripción de la Nueva España en el siglo XVII.* Mexico: Editorial Patria, 1944.

Velázquez de León, Joaquín. *La estirpe vespasiana. Idea alegórica de las pinturas y aparatos festivos del arco triunfal que para la entrada pública y solemne del Excmo. Sr. Don Matías de Gálvez, virrey . . . erigió la Nobilísima, Imperial Ciudad de México el día 8 de febrero de 1784 . . .* Mexico: Felipe de Zúñiga y Ontiveros, 1784.

———. *Explicación breve de los Arcos y aparatos festivos, que para celebrar la exaltación al trono de España DNRC el Sr. D. Carlos III, erigieron los professores de la platería . . .* Mexico: Bibliotheca Mexicana, 1761.

———. *Explicación de los adornos simbólicos y poéticos del arco del triunfo que para la entrada pública y solemne del Excmo. Sr. Frey Don Antonio María de Bucareli, virrey . . . erigió esta Nobilísima e Imperial ciudad de México . . .* Mexico: Felipe de Zúñiga y Ontiveros, 1771.

———. *Ilustración de las pinturas del arco de triunfo que para la entrada pública y solemne del Excmo. Sr. D. Joaquín de Monserrat Currana Criullas, Marqués de Cruillas, virrey . . . erigió esta Nobilísima e imperial Ciudad de México. . . .* Mexico: Imprenta Nueva de la Biblioteca Mexicana, 1761.

Ventura Beleña, Eusebio. *Recopilación sumaria de todos los autos acordados de la Real Audiencia y Sala del Crimen de esta Nueva España y providencias de su superior gobierno.* 2 vols. Mexico: D. Felipe de Zúñiga y Ontivero, 1787.

Vetancurt, Agustín de. *Teatro mexicano. Descripción breve de los sucesos ejemplares de la Nueva España en el Nuevo Mundo Occidental de las Indias.* 4 vols. Madrid: Porrúa Turanzas, 1960–61.

El viagero universal o noticia del mundo antiguo y nuevo. Vol. 26, *Obra recopilada de los mejores viageros por DPEP 1799.* Madrid: Imprenta de Villalpando, n.d.

Viera, Juan de. B*reve compendiosa narración de la ciudad de México . . . año 1777.* Mexico: Edit. Guarania, 1951–52.

Villalobos, Arias de. "Obediencia que México, cabeza de la Nueva España, dio a la majestad católica del rey Don Felipe IV, en su real nombre, con un discurso en verso del estado de la misma ciudad, desde su más antigua fundación, imperio, conquista hasta el mayor crecimiento y grandeza en que hoy está." In *Documentos inéditos o muy raros para la historia de México.* Mexico: Editorial Porrúa, 1975, 282–380.

Villarroel, Hipólito de. *Enfermedades políticas que padece la capital de esta Nueva España en casi todos los cuerpos de que se compone y*

*remedios que se la deben aplicar para su curación si se quiere que
sea util al rey y al público.* Mexico: Bibliófilos Mexicanos, 1979.

Vives, Luis. *Instrucciones de la mujer cristiana.* Buenos Aires, 1940.

Walsh, Vizconde. *Cuadro poético de las fiestas cristianas.* Mexico:
Boix, Besserex, y Cía, 1852.

Zorita, Alonso de. *Historia de la Nueva España.* Madrid: Librería
General de Suárez, 1909.

Secondary Sources

Agovi, Kofi. "A King Is Not Above Insult: The Politics of Good
Governance in Nzema Avudwene Festival Songs." In *Power,
Marginality and African Oral Tradition,* edited by Graham
Furniss and Liz Gunner. New York: Cambridge University Press,
1995, 47–61.

Aguirre Beltrán, Gonzálo. *La población negra de México 1519–1810: un
estudio etnohistórico.* Mexico: Ediciones Fuente Cultural, 1946.

———."The Slave Trade in Mexico." *Hispanic American Historical
Review* 24 (1944): 412–51.

Alberro, Solange. *Inquisición y sociedad en México, 1571–1700.* Mexico:
Fondo de Cultural Económica, 1988.

Alvarado Morales, Manuel. "El Cabildo y regimento de la ciudad de
México en el siglo XVII: un ejemplo de la oligarquía criolla."
Historia mexicana 28 (1979): 489–514.

Anna, Timothy. *The Fall of the Royal Government in Mexico City.*
Lincoln: University of Nebraska Press, 1978.

Archer, Christon I. *The Army in Bourbon Mexico, 1760–1810.*
Albuquerque: University of New Mexico Press, 1952.

Atwell, William S. "International Bullion Flows and the Chinese
Economy circa 1530–1650." *Past and Present* 95 (May 1982): 86–90.

Bakewell, Peter J. *Silver Mining and Society in Colonial Mexico,
Zacatecas, 1546–1700.* New York: Cambridge University Press,
1971.

Beezley, William H., Cheryl English Martin, and William E. French,
eds. *Rituals of Rule, Rituals of Resistance: Public Celebrations
and Popular Culture in Mexico.* Wilmington, DE Scholarly
Resources, 1994.

Bell, Catherine. *Ritual Theory, Ritual Practice.* New York: Oxford
University Press, 1992.

Bergeron, David. *English Civic Pageantry, 1558–1642.* Columbia:
University of North Carolina, 1971.

Bergman, Hannah E. "A Court Entertainment of 1638." *Hispanic Review* 42 (1974): 67–81.

Bernáldez Montalva, José María. *Las tarascas de Madrid.* Madrid: Ayuntamiento de Madrid, 1983.

Beverly, John. *Subalternity and Representation: Arguments in Cultural History.* Durham: Duke University Press, 1999.

Bonet Correa, Antonio. "La fiesta barroca somo práctica del poder." In *El arte efímero en el mundo hispánico.* Mexico: UNAM, 1983, 45–78.

———. *Fiesta, poder y arquitectura: Aproximaciones al barroco español.* Madrid: AKAL, 1990.

Borah, Woodrow. *New Spain's Century of Depression.* Berkeley: University of California Press, 1951.

———. "Race and Class in Mexico." *Pacific Historical Studies* 23 (1953): 331–42.

Boyer, Richard. "Absolutism versus Corporatism in New Spain: The Administration of the Marquis of Gelves, 1621–1624." *International History Review* 4, no. 4 (November 1982): 475–627.

———. *La gran inundación: Vida y sociedad en la ciudad de México (1629–1638).* Mexico: SEPA, 1975.

———. "Mexico in the Seventeenth Century: Transition of a Colonial Society." *Hispanic American Historical Review* 57 (1977): 455–78.

Brading, David. A. "Bourbon Spain and Its American Empire." Vol. 1, *The Cambridge History of Latin America,* edited by Leslie Bethell. New York: Cambridge University Press, 1984, 389–440.

———. *Miners and Merchants in Bourbon Mexico, 1763–1810.* Cambridge: Cambridge University Press, 1971.

———. "Tridentine Catholicism and Enlightened Despotism in Bourbon Mexico." *Journal of Latin American Studies* 15, no. 1 (May 1983): 1–22.

Brandes, Stanley. *Power and Persuasion: Fiestas and Social Control in Rural Mexico.* Pittsburgh: University of Pennsylvania Press, 1988.

Bromley, Juan. "Recibimientos de virreyes en Lima." *Revista Histórica* 20 (Lima) (1953): 5–108.

Brown, Jonathan, and Elliott, John H. *A Palace for a King: The Buen Retiro and the Court of Philip IV.* New Haven: Yale University Press, 1980.

Bryant, Lawrence M. *The King and the City in the Parisian Royal Entry Ceremony: Politics, Ritual and Art in the Renaissance.* Geneva: Librairie Droz, 1986.

Burke, Peter. *The Historical Anthropology of Early Modern Italy*. New York: Cambridge University, 1987.

———. *Popular Culture in Early Modern Europe*. New York: Harper and Row, 1978.

Burkhart, Louise. "Pious Performance: Christian Pageantry and Native Identity in Early Colonial Mexico." In *Native Traditions in the Postconquest World*, edited by Elizabeth Hill Boone and Tom Cummins. Washington, DC: Dumbarton Oaks, 1998, 361–81.

Burkholder, Mark A., and Chandler, D. S. *From Impotence to Authority: The Spanish Crown and the American Audiencias 1787–1808*. Columbia: University of Missouri Press, 1977.

Bush, Barbara. *Slave Women in Caribbean Society, 1650–1838*. Bloomington: University of Indiana Press, 1990.

Buxó, José Pascual. *Arco y certámen de la poesía mexicana colonial (siglo XVII)*. Xalapa: Universidad Veracruzana, 1959.

Cañeque, Alejandro. "Theater of Power: Writing and Representing the Auto de Fe in Colonial Mexico." *Americas* 52, no. 3 (January 1996): 321–44.

———. "The King's Living Image: The Culture and Politics of Viceregal Power in Seventeenth-Century New Spain." Ph.D. diss., New York University, 1999.

Carrasco, David. *City of Sacrifice: The Aztec Empire and the Role of Violence in Civilization*. Boston: Beacon Press, 1999.

———. "The Sacrifice of Tezcatlipoca: To Change Place." In *To Change Place: Aztec Ceremonial Landscape*. Niwot: University of Chicago Press, 1991.

Carrera Stampa, Manuel. *Los gremios mexicanos. La organización gremial en Nueva España 1521–1861*. Mexico: EDIAPSA, 1954.

Carroll, Patrick. *Blacks in Colonial Veracruz. Race, Ethnicity and Regional Development*. Austin: University of Texas Press, 1991.

Castro Gutiérrez, Felipe. *La extinción de la artesanía gremial*. Mexico: UNAM, 1982.

Chance, John K. *Race and Class in Colonial Oaxaca*. Stanford: Stanford University Press, 1978.

Charlot, Jean. *Mexican Art and the Academy of San Carlos, 1785–1915*. Austin: University of Texas Press, 1962.

Chatterjee, Partha. *Nationalist Thought and the Colonial World: A Derivative Discourse?* London: Zed Books, 1986.

Chaunu, Pierre, and Chaunu, Hugette. *Seville et l'Atlantique*. Paris: A. Colon, 1955–59.

Chevalier, Francois. *Land and Society in Colonial Mexico: The Great Hacienda*. Berkeley: University of California Press, 1966.

Clenidinnen, Inga. "Ways to the Sacred: Reconstructing Religion in Sixteenth-Century Mexico." *History and Anthropology* 5 (1990), 105–41.

Cohen, Walter. *Drama of a Nation: Public Theater in Renaissance England and Spain*. Ithaca: Cornell University, 1985.

Comaroff, John and Jean. *Ethnography and the Historical Imagination*. Boulder: Westview Press, 1994.

Connerton, Paul. *How Societies Remember*. New York: Cambridge University Press, 1989.

Cook, S. F., and Borah, Woodrow. *The Indian Population of Central Mexico, 1531–1610*. Berkeley: University of California Press, 1960.

Cooper, Donald B. *Epidemic Disease in Mexico City 1761–1813: An Administrative, Social and Medical History*. Austin: University of Texas Press, 1965.

Cope, R. Douglas. *The Limits of Racial Domination: Plebeian Society in Colonial Mexico City, 1660–1720*. Madison: University of Wisconsin Press, 1994.

Cuevas, Mariano. *Historia de la Iglesia en México*. 5 vols. Mexico: Patria, 1946–47.

Cunningham, J. V. *Tradition and Poetic Structure*. Denver: A. Swallow, 1960.

Curcio-Nagy, Linda. "Giants and Gypsies: Corpus Christi in Colonial Mexico City." In *Rituals of Rule, Rituals of Resistance: Public Celebrations and Popular Culture in Mexico*, edited by William H. Beezley, Cheryl English Martin, and William E. French. Wilmington: Scholarly Resources, 1994, 1–26.

———. "Native Icon to City Protectress to Royal Patroness: Ritual, Political Symbolism and the Virgin of Remedies." *Americas* 52, no. 3 (January 1996): 367–91.

———. "Rosa de Escalante's Private Party: Popular Female Religiosity in Colonial Mexico City. In *Women in the Inquisition*, edited by Mary Giles. Baltimore: Johns Hopkins University Press, 1999, 254–69.

———. "Sor Juana Ines de la Cruz and the 1680 Viceregal Entry of the Marquis de la Laguna into Mexico City." In *Europa Triumphans*. London: Ashgate, forthcoming.

Darnton, Robert. *The Great Cat Massacre and Other Episodes in French Cultural History*. New York: Vintage Books, 1985.

Davidson, D. M. "Negro Slave Control and Resistance in Colonial Mexico 1519–1650." *Hispanic American Historical Review* 46 (1966): 235–53.

Davis, Natalie Zemon. "The Rites of Violence: Religious Riots in Sixteenth-Century France." *Past and Present* 59: 51–91.

——. *Society and Culture in Early Modern France.* Stanford: Stanford University Press, 1975.

Dean, Carolyn. *Inka Bodies and the Body of Christ: Corpus Christi in Colonial Cuzco, Peru.* Durham: Duke University Press, 1999.

Deleito y Peñuela, José. *El rey se divierte.* Madrid: Espasa Calpe, 1935.

——. *También se divierte el pueblo.* Madrid: Espasa Calpe, 1966.

Del Río, Maria José. "Represión y control de fiestas y diversiones en el Madrid de Carlos III." In *Carlos III, Madrid y la Ilustración. Contradicciones de un proyecto reformista.* Madrid: Siglo XXI, 1988.

Denevan, William M., ed. *The Native Population of the Americas in 1492.* Madison: University of Wisconsin Press, 1987.

Dobyns, Henry F. "Estimating Aboriginal American Population: An Appraisal of Techniques with a New Hemisphere Estimate." *Current Anthropology* 7 (1966): 395–416, 425–35.

Domínguez Ortíz, Antonio. "Los gastos de corte en la España del Siglo XVII." In *Crisis y decadencia de la España de los Austrias.* Barcelona : Ediciones Ariel, 1969.

——. *Sociedad y estado en el siglo XVIII.* Barcelona: Ediciones Ariel, 1976.

Dusenberry, William H. "Discriminatory Aspects of Legislation in Colonial Mexico." *Journal of Negro History* 33 (1948): 284–302.

Eliade, Mircea. *The Sacred and the Profane.* New York: Harcourt, Brace and World, 1959.

Elliott, John H. "Poder y propaganda en la España de Felipe IV." In *España y su mundo 1500–1700.* Madrid: Alianza Editorial, 1990, 210–28.

——. "Spain and America in the Sixteenth and Seventeenth Centuries." Vol. 1, *The Cambridge History of Latin America,* edited by Leslie Bethell. New York: Cambridge University, 1984, 287–430.

Elster, Jon. *El cemento de la sociedad.* Barcelona: Gedisa, 1991.

Falassi, Alessandro, ed. *Essays on the Festival.* Albuquerque: University of New Mexico Press, 1987.

Farriss, Nancy M. *Crown and Clergy in Colonial Mexico 1759–1821.* London: Athlone Press, 1968.

Fee, Nancy H. "La Entrada Angelopolitana: Ritual and Myth in the Viceregal Entry in Puebla de los Angeles." *The Americas* 52, no. 3 (January 1996): 283–320.

Feijoo, Rosa. "El tumulto de 1624." *Historia Mexicana* 14 (1964): 42–70.

——. "El tumulto de 1692." *Historia Mexicana* 14 (1965): 656–79.

Fernandez, James. "The Performance of Ritual Metaphors." In *The Social Use of Metaphor: Essays on the Anthropology of Rhetoric*, edited by J. David Sapir and J. Christopher Crockers. Philadelphia: University of Pennsylvania Press, 1977, 100–31.

Fernández, María Auxiliadora. "The Representation of National Identity in Mexican Architecture: Two Case Studies in 1680 and 1889." Ph.D. diss., Columbia University, 1993.

Fernández, Martha. *Arquitectura y gobierno virreinal. Los maestros mayores de la ciudad de México, siglo XVII*. Mexico: UNAM, 1985.

Fernández del Castillo, Francisco. *El tribunal del protomedicato en la Nueva España*. Mexico: UNAM, 1965.

Firth, Raymond. *Symbols: Public and Private*. Ithaca: Cornell University Press, 1975.

Fisher, J. R. "Imperial 'Free Trade' and the Hispanic Economy, 1778–1796." *Journal of Latin American Studies* 13 (1981): 21–56.

Flinchpaugh, Stephen. "Economic Aspects of the Viceregal Entrance in Mexico City." *The Americas* 53, no. 3 (January 1996): 345–66.

Flores Olea, Aurora. "Los regidores de la ciudad de México en la primera mitad del siglo XVII." *Estudios de historia Novohispana* 3 (1970): 149–72.

Florescano, Enrique. *Memory, Myth and Time in Mexico: From the Aztecs to Independence*. Austin: University of Texas Press, 1994.

Florescano, Enrique, and Gil Sánchez, Isabel. "La época de las reformas borbónicas y el crecimiento económico 1750–1808." Vol. 2, *Historia general de México*. Mexico: Colegio de Mexico, 1980, 185–301.

Furniss, Graham. "The Power of Words and the Relation between Hausa Genres." In *Power, Marginality and African Oral Literature*. New York: Cambridge University Press, 1995.

García Icazbalceta, Joaquín. *Bibliografía mexicana del siglo XVI*. Mexico: Fondo de Cultura Económica, 1954.

García Tapia, Nicolás. *Técnica y poder en Castilla durante los siglos XVI y XVII*. León: Junta de Castilla y León, 1989.

Garner, Richard. "Prices and Wages in Eighteenth-Century Mexico." In *Essays on the Price History of Eighteenth-Century Latin*

America, edited by Lyman L. Johnson and Enrique Tandeter. Albuquerque: University of New Mexico Press, 1990, 73–108.

Geertz, Clifford. "Centers, Kings, and Charisma: Reflections on the Symbolics of Power." In *Culture and Its Creators: Essays in Honor of Edward Shils*, edited by Joseph Ben David and Terry Nichols Clark. Chicago: University of Chicago Press, 1977.

———. *The Interpretation of Cultures*. New York: Basic Books, 1973.

Gibson, Charles. *The Aztecs under Spanish Rule: A History of the Indians of the Valley of Mexico, 1519–1810*. Stanford: Stanford University Press, 1964.

Gil Calvo, Enrique. *Estado de fiesta*. Madrid: Espasa-Calpe, 1991.

Gillespie, Susan. *The Aztec Kings: The Construction of Rulership in Mexica History*. Tucson: University of Arizona Press, 1989.

González Obregón, Luís. *México viejo*. Mexico: Editorial Patria, 1966.

González Ullóa, Mario. *La medicina en México*. Mexico: Cyanamid, 1959.

Gosner, Kevin. "Religion and Rebellion in Colonial Chiapas." In *Native Resistance and the Pax Colonial in New Spain*, edited by Susan Schroeder. Lincoln: University of Nebraska Press, 1998.

Gramsci, Antonio. *Prison Notebooks*. New York: Columbia University Press, 1991.

Greer Johnson, Julie. *Satire in Colonial Spanish America: Turning the World Upside Down*. Austin: University of Texas Press, 1993.

Gruzinski, Serge. *The Conquest of Mexico*. London: Polity, 1991.

Guesquín, M. F. "Cities, Giants and Municipal Power." *Ethnología* 17: 117–28.

Gundersheimer, Werner L. Ferrara. *The Style of a Renaissance Despotism*. Princeton: Princeton University Press, 1973.

Guthrie, Chester. "Riots in Seventeenth-Century Mexico." In *Greater America: Essays in Honor of Herbert Eugene Bolton*. Berkeley: University of California Press, 1945, 245–58.

Hamilton, Earl J. *American Treasure and the Price Revolution in Spain 1501–1650*. New York: Octagon Books, 1965.

Hamnett, Brian R. "The Appropriation of Mexican Church Wealth by the Spanish Bourbon Government: The Consolidation of Vales Reales, 1805–1809." *Journal of Latin American Studies* 1 (1969): 85–113.

———. *Politics and Trade in Southern Mexico, 1750–1821*. Cambridge: Cambridge University Press, 1971.

Handelman, Don. *Models and Mirrors: Towards an Anthropology of Public Events*. New York: Cambridge University Press, 1990.

Harris, Max. *Aztecs, Moors and Christians: Festivals of Reconquest in Mexico and Spain.* Austin: University of Texas Press, 2000.

Haslip-Viera, Gabriel. *Crime and Punishment in Late Colonial México City 1692–1810.* Albuquerque: University of New Mexico Press, 1999.

Hoberman, Louisa Schell. "Bureaucracy and Disaster: Mexico City and the Flood of 1629." *Journal of Latin American Studies* 6 (1974): 211–30.

———. *Mexico's Merchant Elite, 1590–1660: Silver, State and Society.* Durham: Duke University Press, 1991.

Ingersoll, R. "Ritual Use of Public Space in Renaissance Rome." Ph.D. diss., University of California at Berkeley, 1985.

Israel, Jonathan. *Race, Class and Politics in Colonial Mexico, 1610–1670.* London: Oxford University Press, 1975.

Jiménez Rueda, Julio. "El certámen de los plateros en 1618 y las coplas satíricas que de él se derivaron." *Boletín del Archivo General de la Nación XVI* no. 3 (1945): 343–84.

———. "Nadie se engaña si con fe baila." *Boletín del Archivo Nacional de la Nación* no. 4 (October–November 1945).

Juegos de ingenio y agudeza; La pintura emblemática de la Nueva España. Mexico: Consejo Nacional para la Cultura y las Artes, 1994.

Kellogg, Susan. *Law and the Transformation of Aztec Culture, 1500–1700.* Norman: University of Oklahoma Press, 1995.

Klor de Alva, J. Jorge. "Religious Rationalization and the Conversions of the Nahuas: Social Organization and Colonial Epistomology." In *To Change Place: Aztec Ceremonial Landscapes,* edited by David Carrasco. Niwot: University of Colorado Press, 1991.

Ladd, Doris M. *The Mexican Nobility at Independence, 1780–1826.* Austin: University of Texas Press, 1976.

Lavrin, Asunción. "The Execution of the Law of Consolidation in New Spain: Economic Gains and Results." *Hispanic American Historical Review* 53 (1973): 27–49.

Leach, Edmund. *Culture and Communication.* New York: Cambridge University Press, 1989.

Lemoine Villicaña, Ernesto. "El alumbrado público en la ciudad de México durante la seguna mitad del siglo XVIII." *Boletín de Archivo General de la Nación* 2d ser. IV, no. 4: 783–818.

León, N. *Las castas del México colonial o Nueva España.* Mexico: Talleres Gráficos del Museo Nacional de Arqueología, Historia, y Etnografía, 1924.

Leonard, Irving, ed. *Alboroto y motín de México del 8 de junio de 1692.* Mexico: Talleres Gráficos de Museo Nacional de Arquedogía, Historia y Etnografia, 1932.

——. *Baroque Times in Old Mexico: Seventeenth-Century Persons, Places, and Practices.* Ann Arbor: University of Michigan, 1959.

Le Roy Ladurie, Emmanuel. *Carnival in Romans: A People's Uprising at Romans, 1579–1580.* New York: Braziller, 1980.

Lira, Andrés, and Luís Muro. "El siglo de la integración." Vol. 2, *Historia general de México,* edited by Daniel Cosío Villegas. Mexico: Colegio de México, 1980.

Lisón Tolosana, Carmelo. *La imagen del rey: Monarquía, realeza y poder, ritual en la Casa de los Austrias.* Madrid: Espasa-Calpe, 1991.

Lockhart, James. *The Nahuas after the Conquest: A Social and Cultural History of the Indians of Central Mexico, Sixteenth through Eighteenth Centuries.* Stanford: Stanford University Press, 1992.

Lopes Don, Patricia. "Carnivals, Triumphs, and Rain Gods in the New World: A Civic Ritual in the City of Mexico-Tenochtitlan in 1539." *Colonial Latin American Review* 6, no. 1 (1997): 17–40.

MacCormak, Sabine G. *Art and Ceremony in Late Antiquity.* Berkeley: University of California, 1981.

MacLeod, Murdo. *Spanish Central America: A Socioeconomic History, 1520–1720.* Berkeley: University of California Press, 1973.

Maravall, José Antonio. *The Culture of the Baroque.* Minneapolis: University of Minnesota Press, 1986.

María de Campos, Armando de. "Las comedias en el Corpus mexi-cano colonial." *Humanismo* 2, nos. 11–12 (May–June 1953): 111–14.

Marroquí, José María. *La ciudad de México.* 3 vols. Mexico: Tip. y Lit. La Europa de J. Aguilar y Cía, 1900–3.

Marshall, C. E. "The Birth of the Mestizo in New Spain." *Hispanic American Historical Review* 19 (1939): 161–84.

Martin, Cheryl English. *Governance and Society in Colonial Mexico: Chihuahua in the Eighteenth Century.* Stanford: Stanford University Press, 1996.

Martín, N. F. *Los vagabundos en la Nueva España, siglo XVI.* Mexico: Editorial Jus, 1957.

Martín Tovar, Virginia. "La entrada triunfal en Madrid de Doña Margarita de Austria (24 de octubre de 1599)." *Archivo Español de Arte* 244 (1988): 385–404.

Maza, Francisco de la. *La mitología clásica en el arte colonial de México.* Mexico: UNAM, 1968.

McAlister, Lyle. *The Fuero Militar in New Spain, 1764–1800.*
Gainesville: University of Florida Press, 1952.

———. "Social Structure and Social Change in New Spain." *Hispanic American Historical Review* 43 (1963): 349–70.

———. "Royal Government in the Indies: Powers and Limitations." In *Spain and Portugal in the New World 1492–1700.* Minneapolis: University of Minnesota Press, 1987.

Mitchell, Bonner. *Italian Civic Pageantry in the High Renaissance: A Descriptive Bibliography of Triumphal Entries and Selected Other Festivals for State Occasions.* Florence: Leo S. Olschiki Editore, 1979.

Moore, Sally, and Myerhoff, Barbara. *Secular Ritual.* Amsterdam: Van Gorcum, 1977.

Moreno Navarro, Isidro. "De la escenificación de lo simbólico a la simbolización de lo escénico." In *Teatro y fiesta en el Barroco, edited by José María Diez Borque.* Barcelona: Ediciones Serbal, 1986, 179–86.

Muir, Edward. *Civic Ritual in Renaissance Venice.* Princeton: Princeton University Press, 1971.

Mullett, Michael. *Popular Culture and Popular Protest in Late Medieval and Early Modern Europe.* New York: Routledge, Chapman and Hall, 1987.

Muriel, Josefina. *Hospitales de la Nueva España.* Mexico: UNAM, 1956.

Nwasike, D. A. "Mexico City Town Government, 1590–1650: A Study in Aldermanic Background and Performance." Ph.D. diss., University of Wisconsin, 1972.

Oliva, César. "La práctica escénica en fiestas teatrales previas al barroco: Algunas referencias a muestras hechas en la región de Murcía." In *Teatro y fiesta en el Barroco, edited by José María Diez Borque.* Barcelona: Ediciones Serbal, 1986, 98–114.

Orgel, S., and Strong, Roy. Inigo Jones: *The Theatre of the Stuart Court.* Berkeley: University of California, 1973.

Orso, Steven. *Art and Death at the Spanish Hapsburg Court: The Royal Exequies for Philip IV.* Columbia: University of Missouri, 1989.

Palmer, Colin A. *Slaves of the White God: Blacks in Mexico.* Cambridge: Cambridge University Press, 1976.

Pan y toros y otros papeles sediciosos de fines del siglo XVIII. Madrid: Editorial Ayuso, 1971.

Partridge, Loren, and Star, Randolph. "Triumphalism and the Sala Regia in the Vatican." In *Triumphal Celebrations and Rituals of*

Statecraft: Art and Pageantry in the Renaissance, edited by Barbara Wisch and Susan Scott Munshower. University Park, PA: Department of Art History, Pennsylvania State University, 1990.

Poole, Stafford, CM. *Our Lady of Guadalupe: The Origins and Sources of a Mexican Symbol, 1531–1797.* Tucson: University of Arizona Press, 1995.

Praz, Mario. *Studies in Seventeenth-Century Imagery.* Rome: Edizioni di Storia e Letteratura, 1964.

Ramos Smith, Maya. *La danza en Mexico durante la epoca colonial.* Mexico: Alianza, 1990.

Rivera Ayala, Sergio. "Lewd Songs and Dances from the Streets of Eighteenth-Century New Spain." In Beezley, *Rituals of Rule,* 27–46.

Rodríguez, Laura. *Reforma e Ilustración en la España del siglo XVIII: Pedro de Campomanes.* Madrid: Fundación Universitaria Española, 1975.

Rojas Garciadueñas, José. "Fiestas en Mexico en 1578." *Anales del Instituto de Investigaciones Estéticas* no. 9 (1942).

Romero de Terreros, Manuel. *Ex-Antiques. Bocetos de la vida social en la Nueva Espána.* Guadalajara: Imp. Fortino Jiménez, 1919.

———. *Torneos y mascaradas y fiestas reales en la Nueva España.* Mexico: Editorial Porrúa, 1918.

Rubin, Miri. *Corpus Christi: The Eucharist in Late Medieval Culture.* New York: Cambridge University Press, 1991.

Schroeder, Susan. *Chimalpahin and the Kingdoms of Chalco.* Tucson: University of Arizona Press, 1991.

———. "Marginal Intellectuals: Nahua Musicians and the Church." Paper delivered at the Rocky Mountain Council for Latin American Studies, Missoula, MT, April 15, 1998.

Schurz, William Lytle. *The Manila Galleon.* New York: E. P. Dutton, 1939.

Scott, H. M., ed. *Enlightened Absolutism: Reform and Reformers in Later Eighteenth-Century Europe.* Ann Arbor: University of Michigan Press, 1990.

Scott, James. *Domination and the Arts of Resistance: Hidden Transcripts.* New Haven: Yale University Press, 1990.

Seed, Patricia. *To Love, Honor, and Obey in Colonial Mexico: Conflicts over Marriage Choice, 1574–1821.* Stanford: Stanford University Press, 1988.

Silva Menduajo, Gabriel. *La Catedral de Morelia: arte y sociedad en la*

Nueva España. Mexico: Comité Editorial del Gobierno del
  Estado, 1984.

Smith, Earl Baldwin. *Architectural Symbolism of Imperial Rome and
  the Middle Ages.* Princeton: Princeton University Press, 1978.

Spivak, Gayatri. "Can the Subaltern Speak?" In *Marxism and the
  Interpretation of Culture,* edited by Cary Nelson and Lawrence
  Grossberg. Urbana: University of Illinois Press, 1988.

Stove, Noel J. "The Tumulto of 1624: Turmoil at Mexico City." Ph.D.
  diss., University of Southern California, 1970.

Strong, Roy. *Art and Power: Renaissance Festivals 1450–1650.* Berkeley:
  University of California Press, 1984.

Taylor, William B. *Magistrates of the Sacred.* Stanford: Stanford
  University Press, 1996.

———. "The Virgin of Guadalupe in New Spain: An Inquiry into the
  Social History of a Marian Devotion." *American Ethnologist* 14,
  no. 1 (February 1987):9–33.

Tepaske, John H. "New World Silver, Castile and the Far East
  (1590–1750." In *Precious Metals in the Later Medieval and Early
  Modern World,* edited by John Richards. Durham: Carolina
  Academic Press, 1982.

———, and Klein, Herbert S. "Seventeenth Century Crisis in the
  Spanish Empire: Myth or Reality?" *Past and Present* 90 (February
  1981): 116–35.

Thompson, E. P. "Folklore, Anthropology, and Social History." *Indian
  Historical Review* 3 (1977): 247–66.

Toussaint, Manuel. *Colonial Art in Mexico.* Austin: University of
  Texas Press, 1967.

Tovar de Teresa, Guillermo. *Bibliografía Novohispana de arte.* 2 vols.
  Mexico: Fondo de Cultura Económica, 1988.

Turner, Victor. *Dramas, Fields, and Metaphors: Symbolic Action in
  Human Society.* Ithaca: Cornell University Press, 1974.

———. *From Ritual to Theatre: The Human Seriousness of Play.* New
  York: PAJ Publications, 1987.

———. *The Ritual Process: Structure and Anti-Structure.* New York:
  Cornell University Press, 1989.

Trexler, Richard. *Public Life in Renaissance Florence.* New York:
  Academic Press, 1980.

Valle Arizpe, Artemio de. *Notas de Platería.* Mexico: Editorial Polis,
  1941.

———. *Por la vieja Calzada de Tlacopan.* Mexico: Tip. Cultura, 1937.

Van Young, Eric. "The Age of Paradox: Mexican Agriculture at the

End of the Colonial Period." In *The Economics of Mexico and Peru During the Late Colonial Period, 1760–1810,* edited by Nils Jacobsen and Hans-Jürgen Puhle. Berlin: Colloquium Verlag, 1986, 64–90.

———. "Who Was That Masked Man, Anyway? Symbols and Popular Ideology in the Mexican Wars of Independence." In *Proceedings of the Rocky Mountain Council on Latin American Studies* 1 (1984): 18–35.

Varey, J. E. "Further Notes on Processional Ceremonial of the Spanish Court in the Seventeenth Century." *Iberoromania* 1 (1974): 71–79.

———. "Processional Ceremonial of the Spanish Court in the Seventeenth Century." *Studia Iberica: Festschrift für Hans Flasche* (Bern-Munich) (1973): 643–52.

Vázquez Mellado, Alfonso. *La ciudad de los palacios: Imagenes de cinco siglos.* Mexico: Editorial Diana, 1990.

Very, Frances G. *The Spanish Corpus Christi Procession: A Literary and Folkloric Study.* Valencia: Topografia Moderna, 1962.

Veyne, Paul. *Bread and Circuses: Historical Sociology and Political Pluralism.* New York: Penguin Viking, 1990.

Viqueira Albán, Juan Pedro. *¿Relajados o reprimidos? Diversiones públicas y vida social en la ciudad de México durante el Siglo de las Luces.* Mexico: Fondo de Cultura Económica, 1987.

Von Barghahn, Barbara. *Age of Gold, Age of Iron: Renaissance Spain and the Symbols of Monarchy.* 2 vols. Boston: University Press of America, 1985.

Von Kugelgen, Helga. "Carlos de Siguenza y Góngora, su Theatro de Virtudes Políticas que constintuyen un Príncipe y la estruc-turación emblemática de unos tableros en el Archo de Triunfo." In *Juegos de ingenio,* 151–61.

Wachtel, Nathan. *Los vencidos.* Madrid: Alianza Editorial, 1976.

Warman, Arturo. *La danza de los moros y cristianos.* Mexico: Sep-Setentas, 1972.

Wisch, Barbara, and Scott Munshower, Susan, eds. *Triumphal Celebrations and Rituals of Statecraft: Art and Pageantry in the Renaissance.* University Park, PA: Department of Art History, Pennsylvania State University, 1990.

Index

acculturation, 5–6, 48–50, 106, 146

Afro-Mexicans: Bourbon era, 99; Hapsburg era, 58–63; and idealized colonial society, 64–66; revolts, 159–60; Spanish conceptualization, 43; and triumphal arches, 59–60

alcaldes mayores, 55–56

Almanza, Viceroy Martín Enríquez, 4

el alza del pendón real, 78–79

Aranda, Simona, 176

arbor (Corpus Christi), 113–16

architectural guild, 100

Argüello, Manuel de, 54–58, 175–76

artists, 10–11

audience, 12–13

Audiencia, 18

authors, 10–11, 162–63. *See also* triumphal arches

auto-de-fé, 95

Azevedo, Francisco, 25

Aztecs, 44–47, 172, 174

Baños, count of, 38

Bentura Ximénez, Juan, 174

Beristáin, José Mariano, 130–33

black hand charm, 59

Bourbon era: and Afro-Mexicans, 99; councilmen, 84–85, 119, 147; demographics, 101; economy, 134–35, 152; entrance ceremony, 79–83, 103–5, 146–52, 183–84; Ferdinand VI's coronation, 67–70; funding of festivals, 74–75; illumination, 69, 71–72, 105, 187; jura del rey, 70–71, 103–5, 118, 150–51, 177–78; and Native Americans, 99, 102–3, 106–7, 110–11, 118, 152–53; reforms, 11, 108–17, 119, 122–23, 151, 188–89; revolts, 111–12; triumphal arches, 71–72, 80–83; viceroy, 79–83; warfare, 163

Branciforte, marquis of, 135

bullfights, 74–75, 82, 92, 181–82

Calancha y Santander, Don Hepicurio Almanancer, 127–29

Calleja del rey, Félix María, 140, 142–43

canopy, 35

carnival, 117

castas, 1, 4–5

caste system, 4, 5, 146

Catholicism: Bourbon reform, 108–11; and Church real estate, 135; Dominican order, 129–30, 133; and festival dancers, 116–17

Cerralvo, marquis of, 1–2, 24, 29–30

Chapultepec, 15–16, 37, 90, 91, 92, 164, 182

Charles II, 169–70
Charles III, 97, 111, 133–34
Charles IV, 97–98
Christianity, 6, 25–32
Cihuacoatl, 45
citizen performances. *See also*
    Afro-Mexicans; Native
    Americans; Hapsburg era,
    6; and idealized colonial
    society, 43–44, 64–66; and
    identity, 42–43, 49–52
Colina, Felipe de, 56
confraternities, 108–10
Conquistadora, 76–78
Constitution of Cádiz, 140–42, 143
Cornejo, Diego de, 30
Corpus Christi: Bourbon era,
    112–17, 151, 188–89;
    Hapsburg era, 147; and
    Native Americans, 113–17;
    the procession, 28–29; and
    revolts, 112; and satire,
    127–29; and the viceroy, 29,
    30, 147
Cortes of Cádiz, 140–41
Coruña, count of, 48
councilmen. *See also* govern-
    ment; and Bourbon reform,
    119; clothing of, 20; in
    Corpus Christi procession,
    29; corrupt, 38–39; criticism
    by Argüello, 55; and
    Ferdinand VII, 141–42; and
    funding, 35–38, 53–54, 75,
    80, 82–83, 105, 175;
    Hapsburg vs. Bourbon,
    84–85, 147; and home rule,
    136–37, 140; and patriotism,
    10; and royal decrees, 34–37;
    spending, 170–71; and the
    viceroy, 18, 28; and Virgin of

Guadalupe, 78; and Virgin
    of Remedies, 31, 75–78
count of Baños, 38
count of Coruña, 48
count of Montezuma, 37
criollos, 119
Croix, marquis de la, 87
Cruz, Sor Juana Inés de la, 25

dances, 129–33
demographics: Bourbon era, 101;
    and castas, 1, 4–5; and
    changes in rituals, 48; and
    disease, 8, 172–73
disease, 8, 172–73
Don Juanism, 59
drought, 76

Easter festivals, 111–12
economy: Bourbon era, 85, 101,
    134–35, 152; and citizen per-
    formances, 63; eighteenth-
    century, 8–9; and guilds,
    103; seventeenth-century, 8,
    161–62; silver boom, 100;
    and triumphal arch symbol-
    ism, 25
education, 109, 187
enramada, 113–16
entrance ceremony: and the
    absent king, 37; Bourbon
    era, 79–83, 103–5, 183–84;
    and the canopy, 36; com-
    pared to the jura del rey,
    33–34; early, 15–19; funding
    of, 35–38, 52–54, 82–83, 165,
    175; Hapsburg vs. Bourbon,
    146–52; and idealized
    colonial society, 43–44,

54–58, 64–66; magnificence of, 19–23

Ferdinand VI, 67–70, 126
Ferdinand VII, 136–43
Fernández Osorio, Pedro, 25, 27
Ferrer Montes, Ambrosio, 109–10
fireworks, 93, 94; and Apollo, 72–73; Bourbon era, 69, 71–72, 105, 187; and triumphal arches, 98
flooding, 26, 55

Galvez, Matias de, 82
Garibay, Pedro, 137
Gelves, marquis of, 1, 36
gender stereotypes, 43, 59–62
Generala, 138–40
Gónzalez Velásquez, Don Antonio, 97
government. *See also* councilmen; essential qualities, 24–27; and home rule, 136–37, 140; and magnificence, 18, 19–23; Native American leaders, 50–51; politics, 6–7, 79, 124–25, 133–35, 153–54; private use of funds, 82–83, 105; and symbolism, 19–20, 23–27, 146, 148
guilds, 68–69, 97–98, 100, 103–5, 185, 186
Gutiérrez, Sebastián, 24

Hapsburg era: and Afro-Mexicans, 58–63; and citizen participation, 6; Corpus Christi, 147; councilmen, 84–85, 147; entrance ceremony, 15–18, 20, 146–52; jura del rey, 70–71, 150–51; morale, 9–10; Virgin of Remedies, 147
Hidalgo y Costilla, Miguel, 138–40
higa, 59
Holy Eucharist, 29

identity: and acculturation, 5–6; and citizen participation, 42–43, 49–52; and Corpus Christi, 29; and morale, 9–10; and patriotism, 10
illumination, 93, 94; and Apollo, 72–73; Bourbon era, 69, 71–72, 105, 187; of triumphal arches, 98
Inquisition, 31–32, 123, 130, 133–35, 189
intendant system, 79
Iturbide, Agustín, 142
Iturrigaray, José de, 136, 137

jura del rey: Bourbon era, 103–5, 118, 177–78; for Charles IV, 97–98; compared to viceregal entries, 33–34; costs of, 169–70; for Ferdinand VII, 136–37; Hapsburg vs. Bourbon, 70–71, 150–51

king: his absence, 32–33, 34, 37, 40; accountability, 85; as Apollo, 72–73, 178–79; displays of loyalty, 105–7, 150;

and Mexican independence, 143–44; and royal decrees, 34–37; his virtue, 72–73, 108

language, 106
López Pacheco, Diego (marquis of Villena), 15–17
Lorenzana, Archbishop Francisco de, 11, 109, 111, 116
love, 59–61

Machete Conspiracy, 135
Marmalejo, Pedro de, 30
marquis de la Croix, 87
marquis of Branciforte, 135
marquis of Cerralvo, 1–2, 24, 29–30
marquis of Gelves, 1, 36
marquis of Montesclaros, 35
marquis of Villena, 15–17, 41
marriages, 5
máscara ridícula, 121
Massías, Nicolas, 56
Melchor de Jovellanos, Gaspar, 117
Mendieta Rebollo, Gabriel, 78
Mexico City, 7, 8–9, 26, 55, 86
mojiganga, 125–126, 190
Montaña, Luis José, 137–138
Montesclaros, marquis of, 35
Montezuma, count of, 37
Morelos y Pavón, José Maria, 140
morenas criollas, 61, 176–177
Morga, Antonio, 159

Native Americans: after the conquest, 47–48; in Bourbon era fesitvals, 99, 102–3, 106–7, 118; and Bourbon reform, 110–11, 152–53; and carnival, 117; clothing, 113; during Corpus Christi, 113–17; the elite, 48–52; funding of festivals, 52–54; and Hidalgo revolt, 138, 144; and idealized colonial society, 64–66; and Pre-Columbian rituals, 44–47; and Saint Hippolytus, 79; Spanish conceptualization, 43, 49–50; triumphal arches, 173 ·
Noche Triste, 78

oath celebrations. *See also* jura del rey; Bourbon era, 103–5; for Charles IV, 97–98; comparisons, 33–34; costs of, 169–70
Ortega de Montáñez, Juan, 126–27
Osorio de Escobar, Diego, 38

Pacheco Osorio, Rodrigo, 24
patria potestad, 5
peninsulares, 119, 134, 137
Pérez de la Serna, Juan, 1
Philip IV, 169–70
Philip V, 186
Pinelo, Alavés, 27
plateros, 97–98
plaza, 7–8, 95; La Plaza Mayor, 86
poetry, 123–24
politics. *See also* government; and Christianity, 6; and festival

space, 6–7; intendant system, 79; and race, 4, 5, 62; and satire, 124–25, 133–35, 153–54
primordial titles, 174

race, 4, 5, 62
Ramírez de Vargas, Alonso, 25
Real Pragmática de Matrimonios, 5
Real Protomedicato, 100, 185
religion, 108–11, 116–17, 129–30, 133, 135
revolts: Afro-Mexican, 58–59; Bourbon era, 111–12; and Corpus Christi, 112; Hidalgo revolt, 138–40; and independence, 135; Riego Revolt, 142; and satire, 133–35; seventeenth-century, 5, 159–60
Riego Revolt, 142
rituals: alternative, 57–58; post conquest, 48–50, 52; Pre-Columbian, 44–47, 172, 174
romance, 59–61
Royal Banner Festival, 78–79, 138, 140–42, 149, 151

Saint Hippolytus, 78–79, 97
Salazar y Torres, Agustín de, 25, 26
San Gonzalo, 129–33
San Juan Nepomuceno, 96
San Salvador, Fernández de, 139–40
satire: and Bourbon reform, 122–23; and Corpus Christi, 127–29; and dance of San Gonzalo, 129–33; and the

Inquisition, 123; parade for Louis I, 121–22, 124–25; and politics, 124–25, 133–35, 153–54; of viceroys, 126–27
silver mining, 161–62
silversmith guild, 97–98
slavery, 3–4, 58, 61–62
symbolism, 19–20, 23–27, 105–7, 146, 148

Tenochtitlan, 47, 48
Tovar, Juan de, 138
triumphal arches: for Afro-Mexican festivals, 59–60; in Bourbon era, 71–72, 80–83; design of, 21–22; dimensions of, 165–66; eighteenth-century, 94; illumination of, 98; Native American, 173; symbolism, 23–27

Valeriano, Antonio, 48
Velasco, Viceroy Luís, 4, 35, 36
Venegas, Francisco Xavier, 137, 139, 140
viceroy: and Afro-Mexican women, 58–63; Bourbon era, 79–83; and cihuacoatl, 45; in Corpus Christi procession, 29, 30, 147; corrupt, 38; entrance ceremony, 15–18, 20; his image, 28, 56–58, 167; and the Inquisition, 31–32; mythological counterparts, 166–67; oaths, 21–22; his religious devotion, 25–26, 27–32; and triumphal arch symbolism, 23–27; and the Virgin of Remedies, 31

Villena, marquis of, 15–17, 41
Virgin of Guadalupe, 78, 139, 140
Virgin of Remedies: after inde-
    pendence, 142; as
    Conquistadora, 76–78;
    devotions to, 30–31, 180–81;
    as Generala, 138–40;
    Hapsburg era, 147; royal
    appropriation of, 75–78,
    137–39, 149, 151
voladores, 41, 88

warfare, 163
women, 43, 58–63

Yermo, Gabriel de, 137

zócalo, 7–8, 95